MANKIND

MANKIND
In Quest of the Self

Sem Topno

KALPAZ

Mankind : In Quest of the Self

ISBN: 978-81-7835-904-5

Published in 2012 in India by
Kalpaz Publications
C-30, Satyawati Nagar,
Delhi-110052
E-mail: kalpaz@hotmail.com
Phone : 9212729499

Lasser Type Setting by: Rudra Computer Graphics, Delhi
Printed at : Chawla Offset Press, Delhi

Dedicated to

The most beloved son
Late Herman Neeraj Topno

Contents

Preface

Evolution or origin of life is a mystery, so also the origin of human being. How the universe originated from void or nothingness during the period of pre-time and pre-space period is yet to be settled by the scientists!.' Mankind in quest of the self is based on these issues of human origin and development. The theory of Big Bang has been proposed by the scientists which is supposed to solve the probable origin of universe, i.e. the physical and chemical world and latter followed by biological origin. There is still some confusion on the method and process without referring to the causative factor for prime cause of origin.

In the initial introductory chapter we considered the concept and theories of origin and Darwin's theory of common origin from the molecule or bacteria which proposed a gradual development of life from lower to higher stage from animal to human. His booll Origin of Species which made great impact on human community, Was discussed by the great scientists against the backdrop of present available evidences. In the second chapter the origin of universe, the planet and the stars as well as dark matter, god's particle, black and white hole have been discussed. Reshaping the planet Earth theory coming into the present form has been discussed.

Origin or strategic origin of life has been discussed in third chapter. Molecular origin of life from soup or ocean vent is supposed to be the possible of life. Some scientists doubted the origin of life from earth and proposed origin from outer space and suggested pans-permia theory planet earth which was bombarded constantly for millenniums of years by steroids and seeds of life came from outer space. For millennium of years molecular biology and natural selection work and higher life form developed species of hominids and homosepiens. Genetic study has now indicated that all human beings belong to the same human species.

In forth chapter we discussed human origin it happened when lower species had already flourished on earth. Scientists have theorized that human developed from hominid, so also the Santhal aboriginals of India one of the most ancient people of austric language speakers say-that human originated from bird's egg when dinosaur ruled the planet earth as dominant creatures. Bird is stated to belong to dinosaurs descendants, so human beings are the descendants of dinosaurs through reshuffling and natural selection of genes. Human beings is also said to have originated from clay of the earth by another group of aborigines of the same language family from clay of the earth like chloroplast from the sun's heat.

In chapter five human origin or better known as homosapienes have been traced out from South Africa. Homosapiens first developed from hominids from Africa. Several missing links were suggested of homesapeins to modern human to hominids but no evidence of missing link was sure to confirm this.

In chapter Human migration from Africa has been dealt with in detail. It is stated that it is the sub-Saharan region of Asia which is supported that modern human developed and headed to European countries first and then Siberia and Asia and America. South America is stated to have been peopled by Australia aborigines. However in recent research finding

Australia itself have been peopled by descendent of Indian aboriginal people. Modern human footprints on the sedimentary rock of Jharkhand, India which is stated to be millions of years old is most ancient modern human footprints found in Earth so far. There are other footprints of fauna which is stated non-existent in Indian scene, such as a horse. The intensive study of pre-history will surely rewrite the ancient history of the world.

Search of human is not over. Earlier Neanderthal and Hobbits have been discussed and doubted to be another species of humans. In the meantime large bodies of Ape like species known as big foot in many parts of the earth have been sighted but so far no identification has been made so far. We also have doubted that we are not alone in the universe and search of life in outer space is on. We are searching alien life in outer space but so far nothing sort of alien have been detected and we are waiting for their communication for better or worse for human being on Earth. But we are still hopeful for their findings. This has been dealt in chapter eight.

Sem Topno

1

Introduction

One of the most elusive idea that made the global impact on rationalist thinkers and scientists during twentieth century was Darwin's Theory of Evolution. It has not only created ripples on the believers of the traditional notion of creation, but wrested the allegiance of both theist and atheist creation by the benevolent and benign creator. This was the prevalent notion till now. The Theory of Evolution wittingly or un-wittingly convinced almost every individual thinker in every field. During Darwin's time naturalist philosophy was in vogue among the intelligentsia . He was also influenced by the view of the thinkers who were analyzing it through the angle of natural theology. The conflict between science and religion had already been disturbing the people. This revealed and inspired view of religion was challenged. The progress of anatomy, geology, paleontology also undermined the static view of religion that had been taken as granted by the believers and scholars. At this stage Darwin put forward the idea that the whole life form of the nature's species hud evolved from a simple form during vast period of time. Dropping of nickel effect from the environment helped enthusion of oxygen 2.4 billion years ago, and the molecular gene evolved into development of higher species and new modern humans. This approach of natural science was later extended to social science in the study of man and society. The debate concerning static Biblical views however, did not stop nor the notion of creation discontinued.

The prevalent thinking and approach of natural science evidenced in observation and discoveries was so great on Darwin that he lost faith on God as creator, redeemer and judge. He dissociated himself from Christianity and became totally an agnostic. He observed (p. 44, J.C. Greene, *Darwin and Modern World View*, 1905).

"There seems to me too much misery in the world. I cannot persuade myself that a beneficent and omnipotent God would have designedly created the Ichneumotnidea with the express intension of their feeding within the living bodies of caterpillars or that a cat should play with mice. Not believing this, I seem necessity in the belief that the eyes were expressly designed. On the other hand, I cannot any how be contented to view this wonderful universe, and especially the nature of man and to conclude that everything is the result of brute force. I am inclined to look at every thing as resulting from designed laws with the details, whether good or bad, left to the working of what we may call chance. Not that this notice at all satisfies me. I feel most deeply that the whole subject is too profound for the human intellect".

All modern scientists follow this idea of Darwin and material approach of human peace and progress, but the animal behaviour of brute force and misery which nature had created has not changed. Ancient people had also formed their own philosophy, world views, myths and stories on the basis of their observations, imagination and perceptions on evolution or origin of life. It became the source materials of our early scientists. These stories are still found in almost all ancient people in different forms and styles throughout the world. Millions of years have passed but there is no controversy regarding the origin of planet Earth or origin of mankind among these people. Modern philosophers and rationalist thinkers are restless and puzzled in seeing the ancient civilization about the genius and ingenuity of these people. The search of reality or truth is in progress. The views and assumptions of these ancient people have now been dismissed. But the modern philosophers and scientists also have proposed assumptions and theories about the origin of universe and life, some of which are equally fictitious and frivolous. But the most accepted and authentic theory is "evolution of life" by Charles Darwin. On this theory he also published a book *Origin of Species* in 1859. This book and his evolutionary theory revolutionized and hyped up the thinking of scientists of the entire world. Its impact was so tremendous and extensive that it almost changed the course of thinking of the modern man. Hendel R. Bird, a prominent American attorney and Yale Law School Graduate argued that simple volume has had a massive influence not only on sciences which increasingly are built on evolutionary assumptions, but on the humanities, theology and government. (p. 40)

In his *Mankind Evolving* eminent biologist Theodosius Dobzhansky observes that the publication of Darwin's book in 1859 "marked a turning point in the intellectual history of mankind" and ushered in a new understanding of man and his place in the universe. He observes that even a hundred years after Darwin, the idea of evolution is becoming an integral part of man's image of himself. The idea has percolated to much wider circle than biologists which even scientists understood or misunderstood. It is a part of mass culture". (p. 40)

Writing in *Scientific American* for September 1978, Harvard scientist Emest Mayr, observed that "man's world view today is dominated by evolution, and he stated in science magazine for June, 1972, that not only eliminated man's anthropocentrisom, but affected every metaphysical and ethical concept, it consistently applied. Rene Dubois observed in *American Scientist* for March, 1965, the "evolutionary concept are applied also to social Institutions and to the arts. Indeed most political parties as well as schools of theology, sociology, history or arts accept these concepts and make them the basis of their doctrines. (p. 41).

Robert B. Downs a former president of the American Library Association, writes concerning the influence of Darwin's book", of these celebrated names (of the 19th century) and infact among all the millions born in the nineteenth century, none with the possible exception of Karl Marx, did as much as Darwin to change the main trends of thought, and to produce a new outlook in human affairs. Viewed in retrospect Darwin's impression on nearly all major fields of learning was and continuous to be profound. The doctrine of organic evolution has been accepted by biologists, geologists, chemists and physicists, as well as anthropologists, psychologists, educators, philosophers and sociologists. Charles Ellsword declared, when one reflects upon the immense influence which Darwin's work has had in practically all lines of human thought and especially on the biological, psychological and social sciences, one is forced to conclude that Darwin must be given seat of highest honour as the most fructifying thinkers which the nineteenth century produced, not only in England, but in the whole world. And the social significance of Darwin's teaching is even yet only beginning to be apprehended. (p. 41)

Anthony West concurred, in writing of the *Origin of Species*, the effect was truly tremendous. Almost by mere statement of a new principle of approach, dynamic not static, he revolutionized every department of study from astronomy to history from paleontology to psychology from embryology to religion (p. 41). Evolutionary theory is so widely accepted and its world view is so dominant in the modern world that every generation accepted it without question, interpreting all facts of the natural world in the light of its alleged truth" (p.73).

Rene Dubois, one of the country's leading ecologists stated in *American Scientist* "most enlightened persons now accept as a fact that everything in the cosmos from heavenly bodies to human beings has developed and continuous to develop through evolutionary process" (p. 73). Noted geneticist Richard Gold Schmidt of the University of California, stated in *American Scientist* "evolution of the animal and plant world is considered by all those entitled to judgement to be a fact for which no further proof is needed" (p. 72). Sir Julian Huxley wrote that "our present knowledge indeed forces us to view that the whole of reality is evolution." This is why Dobzhansky could observe that evolution comprises all the stages of the development of the universe, the cosmic, biological and human or cultural development. Life is a product of the evolution of inorganic nature and is a product of life (p. 43). In these statements we see the impact of evolution, how deep and extensive it is. The birth of *Darwin's Leap of Faith* – p. 72, 73 of first species of every living being is through evolution by itself. The evolution of this species or origin of life cannot be verified because it occurred once and for all, there is no repetition. The second and subsequent generation of the species is not by evolution but by reproductive development. Lineal descent cannot be sustained by unilinear notion of evolution. As there are many contingencies in human life as accident and diseases are surely to occur in life span of an individual. It is supposed that humans were helpless on pre-historic times on these accounts and hence the growth of human population was also slow. Peopling the world by Homonids or Homo Sapiens was not easy as we generally think today. It is after the Neolithic period that humans made rapid development.

What prompted me to write this book on *Mankind in Quest of the Self* is with the object of highlighting the human origin on the basis of our predecesor data surfacing presently in the world. Secondly to explain evolutionary theory against the event and evidencc wherein a human mother gave birth to animal kids, and availability of human foot prints on the surface of a sedimentary rock in Jharkhand, India.

The human origin have also been explained on the basis of a notion of creation prevalent among the descendants of ancient indigenous people. The notion is outside the biblical notion of creation and it is stated to be as old as the evolution of the planet itself. And since Darwin has given new trend of thinking to the world through evolutionary theory all the available data will be explained against the backdrop of this theory.

Some of the events and evidences related to scientific field affected my mind greatly. I would like to mention these how it all happened. Education, communication, and electricity all these modern urban facilities arrived late to my community and are a recent phenomena. Evolution was a strange notion in educational institutions. In my early childhood days, I used to observe women in group of eight or ten holding piglets or goat kids in their lap, visiting one village after another telling women of the household of those kid's birth from human mother. It was a strange story and by custom at that time, was considered a national disease and needed to be warded off from the national boundary. The issue was birth of an animal kid from a human mother which was that they considered as national disease by the people and its repetetion must be stopped. It could have been a great scientific news like "big bang" had it got publicity in the modern media and T.V. In this case, nobody ever tried to confirm or verify the truth, people accepted it as a fact. And remained purely a superstitious belief, but this cannot be examined or tested from the point of Darwinian's evolutionary principle. It may have been a scientific fact, but as all such cases cannot be verified scientifically, it is accepted as a fact. It is an example of Darwin's evolution by mutation or natural selection or genetics function of reshuffling on a case of cross breeding. One such case was reported in TOI in the 5th March 1999 issue in which a human chip hybrid was created through laboratory. The piglet mentioned in the case, however was not a cross breeding and a fit case of origin through para mutation. When an animal species was born from a human mother – a wholly different species from human. Such cases may have occurred earlier also and considered as National disease but no evidence is available due to lack of reporting. In this case, without confirmation or verification the birth of piglet or goat kids from human mother was accepted as a fact through hear say only. Whether it is possible to take birth of a complete different species from another species? This may have happened when modern humans took birth from Homonids. Had this case been proved or verified? Or we simply assume, as true or a fact?

Similarly when Darwin first proposed the evolutionary theory the ideology in principle, spread like wild fire, without its confirmation. Principle of evolution in the initial years was actually a blind or superstitious belief as it was based on observation only.

During the sixties when I was in the university the evolutionary thinking among the scholars of Anthropology Department was immense and accordingly all study materials, laboratories, and museums were designed to meet the objective of study. The idea of evolution and descent of man for students of Anthrology was interesting. The study of man interested me the most, as there was human foot print on the sedimentary rock at my native village whose origin and antiquity had puzzled me and I was desirous to know its reality.

Another interesting event occurred during my childhood days. Radio and Television were not there in those days, and electricity was only found in urban areas.

One evening at about eight or nine o'clock I was sitting for dinner. Suddenly the night turned into day and cock began to crow and the birds on the trees began to chirp as if it has become morning. I ran out to the open courtyard and began to scan the eastern sky towards the rising sun. I was surprised to see a burning ball of the size of rising or setting sun to the south of my house in the sky hurtling away from east to west leaving behind flames of fire about fifteen feet long at high speed silently at thirty to forty degree angle from the earth. And in a moment, it was gone and disappeared from the sight and everything became normal as earlier.

I was amused to see the event and discussed it with my parents. They did not see the event and were unaware of it. As they were rustic and non-literate, they had neither seen nor heard anything like it before in their lives. They were as ignorant as I was then. Next day, I enquired about the event from the village people, but nobody had seen the event and knew nothing of it. There was no science subject in the school those days and I did not get an idea on the matter. The issue vanished in the blue eternally, like its sudden appearance, but it left a deep impact in my mind.

Science and Technology had developed tremendous and extensively. But as far as, the evolution of Homo Sapiens or modern man is concerned, we are still on the dark, as neither the evolutionary theory nor the creation theory have given us concrete proof of origin. The evolutionary theory which is accepted by almost all the modern scientists tells us that humans have descended from ape man or man ape and still are busy in search of missing link. Geneticists now tell us that humans have a distinct species – Human species. But how it evolved is another question to be answered. Whether modern humans have originated from Homonids or African "Eve" who made the Laotian foot prints in Tanzania. We are still in search of the true brand in the evolutionary family tree.

What has made us different from monkeys or great apes or for that matter any other animal is that humans have more copies of a possible important brain gene in their genome than other apes. The new study performed by Magdale – Popesco and colleagues at the University of Colorado detailed in the *Journal Science* called MGC 8902, the gene is implicated in the function of the Neocortex, the region of the brain that in humans is responsible for consciousness, language, and other higher cognitive functions. The researchers compared the genomes of humans to several ape species including chimpanzees, gorillas, macaques and baboons. They found that the more closely related the apes were to humans, the more copies of MGC 8902 they had in their genomes. Humans had 212 copies of the genes, chimps had 37 copies and macaques 30. Scientists also recently linked another gene – called HARI, to the unique cognitive abilities of humans.

They found that HARI, a gene important for brain development in numerous animals, has undergone accelerated evolution in humans, racking up many more mutations than would be expected by chance. (reported in TOI), on this point Darwin wrote that early man was simply an anthropoid animal equipped with a better brain than his cousin anthropoid. (p.86)

Darwinism and Marxism have made great impact on the thinking of modern man. It greatly affected the human behaviour and morality and endangered their peace and security. In twentieth century, Hitler's and communist's brutality were seen as a result of the impact of Darwinism and as is stated that science played a critical role in the age of atrocities. According to evolutionary principle there can be no special sacred character to life since it simply arose by chance. It has no ultimate meaning, no sacred value. "Scientist is not concerned for human existence (survival) or his value. He takes existence for granted (p. 62 J.C. Greene). This view is even found among the modern day terrorists. Dr. Rajat Mitra, psychologist and Director of the *Swanchetan*, NGO, studied terrorist mentality which was reported by journalist Meenakshi in the TOI in the front page on 3rd December 2008, that "the terrorist see humans as objects". It is not only the terrorist mentality but mentality of the modern. Scientists who see every earthly being also ordinary humans as material objects, and not as an intelligent human being worthy of respect hold the same view with terrorist. Similar reporting also appeared on *CBS* Evening News special of 21 and 22 February, 1985, a terrorist communique as life has no special sacred character. Hate is your law and revenge is your first privilege". (p. 36). As humans according to Darwin's view inherit the mentality, character, attitude, and bevaviour of animals, he is still an animal and not human.

Human feeling of love and peace is lacking in Darwin's philosophy and their disciples. For it he blames the creator not of evolving species of this behaviour.

Mumbai like horrific incidence were evident on native people of Tasmania where they were completely exterminated. It was widely believed in the nineteenth century that the Tasmanians were a living link between modern humans and their primitive ancestors. Given the pre-suppositions of naturalistic evolution, the Tasmanian people were often seen as less than human and consequently, many people felt that it was not wrong or immoral to treat them like animals. This attitude eventually influenced behaviour which resulted in the total extermination of the native Tasmanians. Today, it is concluded that they were a distinct racial group similar to Australian aborigines that possessed a unique culture and were fully human. This event is one of many examples of the numerous tragedies that evolutionary naturalism has produced in modern times. (p. 34).

J.C. Greene in his book Darwin and the *Modern World View* (p. 45) sums up in his concluding remarks "we cannot know what Darwin's thought would be if he could survey the course of his ideas and events since he wrote, but we can state our own conclusion. Although Darwin contributed powerfully toward shaping the dominant world view of twentieth century, it settled nothing in either philosophy or theology. This is not surprising in view of the relations between science and world view. Every great scientific synthesis stimulates efforts to view the whole of reality in its terms, and Darwin' theory of natural selection was no exception. But the views of reality that originate in this way are not themselves scientific, nor are they subject to scientific verification. They attempt to make sense not only of the facts "out them" held at arm's length by the observer, but also of facts "in here", facts such as our awareness of our existence, our appreciation of beauty, our sense of moral accountability, our communion with the source of being.

Facts of the latter kind lie close to the heart of reality, but they do not lend themselves to scientific formulation. Attempts to explain them scientifically end by explaining them away. But science itself then becomes unintelligible. A scientist is a person seeking insight into the harmony of things. The harmony and human spirit seeking to comprehend are there first. They are pre-scientific. Darwin seems never to have grasped the implications of this fact. He had a profound intuition of the harmony of nature, of her "endless forms most beautiful and most wonderful" but he distrusted his intuitions. He distrusted them, his autobiography shows, because he feared that they could be explained scientifically as told from man's animal past. Having doubted the reality of spirit, he suffered in spirit the consequences of his doubt. There is no escape from reality, least of all from spiritual reality. In so far as our own world view, deriving from Darwin, Freud, Marx, Comte and innumerable other sources, deny the reality of spirit, whether human or divine, we too must pay the price of that denial."

"Basic thinking of Darwin's evolutionary theory was that the species by themselves may make constant improvement for the better in each generation in morphology, in mental capacity and in behaviour. But neither brutal behaviour of animals nor their mental capacity, nor their morphology improved, which Darwin had anticipated. Its notion of survival of the fittest confirmed in the might is right and brutality of the animals which Darwin had lamented. He had blamed God the creator for creating such behaviour and had anticipated it will be changed through evolutionary process. Darwin had assumed that all living beings are objects and born to animal species. But his evolutionary thinking of improvement could not bring out the desired result.

In writing this book, I was greatly inspired by my late beloved son, Herman Neeraj Topno, who had created a website on "tribal life style" in my name with an avowed objective to make a regular contribution on dying life style of this vanishing human group, in his short span of life, but I could not do so because of my, health problem due to attack of stroke to me. I was both physically and mentally helpless, but assured him to contribute as soon as I get a little respite. In the meantime, he himself got bed ridden and was hospitalized. This made us separated from each other forever as he could not return from Hospital in spite of my ill-health, his memory inspired me to complete the book, though a little late. During all these period my wife Angelina was in constant solace and companion to me and

I am very grateful to her.

Sereng Alva, my eldest daughter agreed to undertake the typing work inspite of her pre-occupation in her various household duties. She spared some time daily in this work and slowly completed the whole book. How diligently she did the typing is worth appreciable. Her dedication besides her engagement, is beyond my imagination. I express deep gratitude to her for all this. While Hazel Nutan, my younger daughter helped me with all correspondence with the publishers and in all my personal works. She deserve all thanks from me.

The assessment of human origin from bird's egg have been from the Santhal tradition of Dr. P.C. Hemrom's book – *Santhali a Natural Language*, 2006, New Delhi. I gratefully acknowledge to him.

Assessment of human origin is a very difficult job when the process is continuous. To arrive at the right conclusion on this issue, references, have been taken from imminent scholars and authors of the world as well as up to date informations available in print media and particularly the scientific journals, without the help of which the "mankind's quest of the self" could not have been completed. I gratefully acknowledges to them all irrespective of mentioning their personal names.

An attempt to link up the event and story in historical perspective have been done, but I am not sure how far this has been achieved. Lacuna may be innumerable but attempt is human endeavour and this is one specimen.

September, 2011. **Sem Topno**

2

Origin of Universe

The question of origin has been the biggest issue for humans since the ancient times. Earlier it was accepted that it was created by one super human being. This view was abandoned by the rationalist thinkers, since then various theories have been proposed for its origin but no one was found satisfactory. No idea is permanent and like creation theory, this also had to face the same fate. The origin entails more questions than answers. The first question that crops up in the mind was where from the materials making up the universe came into existence? and how the material was made? How did it form out of nothing? With a priory notion of creator? The notion of origin is thus shrouded with mystery. Everybody is inquisitive to know the basic question. The natural science was not concerned with explaining the origin of things. Its task was to name, classify and describe, to investigate the uses of things to discover natural systems like the solar system and display their structure and design. Till now nobody has ever suggested satisfactory answer or presented a clue to this effect. As every thing to be constructed by observation and perception, the answer lies in human ideas and is approached by only through the assumption which also takes a round about turn on the question of origin. Astronomers and physicians were vigorously engaged in debate on this issue till today. It was now generally agreed on the assumption that either the material making up the universe came into existence automatically out of nothing at some particular moment of time or else, it has always existed in which case the universe has infinite past. Some of the scientists assume that the universe came into being of out of nothing. Scientists also hold this view with respect to origin of life that it always existed.

There are two basic theories regarding the origin of universe – (1) evolutionary and (2) cyclic. According to evolutionary idea, all the matter of the universe was suddenly automatically created at certain point of time out of nothing in the form of primeval "fire ball" or "atom". This atom exploded with great force called "big-bang", like volcanic eruptions, sending materials outward in all directions. At the big bang itself, the universe is thought to have had zero size and so to have been initially hot. But as the universe expanded the temperature cooled, the fire ball or gas cloud cooled an observable phenomena like planets, stars, and galaxies were formed. Notion of life also existed with big-bang associated with cloud of dust and gas. The universe, thus, had a definite beginning and went on further exploding and expanding forever without limit. There were several big and small big bangs or hissing type of eruptions. In this process, innumerable stars and galaxies were formed successively.

The big bang has given birth to Physics and Chemistry and the physical world. It is also assumed if the energy of big-bang can overcome or equal the force of all the gravity, the universe will soon expand forever, but if the gravity dominate the receding Universe, the expansion may slow down and start coming closer and closer until they are all clumped together in catastrophic. Thus, collision producing another big bang after which the expansion starts a new and the whole process of creation repeated again. On this cyclic pattern the universe will never end but will be reborn periodically.

The 'steady state' theory of the universe though now in disfavour, also postulates the "white hole" concept. The theory implies that matter is constantly created "out of nothing" elsewhere in the universe. It was initially pictured that matter some how is formed uniformly through the space, but the "white hole" idea would allow for matter to be created in numerous localized spots. Thus, the theory hypothesized that the universe has always existed and it will exist forever so that old stars and galaxies die out turning into "black hole" and they are replaced by new system formed from materials which was spontaneously created out (spewed out) of nothingness in some unexplained manner. The "steady state" theory is philosophically satisfying, but unfortunately as with other theories, it has not stood up the observational tests. If it were true, then the galaxies would always have had the same sort of average distribution and if we could have looked at the universe thousands of millions of years ago, it would have seemed specifically very late from the universe we see today.

Geoffrey Barbidge and Jayant Narlikar, on the other hand believe on "Quasi Steady State" cosmology. They attribute, the universe to a series of mini-bangs in which creation and destruction are a constant process. They say that the beginning and the end of the universe are determinable. Hawkings speaks of an "imaginary time" which runs in perpendicular direction to rear time follows from past to future a dimension of space time running in a different direction. Time, has such, as no beginning or end. Cosmic time may have no beginning or end.

Where from the matter comes is one of the vexed question often asked for which three possibilities may be suggested. It is assumed that nature is always there in existence visible or invisible in the form of gas and dark matter or God's particles. Matter in the universe is concentrated in gas clouds and mineral dust or atom ingress with their refinement of planets and satellites in neutron stars and in black hole. It may be that our universe co-exists with other universe, as it is believed several other universe also exist, with which in normal run of things, we have no contact except the energy of space time singularities, or either the matter disappear into black hole and reappear elsewhere in our universe. Matter disappearing though black hole may emerge out in white hole in another universe and vice versa. Matter from another universe may enter ours. In other words we might regard the big-bang as the ultimate white hole (p. 110, 1979 Moor & Nicolson). This big-bang was actually a black hole of some other gaseous or vice versa which turned into white hole originating our universe.

There is a fascinating possibility that the universe itself is a black hole even now. Also, there is no logical objection to the concept of universe within or upon universe, just as there is no objection, in principle, to the co-existence of two or more universe with communication between them via black hole and white hole. (p. 112, 1979 Moor & Nicolson). However, having ranged from concept of a microscopic mini black hole to considering the entire universe as a black hole, the speculation needs further probing. These are just hypothetical ideas.

Whatever may be the assumption, however, facts favour an evolutionary universe beginning with a big bang many millions years ago, about 15 million years, let us look ahead. On this assumption we try to assess the turn. There are two possibilities, either the universe continues to expand forever without limit, or the expansion totally ceased, in which case mutual gravitational attraction, will cause the universe to collapse. The galaxies will begin to move toward, each other until they are all clumped together or they come to the state of singularity. At this stage, a new big bang or mini-big-bang will occur and a new expansion begins. This cyclical expansion and contraction may continue forever, and may have been going on forever, since the original big-bang, here on this universe or else on other universe.

The imminent author of "cosmos" Carl Sagan says, "that if the general picture of an expanding universe and a big-bang is correct, we must then confront still more difficult questions. What were conditions like at the time of big-bang? What happened before that? Was there a tiny universe, devoid of a matter and then, the matter suddenly created from nothing? How does that happen? In many cultures it is customary to answer that one of the ancestors or one super nature's power or God or presently an intelligent designer created the universe and everything in it out of nothing. Greeks, Hebrews, Hindus and most of all ancient people of the world have this view. Then, our immediate next question, will be where from God comes from?"

And the answer will be in the same fashion that he is the "Sui-generis". And that He, and the universe always existed. These questions were answered at the time when humans were at the evolutionary stage of developmental process economically, philosophically, linguistically, and socially and had attained less sophistication in these fields. Conceptually, "creation idea was most suitably used by ancient authors and almost all ancient human society has formulated creation story initially either from their own body, or through cosmic egg or through clay images. It is not that the ancient people did not perceive or conceive evolutionary process of development like origin automatically out of nothing. If research is to be done on linguistic vocabulary of the ancient people, word of creation or evolution or word denoting to origin may be available. Generally, the first creator of human being is treated as one of their own people and addressed as "father" and acts as teacher, guide, and leader and is considered as the first progenitor of the people. But it is strange that this first creator of human beings is always found missing at the end of the event among all human beings wherever the creation story is told. So, the ancient human always did habitat in family and community and lived a life of peace and harmony at the hidden presence of the "father" or "leader". Evolutionary theory does not teach living with solar in harmony but sees the ancients as brute. As the worm or cell is the first life who by self origin or sui-generis so also the decision being identified as God or designer was by sui-generis.

Astronomers using X-ray satellite called "Chandra" have revealed that "the expansion of the universe seem to be according to galaxies flying apart faster with time, under the influence of anti-gravitational force – the dark energy". Dark energy acting as an anti-gravity force drives the turbo-expansion of the universe at a run-away rate, believes particle physicist Michio Katy. Finally, it will wind down, as temperatures drop uniformily to zero. It seems indisputable that unless we can escape from the earth all intelligent life must die he intones.

So where does the parallel universe spring from? They are part of the M-theory cosmology which assumes that our universe is an infinite membrane floating in higher dimensional space occasionally gravity attracts a nearby membrane and two universe collide in an explosion of energy that Kaku terms "the big splate". This creates a new universe like a budding soap bubble.

At the moment, we have no other alternative but to accept the modern scientific myth or theory of big-bang till it is proved wrong some day. Those creation stories too, are worthy of our deep respect. One of the creation stories belongs to Eastern philosophy is that there are cycles in nature. The God created being and the cycles. The Hindu faith is the only one of the world's great faiths dedicated to the idea that the cosmos itself undergoes an immense indeed an infinite number of deaths and births. It is the only faith in which the time scale correspond, no doubt, by accident to those of modern scientific cosmology. Its cycles run our ordinary day and night to a day and night of Brahma, 8.64 billion years long, longer than the age of the earth or the sun and about half the time since the big-bang. And there are much longer time scales still.

Since the big-bang, the universe has been expanding and will continue to expand forever. The expansion may gradually slow, stop and reverse itself if there is less than a certain critical amount of matter in the universe, the gravitation of the receding galaxies will be insufficient to stop the expansion, and the universe will run away forever. But if there is more matter than we can see, hidden away in black hole, say or in hot invisible gas between the galaxies – then the universe will hold together gravitationally and particle of a very Indian succession of cycles, expansion followed by compression, universe upon universe, cosmos without end, if we live in such an oscillating universe, then the big-bang is not the creation of the cosmos but merely the end of the previous cycle, the destruction of the last incarnation of the cosmos.

Neither of these modern cosmologies may be altogether to our liking. In one, the universe is created, some how, ten or twenty billion years ago and expands forever, the other galaxies mutually receding until the last one disappears over our cosmic horizon. Then the galactic astronomers are out of business, the stars cool and die, matter itself delays and the universe becomes a thin cold haze of elementary particles. In the other, the oscillating universe the cosmos has no beginning and no end and we are in the midst of an infinite cycle of cosmic deaths and rebirths with no information trickling through the cusps of the oscillation. Nothing of the galaxies, stars, planets, life forms or civilizations evolved in the previous incarnation. The universe oozes into the cusp, flutters past the big-bang to be known in our present universe. The fate of the universe in either cosmology may seem a little depressing, but we may take solace in the time scale involved. These will even occupy tens of billions of years, or more.

The universe is not static, it is a congeries of growing organisms, each one which is an absolute creator. There are indeed as many universe – that is to say fluctuating temporary adjustment of "selves" and "not-selves" as there are living organisms, and it comes more and more to be evident that there are no lacunae of chemical or magnetic energy, no blind oasis of matter-that are not portions of the mysterious organisms of living things. (Powys p. 168)

"All argument is based upon an illusion that there exists in space-time or behind space-time, some static objective system of relations and values, some arrangement of forces, colours, laws of human nature, process of imagination chemistry, electricity, working of psychology, methods of evolution which taken together constitute the truth. There is no such thing what we can call nature or the universe is a congeries of mysterious units of energy each with a material side and a psychic side, which are perpetually, by an ultimate and absolute movement of sheer essences, creating new worlds. (p.176, Powys, 1960)

The Planet Earth

Geologists entered the twentieth century beset by mysteries enigmatic pattern of earthquakes and volcanoes, continents shaped like puzzle pieces and beds of the same fossils on opposite sides of the oceans. By the mid- 1960's enough evidence had been collected for most to accept a revolutionary answer for a multitude of questions – geology's grand theory of Plate tectonics. Using this theory, earth's scientists explain charning in Earth's inner layers, prehistoric climates, drifting continents and spreading seas. As before their work is grounded in the physical make up of the planet. But new technologies allow them to drill over deeper into ice caps and sea floors, gathering data about the distant pass.

Six hundred and fifty million years ago (*National Geographic*, May 1998) on a planet already four billion years old, a super continent was fragmented into pieces that were half submerged under high seas. Over several hundred million years, the pieces re-assembled then broke apart again migrating thousands of miles to become the continents we know today. The magnitude of this transformation has become clear only in this century, with the theory of plate tectonics.

First attempt at reconstructing past worlds based on the incomplete theory of continental drift relied on geologic formations and the shapes of continents. "It is just as if we need to refit the torn pieces of a newspaper by matching their edges and then check whether the lines of print run smoothly across," wrote Alfred Wegner who in 1915 used the coast of Africa and South America to construct the super continent Pangea.

The reconstruction on the map created by Paleographer Christopher R. Scoteses of the University of Texas at Arlington, Synthesis recent work. Like Wegner, Scotes considers the evidence of ancient fossil beds and races that have been split along complementary coastlines by younger begins. Unlike Wegner, Scotese uses radio active isotopes to date informations and plot their positions in relation to the poles by measuring ancient magnetic fields. The current technique reveals the latitude but not the longitude of past continents, so these reconstructions involve informed guesses. The most distant evidence sketches back to 1.1 billion years ago when all land but north central Africa was gathered in a super continent called "Rodenia", which what is now North America at its centre.

The earth was born like other planets from gas and dust of the early solar system. It was then bombarded for its first 700 million years by countless smaller bodies and threw enough debris into its orbit to have created a disc like around the planet from which the moon was created.

Glowing from energy of millions of impacts and radioactive decay, the young planet earth would soon be covered with oceans of magma and rafts of solid matter. As the surface cooled, these rafts cohered into a solid crust over a molten mantle.

Meanwhile the planet's interior was busily sorting itself out. Iron and nickel sank to the core, while lighter elements rose to the surface. An atmosphere formed rich in water and carbon dioxide, but lacking free oxygen, water returned to the surface as rain, forming the first ocean.

Enriched by meteorites and comets, the shallow water around thousands of volcanic islands were laden with chemical compounds especially of carbon, the most essential element for life. From this primordial soup, life would emerge in the form of single celled bacteria capable of reproduction. Vast communities build up semi-submerged mounds called stomata lites. Formation of successive layers of sediments happen by microorganisms from structures dominating the tidal flats ringing Earth's developing continents.

While life evolved at sea, earth's continents formed. Riding crusted plates over a plastic mantle, they would assemble into super continents, only to split apart and reassemble in new ways.

After the earliest known super continent "Rodinia" began to split apart 750 million years ago spreading centres opened huge ocean basins pushing one group of pieces north and the other south over the pole. Mountains rose and glaciers grow on high peaks even at the equator as the northern fragment collided with what is now Africa. By 600 million years ago, all the fragments had reunited forming another continent, "Pannotia".

Laurentia (North America) collided with Baltica (Northern Europe) and later with Axatonia (Britain and New England) a fragment of Gondwana 390 million years ago. The Caladonian mountains and northern Appalachians were thrust upon along the boundary. As the continents squeezed together, ocean basins widened and sea levels uncovering more land and withdrawing self water barriers between rivers and lakes. Fresh water fish migrated freely, and plants colonized land. Later as carbon rich vegetarian was buried, carbon levels in the atmosphere fell, allowing earth to cool.

A chunk of Pannotia tore off and drifted north, leaving the continent of Gondwana at the south pole. As the fragment approached equatorial latitudes, it splintered into three parts that were mostly submerged between lazy worm, shallow seas – when multi-cellular animals with exoskeletons first appeared

570 million years ago. The sudden abundance of fossil evidence, after three million years of primitive life is called the Cambrian explosion.

About 300 million years ago, Gondwana and northern continents collided creating Pangea, a landmass that stretched from pole to pole. Within opened Telhys, ancestor of the Mediterranean around the super continent lay the Panthalassic ocean, ancestor of the Pacific. The enlarged ocean basin caused sea level to fall, withdrawing the north-south land barrier which blocked ocean current that circulated oxygen. Scientists speculate that those events and a vast outpouring of lava in Siberia may have caused earth's largest extinction, 250 million years ago, surviving reptile spread across Pangea, evolving into diverse forms that gave rise to the dinosaurs.

During late Paleozoic times (255 million years ago), the continent of Laurentia, Siberia, Baltica and Gondwana moved closer together until by the early Permian, they were fused together to form the super continent "Pangea". Centered on the Equator, Pangea stretched from north pole to south pole and separated the Palao – Tetheys ocean to the east from the Panthalassic ocean to the West India was nestled in the Pangea at high southerly latitutde. Pangea began to break up rifting into three parts : (1) Eurasia – North America, (2) Africa-South America and (3) Antartica, Australia and India. Next, about 170 million years ago, each of these pieces divided, perhaps pushed apart by hot plasma rising from mantle. The fragmentation isolated land such as, marshy plains and created a warm climate for dinosaurs. Nearly formed mid-ocean ridges displaced seas, flooding continents with heat absorbing waters, while shallow seas between continents carried equatorial currents towards poles.

During the Silurian and Devonian (439 – 462Y) the land mass that occupied southern hemisphere consisting of Africa, South America, Antartica, south Australia, and all waded to each other as stated above, had been moving northward. During the late 290 years BP this landmass hit north America and Europe. The collision created mountain ranges in southern and eastern North America, in North West Africa and across, central Europe. Meanwhile, Siberia moved westward and collided (p. 448 *Planet Earth*) with Europe, from the east forming the Urals. By the end of this period, all landmass, except China formed a single super continent that stretched from pole to pole. This super continent was called Pangea. Pangea thus surrounded by single ocean called Panthalass. On the eastern side of Pangea, Panthalass extended eastward into the broad gulf called Telhys, bounded on the north by China and on the south by Australia.

Glaciation started at the beginning of the 322-296 million years ago, around the south pole and extended northward to cover eastern south America, South Africa, Madagascar, India and Western Australia. A much smaller ice sheet, probably developed over north eastern Siberia, which was located to the north pole. Meanwhile, north America and Europe enjoyed a tropical climate. Ice advanced and retreated many times during the glaciation. Each ice advance caused a drop in sea level.

During the last glaciation, temperatures and sea levels dropped across the central part of India, which was still drifting away from what had been Gondwana. Volcanic eruptions released huge floods of lava as well as dust and aerosols that blanketed the planet blocking solar radiation and mixing with water vapour to fall as acid rain. But the reason most scientists give for why half the world plant and animal species, including all the dinosaurs became extinct lies on the Yucatan peninsula and in the Gulf of Mexico, where a trillion ton asteroid or cornet moving at 100,000 miles per hour, left the 173 mile wide Chicxulub crater. Far more powerful than any volcanic eruption, the explosive impact set off storms, tsunamis and global forest fires. Dust and acid gas rising high in the atmosphere left earth cold and in darkness.

The stratigraphy of Gondwana, the southern half of Pangea, was markedly different from that of the northern half.

From the beginning of the carboniferrus to the end of the Triassic, thick continental deposits accumulated in South America, south Africa, MaDagascar, India, Australia and Antartica. These sediments are largely fluvial, lacastrine and deltaic formed by the rivers that emerged from the huge ice cap that covered the south polar regions. These rivers had a long way to go before finally reaching the ocean. To the south there was the ice cap and the continental margins to the south – west and the south-east were active. The rivers could flow only toward the north-east away from the active margins, filling basins and erupting into the Tethys gulf.

The Gondwana deposits are characterized nearly every where by Tillits at the bottom. There are followed by sand stone and sholes several kilometers thick, with coal beds. They are capped by basaltic flows of Jurassic age upto one km thick, the result of the breakings of Pangea. The Gondwana deposits attain an aggregate thickness of upto 10 km. These form the Gondwana Geo-system of India and the Karoo system of Africa. In Madagascar and Australia there are marine interculations within the thick continental depths and there is no basalt at the top.

From Permian to Triassic (246 – 245 million years ago) the eastern Gondwana remained as a great Gondwana landmass. Consisting of South America, South Africa, Antartica, MaDagascar and Australia and greater India. Indian ocean was non-existent during this period.

The middle and large Jurassic (241-160 million years age) widening of the north Antic rift and the creation and widening of the rift between Gondwana (South America-Africa) and Eastern Gondwana (Madagascar) Sychells-India-Antartica-Australia.

Africa Separated from India-Malagascar Block during 150-160 Million Years Ago

India – Madagascar block broke-up from Antartica-Australia block around 120-130 million years ago and South

America also separated from Africa during this time. Madagascar separated from India around 135 million years ago. India remained an island continent for 100-180 million years. During the end of cretaceous (70 million years) India moved northward and collided with greater Somalia. Sometimes in early Eocene (55-35) India made contact with Asia. A rift was formed between Indo-Somalia and Syehelles at K.T. boundary 65 million years ago.

Australia and Antartica Separated 55 Million Years Ago

The middle cretaceous was characterized by widespread anoxic conditions in the world ocean. It dropped that many times between 125 and 85 million years ago, the ocean had no dissolved oxygen below a depth of 30 cm. or so. During anoxic period the ocean simply was not overturning that is there were no waves.

When India moved to north, Indonesia i.e. Eastern part of Asia also moved to the east. Collusion of India with Asia or

Table 2
Continental land Masses Containing India

	Landmasses	*Events*
1.	Pangaea	Formation of the Super Continent Pangaea with Paleo Tethys-225 Ma
2.	Gondwana	Rift in Pangaea to form Gondwana and Laurasia, 180 Ma.
3.	East Gondwana	Rift between West & East Gondwana, 160 Ma.
4.	Africa	Break up of Africa from Indo-Madagascar Block, 150 -160 Ma
5.	Antarctica	Break up of Indo-Madagascar from Antarctica and Australia, 125-130 Ma
6.	Indo-Madagascar-Seychelles	Indo-Madagascar-Seychelles separates from Antarctica-Australia, 120 Ma
7.	Indo-Madagascar-Seychelles-continent	Brief isolation of Indo Madagascar Seychelles, 100 Ma

(Contd.)

(Contd. Table 2)

	Landmasses	*Events*
8.	Indo-Seychelles island	90 Ma
9.	Indo-Seychelles	Separate from Madagascar, Brief Isolation, 88 Ma
10.	Indo-Seychelles-Greater Somalia	Collision of Indo-Seychelles with Greater Somalia, 70 Ma Contact with Africa
11.	Indo-Greater Somalia	Indo –Greater Somalia Separates From Seychelles, 65 Ma, Shiva impact
12.	India	India, separates from Greater Somalia, 60 Ma
13.	India contact Asia	Collision of India with Asia, disappearance of Tethys Ocean,51 Ma, Arabian sea formed.
14.	Indo-Asia	India collided with Asia, Sub Duction of Greater India, Rise of the Himalayas, 20 Ma, Indian Ocean Formed.

Tibet took place 35 million years ago. The water of the Tethys sea found its way to the Arabian Sea as well as to the Bay of Bengal and formed Indian Ocean in the vacant region between Africa, Antartica, India and Australia. Rest of the Tethys water in the west flowed down to the Mediterranean sea and in the east to the Pacific ocean via China.

Off shore deposition on Sind-Ganga Plane was made 17-20 million years ago and Himalaya uprising was completed by 15 million years ago.

Changing face of the Earth

Geologists have long prided themselves on their ability to peer into the distant past and discern the slow movements of land and sea that have continuously revised the planet's face over eons. Now drawing on new insights, theories, measurements and technologies they are forecasting the shape of terra firma in the distant future.

The maps and animations by these scientists are helping explain core principles of geology to increasingly wide audiences.

Text books, museums and T.V. shows now routinely feature images of what forecasters say earth will look like and geologists are using the forecasts to deepen their own probe of plate tectonics.

Practitioners acknowledge that their predictions, however intriguing become more theoretical when pushed far into the future, as with advanced weather forecasts. Their most ambitious efforts peer 250 million years ahead. But their more short term predictions, they note, draw on mountains of geophysical data and involve relatively small extrapolations of current trends, like the steady northward march of Southern California.

Despite uncertainties, the field of geology predictions is booming. One website has received almost 30 million hits since its debut in 1998 and the field's admirers now include top scientists. Among other things, the snap shot shows that Africa has drifted to the north, plowing into Europe and fusing the two land masses, eliminating the Mediterranean sea and replacing it with the Mediterranean mountains. The rugged range runs down the middle of a continent far bigger than current day Eurasia, a giant new agglomeration that might be called Afrasia.

In 1982, Scotese got a call from *Discover Magazine* asking if he would consider a bigger project envisioning earth not 50 million years from now but 200 million.

Scotese drew a series of futuristic maps and in the 1990s, found an ideal way to communicate his increasingly detailed vision of the terrestrial past and future over the internet. Today, Scotese's Website, www.scotese.com show cases his work called the paleomat project. His long term forecast portrays a distant time when the world's continents come together again to form a new super continent, which he calls Pangea Ultima.

An animated depiction of Pangea Ultima demonstrates a bold exercise in futuristic thinking. First, the Mediterranean closes, then 25 million to 75 million years from now – Australia moves north slamming into Indonesia and Malaysia before pirouetting counter clock wise to smash into the Philippines and then Asia eventually merging with it. Antartica also moves north scheduling its ice cap. Roughly 100 million years from now, it plows into the Indian Ocean and 50 million years later wedges itself between Madagascar and Indonesia. The Indian Ocean becomes a virtual inland sea.

Zillions of Universe

Cosmology used to be a heartless science, all about dark matter lost in mind bending abysses and exploding stars. But whenever physicists and astronomers gather, the subject that rolls during lunch, coffee breaks or cigarette breaks is not dark matter or the fate of the universe. Rather it is about the role and meaning of life in the cosmos.

According to a controversial notion known as the Anthropic principle, certain otherwise belting features of the universe can only be understood by including ourselves in the equation. The universe must be suitable for life, otherwise we would not be here to wonder about it.

The features in question are mysterious numbers in the equations of physics and cosmology, denoting say the amount of matter in the universe or the number of dimensions, which don't seem predictable by any known theory yet. They are like the Knobson God's control console and they seem almost miraculously tuned to allow life.

A light tweak one way or another from the present settings could cause all stars to collapse into black hole or atoms to evaporate negating the possibility of biology.

If there were only one universe, theorists would have their hands full trying to explain why it is such a lucky one. But supporters of the anthropic principle argue that there could be chance. Their view has been bolstered in recent years by a theory of the big-bang, known as inflation which implies that our universe is only one bubble in an endless chain of them, and by string theory the so called theory of everything whose equation seems to have an almost un-accountable number of solutions each representing a different possible universe.

Only a few of these will be conducive to life, the anthropic argument goes, but it is no more surprise to find ourselves in one of them. It is to find ourselves on the most warm earth rather than in Plate.

In short, we live where we can live but those can be fighting words. Scientists agree that the name "anthropic principle" is pretentious but that's all they agree on. Some of them regard the idea as more philosophy than science. Others regard it as a betrayal of the Einstenian dream of predicting everything about the universe.

David Gross regard it as a virus, "once you get the bug you can't get rid of it", he said.

Called the cosmological constant, anthropic principle is a number that measures the amount of cosmic repulsion caused by the energy in empty space. That empty space should be boiling with such energy, is predicted by quantum theory, and astronomers in the last few years have discovered that some cosmic repulsion seems to be accelerating the expansion of the universe. But theoretical attempts to calculate this constant, also known as lambada result in numbers 1060 times as high as those astronomers have measured. (TOI, Sunday, 6 December, 2003).

Universe

A *NASA* robotic probe analyzing the oldest light from the beginning of time, found the most amazing evidence discovered so far which showed that an instant after coming into existence, the universe suddenly expanded from sub-atomic to cosmological size in less than a blink of the eye.

The Wilkinson Microwave a Anisotropy Probe, found after three years of continuous observation of 13.7 billion years old cosmic microwave background radiation, the after glow of the big-bang when the universe was less than a million years old. Scientists now know that after this initial inflation, the universe carried on expanding thought at a much more leisurely pace. This means the actual universe has to be much larger than what can be observed from earth. In fact, the observable may merely be a point compared to the whole. And this whole, scientists also know, is composed of about 4 per cent real or normal matter 22 per cent so called "dark matter" that is not made of atoms and 74 per cent "dark energy" an unknown mysterious "anti-gravitational force" which makes the universe keep on expanding. The new image of the microwave background is also a giant stop closer towards ultimately witnessing time zero the exact moment of universe began.

Space Odyssey

The largest explosion ever seen in space reveals black holes to be more influential than expected sometimes stifling star formation in a galaxy while globing up trillions upon trillions of gas and creating gas bubbles.

The black hole has blown two huge bubbles into the galaxy showing aside a colossal amount of gas equal to the mass of a trillion suns, or more than all the stars of our own milky way galaxy.

The explosive event is the sort of thing that most likely occurred frequently early in the history of galaxy construction at a time when the universe was smaller and more crowded.

Scientists are surprised that there was enough gas available to this relatively modern black hole to fuel such an outburst.

Studies supporting super massive black holes have not grown so significantly or rapidly in the recent past. The observations could help solve a puzzle over, why some galaxies don't form stars.

As a galaxy matures and cools down, star formation should increase. The scientists figure out why expanding space bubbles continiously replenish the galaxy and its surrounding cluster with energy.

The main effect of eruptions like this is to stop stars from forming the preventing hot gas from cooling down.

Cycle of Creation

The NASA scientists observing Chandra X-Ray telescope reckon the most powerful eruption ever witnessed in the universe to date. The event which has lasted more than 100 million years and generated energy equivalent to hundred of millions of gamma – Ray bursts has enormous amounts of matter have been falling into a super massive black hole. Since astronomers are not sure where such a colossal amount of matter equal in mass to about 300 million suns could came from, they theorise it may be steller gas from the black holes host galaxy itself which, for reasons not fully understood cooled down catastrophically and was wholly cannibalized thereafter.

But to paraphrase an old saying, what goes in must come out. And one way it does is by means of what is called "Hawking radiation" – a construct fashioned by British physicist Stephen Howking in 1976 due to this, a black hole gradually shrinks and it turns out that the rate of radiation increases as the mass decreases, so the black hole continues to radiate more and more intensely and shrink more and more rapidly until it snuffs itself out entirely in the end. So what happens to all the matter previously sucked inside? Scientists think the interior of certain black holes could be connected with a corresponding "white hole" in such a way that matter which has fallen into the black end could pop out of the white one through a link called a "worm hole" where it pops out though is any one's guess. It could be some place billion of light years away from where it entered in a totally different region of the space time continuum or in a past dimension. It could even be in another universe altogether. Whatever, it might be though it initiates yet again another cycle of its continued eternal existence, because in its end is always a new beginning. (TOI January 12, 2005)

The Big Crunch Theory

According to Varun Sahni, Prof. at the interuniversity Centre for Astronomy and Astro-physics, Pune, Right how only the universe is expanding, as galaxies move away from each other. But there may be a time when galaxies move towards each other, then the universe will collapse. This is the Big Crunch Theory. The other theory says that if the universe keeps expanding forever, the sun and stars will exhaust their energy content and collapse into giant black holes.

Jaleel Akhtar, Scientist, Institute for Pulsed Power and Microwave Technolgy, Germany, says, "according to the theory of continuity of the universe, matter creates more matter and the cosmos goes on expanding forever. However, this view has been rejected by an equally large number of scientists who believe in a finite universe, both in terms of span and time."

God, the Uncaused Cause of the Universe

We, the human beings, instinctively sense deep down into our minds and marrow, the existence of a deeper power governing the destiny of the universe. Somewhere in a manner in which our giant telescopes initially glimpsed the fact that the distant galaxies in the universe were receding and that the universe itself was therefore expanding. We seem to catch a fleeting glimmer of a power beyond and behind all that we perceive, a power that guides the course of all that is around us and determines all that ever will be.

It is this universal back drop that has been traditionally referred to as God – the intelligent designer. It is this universal that Albert Einstein tried to explore in its search for a unified field theory, such a unified field theory, the famous scientist thought would explain all gravitational and electomagnetic phenomena. All that we see in the universe could be explained as a result of the inter play of the forces of gravitation and electro magnetion. It is a similar theoretical and logical framework that Stephen Hawking attempted in his "theory of everything". It is this underlying spirit of universal governance that Befram Russel fixed to reach through his enunciation of the principle of deductive logic and mathematics.

But can God be understood, comprehended or even vaguely glimpsed by the human minds. Can the sensors of the most furtile mind even tentatively arrive at a Aoran evanescent moment or the dubitable patent of that universal essence that we call the Divine?

Historically one of the argument that the rationalists have advanced for proving the existence of God, is what is called the first cause argument. Every event we find is a caused event, and the cause itself is the result of a prior event. The destiny of the universe can therefore be traced back in an effect cause sequence. Going back thus in time from effects to cause, we should, theoretically be able to arrive at a first cause. The first cause is the original cause, which is God.

However, this historical and intuitive argument poses an interesting and serious problem. The problem is that it makes out God to be as much a creature of time and space as anything else. God as the culmination of the progress of going backwards down the history of the universe in a temporal effect cause sequence is circumscribed by the boundaries of universe of time and space. But should not God be beyond time and space? If everything around us is God's creation, are not time, and space as much God's creation as everything else? If we recall the profound lines that T.S. Eliot penned in childhood,

If time and space as sages say/ Are things that cannot be/ the butterfly that lives a day/ has lived eternity".

It is this transcendental nature of the divine that the Upanishads evoke in vivid metaphor. "The universal spirit the Pavasha is all this, what has been and what will be, he is also the lord of immortality", says the Svetasvatara Upnishad. The human symbolism is carried further. Its hands and feet are everywhere, its eyes and head are everywhere, its ears are everywhere, it stands encompassing all in the world".

But magically, this human metaphor, metamorphoses into something that Sri Aurbindo called "supramental." Grasping without hands, hasting without feet, he sees without eyes, he hears without ears. He knows that can be known, but no one knows him." As the Svetasvatara Upnishad further elucidates. "He is the beginning producing all the causes, which unite the soul with the body, and being above, the three kinds of time, past, present, and future. He is seen as without parts, after we have worshipped that adorable God, who has forms and who is the true source of all things, as dwelling in our mind."

"Therefore, while God may be immanent, he is also transcendent. He is beyond all the forms of the world and of time, he is the other, from this world moves around." To adapt what Albert Camus said in a different context "God may be with the world, but he is not of the world." Albert Einstein general theory of relativity makes the rare found point that to understand the effect of manifestation, we need to view the universe as a four dimensional space time continuum. We need to transcend our traditional history perceptions of the universe as a three dimensional world coursing through time. Similarly to experience the divine, we need to grow into a supramental and spiritual dimension.

Cosmic Scale

Recently, astronomers shared a unique and uplifting experience as they gazed in reverential silence at an infant universe, barely 300,000 years old. Peering through the powerful lens of a radio telescope – the cosmic background imager with its array of microwave antennas the scientists were taking a peek into our collective cosmic past. The Universe that was about as hot as a cool star, with faint and cool patches. Confirming theories that it all began in a fiery blast some 14 billion years ago, in what cosmologists call the Big-bang.

This newest picture of the cosmos confirms the theory that the cosmos is geometrically largely flat, that it went through an initial inflationary phase that later reduced in intensity, and that it is dominated by mysterious “dark matter” and “dark energy” that are pushing the cosmos and its constituents further apart. The observation from the Andes also helps to buttress theories of galaxy formation with observational data. The cosmic background is believed to be made up of microwave radiation which originated in the aftermath of the Big-bang when the fire ball universe “vary like a ball,” sending out acoustic waves. This heavenly harmony has been detected at different times by researchers who say that on a cosmic scale, the notes are valuable indicators that could explain the geometry of space – time and also help us to gauge if space is indeed warped in parts. As Einstein doubted or if the cosmos is uniformly flat as the proponents of standard cosmological theories would have us to believe. Astronomers might eventually find answers to questions on space – time, the density of the universe and its rate of expansion. But the most crucial question of all is, will we as a species, survive long enough to discover the answers the universe unfolds for us?

Cosmic Challenge

The universe is precisely 13.7 billion years old give or take a few hundred years – reveal computer generated simulation of the first ever cosmic event. In the most awesome instance of cosmic reverse engineering NASA scientists have recreated the birth of the universe by transposing information got from radio wave readings of the Wilkinson Microwave Anisotropy Probe (WMAP). The satellite operating some 1.6 million km from earth, has been relaying valuable information over the past year. The discovery of the most enduring secret – the unique recipe of the primordial soup is bound to revolutionize cosmology. What is the universe made up of ? Just 4 per cent atoms, 23 per cent dark cold matter, composed of undiscovered elementary particles and a huge dollop (73 per cent of dark energy, the mysterious component Einstein chose to call this cosmological constant. Most significantly the findings confirm the Big-bang theory of the origin of the universe, that it is inflationary and expansionist by nature, that the first light dawned 700 million years after the Big-bang, that there is more to know than earlier generations ever dreamt of and that cyber span can effectively be used to project anything from the beginning of time and space till date.

Reconstruction of the past – whether cosmic or terrestrial is becoming increasingly credible because of the quantity and quality of the information we are able to derive with the help of technology. That is how extraordinary scientific breakthrough over the last few decades have occurred from the mapping of the universe, charting the blue prints of the human and other genomes, to highly sophisticated robotic surgery techniques.

Cosmic Karma

Starvation and survival struggles, it seems are not the sole presence of life on earth. Black hole and infant star systems, among other cosmic phenomena are vulnerable too. The colossal black hole in the centre of our galaxy, the milky way is actually starving say scientists, who have been studying it closely, with a mass that's calculated to be three million times that the sun, the hole has been devouring everything around it, and is craving for more. The Chandra – X-ray observatory shows that the deprival black hole is given to regular outbursts visible as flares near the event horizon, the point of the return, past which matter gets sucked into the hole. X- ray emitted by the flares are getting locater indicating that the hole needs more "nourishment", past explosive flares, say researchers. Research shown many of the gases in the neighbourhood, leaving the hole with little to feed on. Would the earth along within solar system end up as black hole feed one day? Charles Tower, the noble laureate who directed the team that discovered the black hole in the centre of the milky way says, we don't have to worry about that for the next hundred million years at least.

Immortality, it seems eludes all cosmic constituents which are as much a part of the Karmic birth – death cycle as we are.

Infant solar system too are facing teething problems reveal telescopic studies of the star groups Orion and Carina Nebulce. While the new stars nearby alongwith universal forces, work out an optimum cosmic birth – death ratio, we, obsessed with self importance continue to believe that we are at the top of the evolutionary peeking order. But our exalted self esteem sadly has not helped us cultivate a cosmic perspective. Every technically advanced country for instance is pre-occupied with nuclear argchais and haggling over natural boundaries, while individuals wage mundane equally pointless battles of their own. Who has the time or the inclination to look to the heavens for inspiration? Since we are much a part of the intricate cosmic design as are amoebas or black holes. It would be intensity to learn a few cosmic lessons. As Carl Sagan puts it what else can be exploration of the cosmos to be other than a Journal of self discovery.

31.01.2002 TOI Black Hole

Nature magazine reports that scientists plan to artificially create a cosmic black hole event on the computer desktop using frozen light to mimic this cosmic phenomenon. This is a natural follow up of astrophysicist and cosmologist Stephen Hawking's theory of black holes which states that radiation is emitted around the event horizon born of sparks created by friction from disappearing objects. Hawking has been saying for the last 30 years, that black holes are not readily black. Now by attempting to uncover the dark secrets of black holes on the desktop, scientists hope to be able to understand the quantum effects of gravity, taking us closer towards "resolving conflicts between general relativity (or the theories of biggest bodies in the universe) and quantum theory (or the rules governing its tiniest constituency)." Those holding up the concept of "Hawking radiation" believe that around the event horizon there is radiation present, due to the enormous friction generated by cosmic objects falling into the black hole. Those sparks in fact help us even locate these celestial bottomless pits. NASA Chandra X-ray observatory has recently captured in pictures, what scientists say is the centre or pinwheel of our galaxy, the milky way, teeming with cannibalizing, exploding and collapsing stars black holes of different shapes, sizes and stages. It is indeed awesome that over a small constituent of such galactic phenomena could be simulated on a computer.

The greater the death throws of disappearing matter, the higher the visibility of the collapsed star and the stronger and more powerful the radiation. The Hawking radiation, if it can be made palpably would be tremendous energy source, ever generating ever present. Allowing for some kite flying if we could only hitch our wagon (earth) to a collapsed star (black hole) it will tantamount to ending our search for renewable sustainable power. However, the universe "through reverse engineering". The Cosmo geeks are after all only trying to fit in the pieces of a cosmic puzzle which sounds realistic search for the philosophers.

Black Hole Among Cluster of Stars

For the first time, experts have spotted a black hole nestled in the middle of a packed star cluster a place that is generally not associated with them.

About 10 times more massive than our sun the black hole was found inside a globular cluster in the elliptical galaxy NGC 4472, located some 50 million light years away from earth in the virgo cluster a black hole is an object whose mass is so concentrated that nothing not even light can escape the strong pull of its gravity from within a certain distance.

The discovery is surprising because some theories predict that gravitational interactions among black holes inside a cluster would simply kick most or all of the black holes out of the cluster.

Scientists think the ejection process works like this because black holes are usually among the facts of life. One of the experiment micro organisms living is marhan top soil. In this test, no organic compounds were ever detected.

Black holes are most massive objects in a globular cluster, they sink to the cluster's centre. There they typically pair up with either a star or with another black hole that has also happened to meander into cluster's middle. A binary system made up of a black hole and a star can be stable, but when two black holes pair up, a strong gravity interactions between them are thought to give one or both the boot.

The fact that NGC 4472 black hole has started ejection suggests it is paired up with a star and not another black hole, the researchers say, "if you look at the numerical simulations that say it's hard to keep black holes in clusters, what they generally say is that the ejection happens because of binary black holes, said study leader Thomas Maccatom an astronomer at the University of Southampton in U.K.

Black Holes are an Enigma

Yet theories of collapsing stars add value to Physics and Maths. The suggestion that light cannot escape an exceptionally strong gravitational field is about 300 years old. Scientists believed that light was particles and that very large, compact stars would not allow light particles to escape. In the 1910s light was seen as wave. The term Black hole emerged later. Relativity stipulates that time and space are interrelated and that space has multiplicity. However, space is one in Eulidean geometry, Relativity adopts Riemannian geometry that is created on the rejection of two Eulidean axioms :parallelism of lines and indefinite extension of a straight line at both ends.

Johann Gauss (1777- 1855) proposed non Euclidean geometry. However, Gouss neither approved nor disapproved that hyperbolic geometry was established using imaginary trigonometry and imaginary geometry George Riemann (1826

– 66) had proposed a variant to hyperbolic geometry based on geodesic or closed space, where the square of the elementary space conformed to curvature. Geodesic forms the mathematical base for relativity.

Euclidean space is valid. The two Euclidean Axioms that are excluded from Riemannian geometry hold when infinity is excluded from the system. The studies of manifolds have established that Euclidean geometry is valid upto the distance of 1027 km in all directions. This limit exceeds what telescopes can observe. The associate of observation is conscious time.

What is conscious time? There is a meta concept of time, meta times which is inert and unusable except as the argument of a multitude of temporal functional firms, time forms like conscious time of every day use. Conscious time is composed of instants and at stream of conscious time that is composed of instants of equal duration is called time form. The time forms that are not conscious time are presently grouped and collectively called para-time.

At the heart of the concept of black holes is the belief that an inert neutron star with greater than critical mass would collapse into itself. There are non-relativistic alternations to the theory. One is that a collapsing star may also fragment or its matter may chip away.

However, in relativity literature, the star collapses to a point and creates mathematical singularity where the density and gravitational force become infinite, and temperature, absolute zero. At that point, time dies. There is an event horizon around that point which is the operative black hole wherefrom nothing can come out. However, the laws of thermo-dynamics work against that and eventually, it is conceded, something must come out from the event horizon or, the black hole cannot stay black and time, does not die. Also, fortunately, the infinite gravitational form created by black holes has not yet denuded the universe of all energy and matter.

In the space time continuum light is wave, its velocity fixed and also unsurpassed. So light is reference velocity to all other local motions. However, that is not defendable. The fixed velocity of light entails that the shortest duration of time is fixed and unvaried and measurable in a perfect clock, which unfortunately cannot exist in the exteriority of mind or be placed in the physicality of space. To observe that the velocity of light to fixed light must pass through a perfect but non-existent medium, like other that is uniform in all optional properties.

It is not established that nothing moves faster than light and that outdates and rejects relativity from its use in observation experimentally. The properties of light show that relativity is not a valid concept for past or present. The opposite of light is darkness or the absence of light. Light has no negative identity. Light his always progressive. It cannot go backward. Light cannot stay still, or it cannot be understood at present. Therefore, light, time and light space relationships are always positive. The meaning of relativity always remains in the future, for there is no meaning of relativity in past or present. The analysis of the properties of light unsettled the observational applicability of the special theory of relativity.

Einstein's field theory rests on the supposition that acceleration due to gravity is a purely geometric consequence of the properties of space time in the neighbourhood of the attracting masses provided that 1) local physics is governed by the special theory of relativity and (2) there is no way for an observer to distinguish local gravity and acceleration. The second condition is true. The first condition remains unfulfilled. So space does not warp in a real situation and mass cannot be imagined to have created the field lines that are vertical to create non-relating or rotating black hole. Black hole literature has value. Despite theories questioning the idea of a black hole, literature on black hole theories with its ramifications in topology and intuitionism have immense value for physics and applied mathematics. They indicate how the mathematics of idealized space and para time can be developed.

Ancestors of Mundas detected the Black-hole

Mundas are not the scientists nor the cosmologists or Astronomers but tell the reality and truth of the cosmos according to their own cultural way of presentation. The detection of Black-hole clearly presents serious problems. We cannot see them for no light can escape from within their event horizon. In fact no signal of any kind can reach us from a black hole (p. 79, 1979 Moore and Nicolson). How did the ancestor of the Munda aboriginals detect the black-hole? It is said that all star events have been presented from cultural angle of the Mundas, otherwise it was difficult to conceptualise the event when modern learning was totally absent in human beings. It was the result of constant and regular observation or star gazing that bore fortuitous results. It was the constellation of stars in the galaxy and their blinking and extraordinary movement and shooting attracted the attention of the aboriginals most who used to spend their nights in the open.

The Black-hole is explained through the children's play of hide and seek or cat and mouse. The play is organized by the children throughout the year. The children organized themselves in two groups, one group hid and other seeks. When all the hidden children are found out by the searching group the latter goes on hiding and the play goes on.

It is told that the sun and moon were once neighbours and good friends. Helping each other and making friendly visits was a usual affair. The sun had many sons and daughters so also did the moon. Modern day scientists say that sun had thousands of brothers and sisters. The sons and daughters of the sun and moon were also good friends like their parents and whenever they got time to visit each other, they spent their time in various types of entertainment and enjoyed their time most together.

Once, the moon decided to organize a grand feast and invite all friends and relatives in it. He also sent an invitation to the sun and all his children. The sun was too glad and accepted the invitation. It was good for an outing as well as an occasion to meet the friends and relatives he thought. So on the appointed day he arrived at the moon's residence along with all the sons and daughters. After sending out invitation, the moon was busy in making arrangement for the grand feast and comfort of the guests. For the feast he prepared curry of the pumpkin vegetable which he had planted. There was all sorts of merry making in the gathering. The guests were happy meeting their long lost friends and relatives also to made friendship with unknown persons. The children on the other hand were busy in their own business of entertainment and merry-making. The children of the moon, who otherwise were abundant in number, however seemed missing as there were only few to be seen. The moon had hidden most of his children from the sight of gatherings. The persons who had came for the first time to the moon's residence, were surprised to find that the moon had maintained a perfect small family norm. However, there was great gathering of children who played thier most favourite game of cat and mouse or hide and seek in which there was in good running after each other. Some children were busy organizing dance holding each other or holding each others hand in a long line, and so on.

At the completion of the feast, all were too happy to praise the moon for nice arrangement and his delicious dinner. The sun was the last person to bid farewell to the moon. While leaving his residence he thanked for the delicious curry and dinner and wonderful arrangement of the feast. He however asked the moon that he did not see his children in the feast. The moon told him he actually killed his children and cooked them as curry. The moon was envious of the brightness of the sun's children and secretly planned at eliminating them. The sun courteously once again thanked him and departed with a happy memory.

After many months or year, the sun also decided to host a feast and sent out invitation to all relatives and friends. He however was envious of the curry he had taken at the feast of the moon and according to the process of curry preparation told by the moon, he killed his sons and daughters and prepared the curry. Thus, all the sons and daughters of the sun were killed by the sun. The feast was organized and all friends and relatives came. The moon also attended the feast with all his children. The sun seeing the moon's children in good numbers he understood the fraud of the moon that he was cheated. Since then the sun and moon are staunch enemies of each other and try to harm each other. The eclipse is said to be the indication of such infliction.

The feast is the occasion of gathering of people, so the feast of the moon and sun was also a big gathering. The constellation of stars is an indication of such gathering. During such gathering play and dances are organized and various grouping of people stars are seen. The constellation of stars made various combination, groups and pairs.

It is easy to detect the sons of the sun from the moon's. The sons of the sun were large in size and brighter than the moon's. As the sons of the sun were large they were of heavy mass and gravity also relatively great, hence they would drag on or pulled the smaller size and mass stars towards them. This motion seemed to be running away or chasing each other.

As the sun had filled and consumed all his sons which in scientific language is called swallow up and a case of cannibals, it is the gravity of the sun that dragged in and destroyed and in the eyes of observer vanished or hidden. It is stated that when the star or stars come closer to the sun, the gravity of the sun attracts the star or dragged the stars in it and is burned with the energy of the sun and assimilated or consumed. The more massive star became more brighter and brighter when its energy was burned out and exhausted, they vanished or became black hole and dragged the nearest star which seemed running after it.

Quite often we find the ancestor in a binary is bright while the other is faint – too faint perhaps to be seen. The Mundas identify large and bright star as the son of the sun and small or faint star or the son of the moon. In binary situation, tall stars are moving round their common centre of mass, neither approaching nor receding. The motion of the two continuum movement in the respective lines will repeat themselves in a regular manner. The bright one moving ahead of the faint one and used up its gas of energy and its light faded away and became invisible. All stars rotate, with the more massive rotating more rapidly than less massive ones. Consequently, the central line will be rotating and as many collapse to smaller and smaller size, they rotate faster and faster. There is much dragging and pulling and running like in play of hide and seek, with the seeker in black hole.

Sun had Sisters when it was Born

The sun had sisters when it was born according to new research, they were hundreds or thousands of them.

And at least one was a supernova, producing further support for the idea that there could be lots of planets around other stars since our solar system emerged in such an explosive environment.

"We know that the majority of stars in our galaxy, were born in star clusters" said Leslie Looney, who arrived at the solar sibling finding along with his colleagues at the university of Illinois at Urbana Champaign. Now we also know that the modern solar system, not only arose in such a cluster, but also survived the impact of an exploding star. This suggests that planetary system are impressively rugged and may be common in even the most simultaneous stellar nurseries.

The evidence for the solar sisters was found in daughters, such as decayed particles from radioactive isotopes of iron trapped in meteorites which can be studied as fossil remnants of the early solar systems.

These daughter species allowed Looney and his colleagues to discern that supernova with the mass of about 20 suns exploded relatively near the early sun when it formed 4.6 million years ago, and where there are supernovas or any massive stars. You also see hundreds to thousands of sun like stars, he said.

The cluster of thousands of stars dispersed billions of years ago due to a lack of gravitational pull, leaving the sisters "lost in space" and our sun looking like an only child ever since, according to Looney.

New Physics – the Cosmic Spirit

Time Magazine in its cover story published in 1960 that "God is dead" and held science responsible for it. But by 1990 were talking about "can spiritualist promote health". The same science which once killed off the notion of God is now strengthening humankind's belief in a supreme power. Latest revelation in cosmology and quantum physics are testing this paradigm shift.

Transcending theories and denominations, there is a conviction in a creator divinity which having spawned the universe is present throughout it upholding and administering the universe. People have always accepted that God will never be releaved to us empirically. Yet for eons we have deemed his entity worthy of adoration and have directed ardent prayers to it many in the vessel of our hope.

Now for the first time, in human history, we have objective knowledge of anentity that fills space and time throughout the universe representing primary elements of reality. This entity existence, comprising a quantum field and processing the elemental blue print of everything physical rest on a solid scientific base. Physicists and cosmologists are close to proving that all these fields arise from a common source that was present in an infinitesimal nugget at the inception of the universe. The source sequentially unfolded to create the universe and everything in it. We already have semi-quantitative proof even in the absence of a complete mathematical theory. The elegance of the incredible precision of the blueprint possessed by the source predisposes us to believe that it mirrors the intelligence of a lighter power and amounts to a veritable experience of the spirit.

The source is active through the universe. This is so because physics at extremely high temperature of that existed at the onset of the universe is equivalent to physics at fundamentally small distances. Therefore, the manifest condition at the onset of the universe, is presumed to be the same in an unmanifest quantum physical way at or near the fabric of space. The existence of the common source at the fabric of space would be no less real than the elusive denizens of empty space known to scientists as virtual screening charges.

Persuasive evidence points to a source, which having spawned the universe, is now present in all space and time. This entity is uncannily representative of the Brahman of Vedanta and also accepted in Christian theology. What is missing in credible evidence of awareness in this entity. The necessity for embracing a simultaneous existence of complementary properties explain the quantum world paves the way for contemporary scientists to find an essential link between the seeming complicated mind and mother. From this view point irreducible primary reaction of field and consciousness are inseparable aspects of the same elementary process of our universe. United through mutual participation, the biological nervous system is a process of a material structure for unfolding consciousness in each individual.

So plausible argument can be made to suggest of an inherent quality of awareness, thereby living credence to the existence of a cosmic spirit.

Spirit (Soul) and Matter

Every day thousands of incidents connected with telepathy dowsing pre-cognition of future events takes place. Poart Yeat's occultist response to these occurrences was that there is a far deeper and intimate connection between us and nature than we realize. The cosmos is active on many levels. There could be something that works behind the visual and physical phenomena.

Occult Science recognize even cosmological elements as entirely physical and as fifth element. Semi-material which reigns supreme over the others . They cover the whole of the earth. The sixth and seventh are yet completely beyond the range of human experience. These seven elements have numberless sub-elements which are still not known to science. The other hypothesized by Sir Isaac Newton are imbedded in the grand design of nature. According to Newton, nature is a perpetual circulatory worker generating fluids out of solids, fixed things out of volatile and volatile out of fixed subtle out of gross and gross out of subtle.

The *Secret Doctrine of the East* by H.P. Blavatsky lays down three fundamental propositions. The first and foremost is an omnipresent eternal principle in which any speculation is impossible. Since it transcends the capability of human perception, it is beyond the research of thoughts. Quoting from Mandakya Upanishad Blavetsky terms it “unthinkable” and “unspeakable”.

The reality according to the Secret Doctrine is be-ness rather than being. The be-ness according to Blavatsky is absolute abstract space representing the bare subjectivity. It is also absolute, abstract motion representing unconditional unconsciousness. The fundamental axiom of the secret doctrine is the metaphysical one. Absolute be-ness symbolized by finite intelligence is known as theoretical trinity.

Absolute reality is absolute consciousness which is free from any kind of conditioned existence. Spirit and matter are two aspects of the absolute parabrahm whose breath assume the character of pre-cosmic ideation. It is the force of all individual consciousness paralled to this pre-cosmic substance which is the substantive of matter in various grade. Absolute is essential for the manifested universe. At this juncture duality rises and the earth greets Vishnu in his first Avatar.

To sum up, the absolute is the parabrahm. Western Philosopher Hegel calls it absolute being and non-being. This is the first cause, in the conscious of European Panthesis. This can also be termed as unmanifested logos. The second logos is spirit of universe i.e. Purush and Prakriti. On the third stage comes cosmic ideation, the basis of the intelligent oxoration is and of nature which can be called Mahabodhi.

What's Wrong with Evolution

The proponents of intelligent design do not claim to have a coherent scientific theory about how life actually changed over time on earth. They conclude that a designer is the best hypothesis.

Irreducible Complexity

Much of the biological machinery in cell, like the motor tails or flagella, at the back of the bacterium Helico bacterpylor and other bacteria is similarly complex. Taking away one piece breaks the machine. Because evolutionary makes slow incremental improvements, it would not have produced all these separate piches that would have had no use until they were assembled into the final working mechanism.

The Response

Evolutionary biologists agree that evolution would never have produced the biological structures all at ones, rather what likely happened was that evolution borrowed existing structures for new purposes, like taking the spring of a clothes pin for use in a mouse trap.

The Place of Change

The criticism :- Since natural selection deals with changes in DNA, it cannot creat new forms of life as occurred during the Cambrian explosion a half billion years ago. The trilobite lived half a billion years ago in what is New Wales. The crab like trilobite which lived on the ocean floor, is one of the major groups of advanced animals that appeared sudden in the Cambrian.

The response :- Some very powerful genes control what other genes do. These control genes switch on and off early in the life of embryos and mutations in these genes can make major changes, giving rise to new species. More fossils from the era leading up to the Cambrian are being discovered, and evidence shows earth's environment might have been undergoing major changes, making complex life possible. Further, the changes leading up to the Cambrian, may have taken up to 100 million years.

Information Theory

The criticism : Look at a cell and you should think it must have been designed. Scientists in this field are looking for erosion and tectonic explanations.

The response : The point of science is to discover how natural process work ? Moreover, intelligent design theorists have failed to show calculations that can convincingly differentiate a designed object from natural occurring one.

Man is Just Another Kind of Animal

Recent advances in genetics, evolutionary biology, psychology and neuroscience seem to suggest that what were once thought to be intractable philosophical conundrums have straight forward scientific answers. Human minds, human behaviour, human artifacts and human culture are all biological phenomena. Claim John Tooby and Leda Cosmides, two of the founders of evolutionary psychologists.

For such thinkers the question of what it means to be human will eventually be solved like any other question about nature science, the evolutionary biologist Rob Fleg arguement, turns every large philosophical and metaphysical question into what are often straight forward and boring technical ones.

Darwinists deal with the question what is it to be human by comparing human anatomy and behaviour with those of non-human animals.

Yet, however much we learn about our brain, our genes or our evolutionary history, we will not learn fully what it is to be human. Because, humans are not simply natural creatures, and cannot be understood in their present state. A paradox of science is that its success in understanding nature has created problems for its understanding of human nature.

The success of science derives from the way that it has disenchanted the natural world. Whereas the pre-scientific world viewed the world universe as full of purpose and desire, the scientific revolution transformed nature into an inert mindless entity and shattered the peace of mind into chaotic state of fear and insecurity.

Virtually every scientist today accepts that the natural world can be fully understood using physics, chemistry and biology. In this sense, mammals are like machines – not because ants and apes operate like cars or computers, but because, they lack consciousness and will. Most of us are happy to view human bodies as machines, but what we value about our fellow human beings is that they do not act as animals or machines, but as people. Humans are unique because alone among organisms, we are both objects of nature and subjects that can shape our own fate. We are biological beings, and under the purview of biological and physical laws.

But we are also conscious beings with purpose, and agency, the possession of which traits allow us to design ways of breaking the constraints of biological and physical laws.

This is another way of saying that human beings are transcendent not in a religious but in a very human way. We are able to transcend our immediate circumstances, breaking free both of our culture and our nature. We are shaped by our genes, as we are shaped by our environment. But we also have the capacity to transcend both our genetic and our cultural heritage.

It is this transcendental quality that makes us human not animal.

All non-human animals are constrained by tools that nature has bequeathed them through natural selection. They are incapable of sharing words of truth, they simply absorb information and behave in ways useful for their survival. Both their knowledge of the world and their behaviour towards it, has been largely preserved by evolution. When an animal builds a dam like structure, it does not ask itself why it does so, or whether there is a better way of doing it. Human do ask these kinds of questions. Because we are social creatures bound together by language. Language takes us beyond a purely personal sophistic view of the world. It allows us to understand other people's perspectives and experiences. It enables us to think of the future and the past, about the present and the absent, about the has-beens, and the might have been. It emancipates thinking from there, here and now, and causes it to range freely over the actual, the probable, the possible and even the impossible. It permits debate and criticism, hopes and aspirants, fears and longings.

The relationship between humans as physically determined beings and humans as social beings and moral agents is one of the most difficult problems for scientists and philosophers. But denying one or other aspects of our humanness is not a way of solving the issue.

That however, is just what many scientists in effect do. Few would dispute that human beings possess consciousness or free will. But by insisting that humans can be understood in purely naturalistic terms, they are forced to give up on the attempt to understand humans as subjective beings, and compelled to view us simply as objects.

The peculiar place that humans occupy in the natural order means that we require special intellectual tools to understand our societies. We require not just the tools of natural science which have been developed for the understanding of inert objects (animals included), but also those of other disciplines, the social science, history, philosophy. None of these is any less valuable or less rational than physics, biology, or chemistry. They are simply more or less, useful in different circumstances.

Cracking Cell Riddle

For three billion years, life on earth consisted of single celled organisms like bacteria or algae. Only 600 million years ago did evolution hit on a system for making multi cellular organisms like animals and plants.

The key to the system is to give the cells that make up an organism a variety of different identities so that they can perform many different roles.

So, even though all the cells carry the same genome, each type of cell must be granted access to only a few of the genes in the genome with all others permanently denied to it.

People for instance, have at least 260 different types of cells, each specialized for a different tissue or organism, but presumably each type can activate only some of the 22,500 genes in the human genome.

The nature of the system that assigns cells their various identities is a central mystery of animal existence, one that takes place at the earliest moments of life when all the purpose cells of the early embryos are directed to follow different roles. Biologists at Cambridge have now derived deep into this process and uncovered what seems to be a crucial feature of how a cell's fate is determined, even though much remains to be understood.

They have discovered a striking new feature of the chromatin, the specialized protein molecules that protect and control the giant molecules of DNA that lie at the centre of every chromosome.

The feature explains how embryonic cells are kept in a poised state so that all the genomes many development programmes are blocked, yet each is ready to be exerted if the each is assigned to that developmental path.

The developmental programmes directing a cell to become a neutron, say or a liver cell are initiated by master regulator genes. These genes have the power to reshape a cell's entire form and function because they control many lower genes. They do so by producing proteins known as transcription factors that bind to special sites on the DNA and control the activity of the power level target genes.

A question of interest for biologists studying cell identity is what regulates the master regulator genes. The answer has long been assumed to lie in the chromatin which determines which genes are accessible to the cell and which are excluded. The chromatin consists essentially of millions of miniature protein spools around each of which the DNA strand is looped some one half times.

The spools, however are not mere packaging. They can lock up the DNA. They are carrying so that it is inaccessible or they can unwind a little, so that the strand becomes accessible to the transcription factors seeking to copy a gene on the DNA and generate the protein it specifies working backward from that knowledge, biologists have spent much effort trying to learn how the state of the spools is determined.

They have learnt there are protein complexes essentially sophisticated cellular machines that travel along the chromosome and mark the spools with chemical tags placed at various sites on the spools. (Nicholas Wade – Nyf News Service)

3

Evolution Strategy of Life

Oxygen Theory

The discovery that science has found that oxygen generates life might have enriched the earth far earlier than generally supposed. The discovery is sure to trigger controversy. It suggests life could arise earlier than thought on alien planets too. Reports live science.com.

Currently scientists widely believe photosynthesis microbes helped oxygenate the plan it roughly 2.4 billion years ago, and that oxygen was scant in the atmosphere before then. They base this idea on isotopes of sulpher an ancient rock. Isotopes of sulpher behave virtually the same chemically but with slightly different masses.

Rocks older than 2.4 billion years contain abnormal ratios of sulpher isotopes compared with younger rocks. The only way known to generate these abnormal rocks are reactions between sunlight and sulphrous volcanic gas in the absence of an ozone shield that would normally help screen out ultraviolet rays.

Ozone is a form of oxygen, and if the atmosphere has no ozone, it is assumed, it has no oxygen. Geo Chemist Hiroshi Ohmoto, Director of the Penn State Astrobiology Research Centre and his colleagues examined rocks from Western Australia laid down as sediments on a lake bed and the ocean floor between about 2.76 and 2.92 billion years ago. These displayed Sulphar isotope ratios like those of more modern rocks from higher oxygen eras.

When did the earth's atmosphere became oxygenated, has been an important question for earth scientists and biologists this question became closely linked to those related to the biological evolution of earth and other planets, according to Ohmoto.

An application of the new findings is that an oxygen rich atmosphere generated by oxygen producing organism may be found in young as well as old pignut and other hidden star.

Earth formed about 4.5 billion years ago. Nobody new exactly when and how life began or how quickly it altered the planet's chemistry.

The new findings could mean oxygen levels on earth were "uniformly high since 3.8 billion years", said Ohmoto.

They could also mean oxygen levels went through 40 – 40 fluctuations between high and low. Alternative ultraviolet radiation from the sun might not be the only way that can generate the abnormal ratios of sulpher isotopes seen in older rocks.

There is going to be a howl, even outrage, over these findings, geologists and isotopes geochemists Paul Knuth at Arizona State University said, TNN.

How the pre-historic earth atmosphere developed. Till now, it has been generally accepted that earth atmosphere was devoid of oxygen for some 80% of its existence. "The popular notion was that there was little oxygen in the earth's atmosphere before about 2.4 billion years ago" said Hiroshi Ohomoto of Pennsylvania University.

But Ohomoto team has cast doubt on the theory after finding sulpher isotopes indicating prevalent oxygen, that predated the accepted start of atmospheric oxygenation. The key lies in the fact that while all isotopes of sulpher behave the same chemically, they have slightly differing masses according to the amount of atmospheric oxygen at the time.

Isotopes from two sulphuric samples were analysed by a team. One 2.76 billion years old from a lake bed and the other 2.92 billion years old from sea bed did not indicate an oxygen starved atmosphere. We analysed the sulpher composition and could not find the abnormal sulpher isotopes ratio (indicating no oxygen) Pltando said.

The team concluded that there are two possible explanations – either that pre-historic oxygen levels fluctuated widely or that sulpher showing no oxygen might have been produced in an oxygenated atmosphere as long as 3.8 billion years by violent Volcanic activity. Either way, they said, the accepted theories needed to be re-evaluated Reuters.

Evolution Strategy of Life

Among popularisers of Evolutionary biologist perhaps none was as prolific or as friendly as Stephen Say Gould, an evolutionary biologist, who succumbed to cancer recently. His columnists view of "life" in the magazine N*atural History* attracted wide readership with its engaging style and explanations of evolutionary theory, using analogies drawn from a wide range of disciplines, including sports and pop-culture. Gould was to evolutionary biology, what Carl Sagan was to cosmology. If Sagan's writing brought the universe within our comprehensive reach, Gould did much the same with evolutionary biology. As a paleontologist, Gould theory of evolution was founded on the notion of "punctuated equilibria". Evolution occurs in short – growth sport triggered by exogenous factors measurable in thousands of years connected by long periods of stability, thereby departing from Darwin's theory that evolution is a slow process, measurable in million of years of natural selection. He believed that science does not make moral implications, it merely raises them. Science makes certain things possible like cloning and gene engineering. But we have to debate ethical issues as human beings, not scientists, he said. Neither did he denounced creation theories, as an evolutionary scientists, he preferred that school taught both. He believed in the "beauty of non predictability", and would like the instance of the extinction of dinosaurs following a random extraterrestrial impact that make room for mutation seen long back but he also stressed the importance of accountability because there is enough contingency even in randomness in complex systems, that might be unpredictable but nevertheless, explicable.

Recently, two new theories of evolution have been proposed – punctuated equilibrium and extinction evolution, considering that established speeds comfortably persist through time (stasis), for upto several million of years, the punctuated equilibrium model simply combines allopathic speculation with stasis. The model is thus more a new name than a model for both allopatric speciation and species longevity had been known for a long time. Further more, the model does not explain extinction without replacement.

The extinctive evolution model makes extinction an integral part of the process of evolution. This model maintains that established population exhibit considerable inertia to change and change only in environmental threshold conditions are violated. Peripheral to the established populations are marginal population living under conditions of continued environmental stress.

These populations are the store house of genetic variability. Occasionally, the evolution of virus that fits the genome of an established species will lead to extinction of that species is the theory available. The new species will not necessarily be better adapted than the extinct species. If no suitable species is available from the marginal environment, the niche vacated by the extinct species remain vacant, and diversity is reduced. Extinction is abrupt. Speciation is not abrupt, but the appearance of a new species in the stratigraphic record is abrupt. According to this model, the "missing link" has never existed in the environments occupied by established populations.

There is no fossil record of missing link. The modern theory solve the missing link problem by claiming that speciation occurs in small population in limited isolated areas greatly reducing the chances of leaving a detectable or discoverable fossil record. The modern theory of evolution incorporates modern genetics and a few accruements.

The extinctive evolution model requires the chance evolution of a virus fitting a specific genome. That should be easy, for viruses mutate a million times faster than cellular organisms prokaryotes or eukaryotes – because viruses lack mending enzymes to correction made during nucleic acid duplication. In addition, the virus must be able to spread rapidly throughout the range of the genome under attack.

Speciation is the process by which new species come into existence. According to Darwin, species come into existence because, (1) natural population are variable (2) The environment continuously and slowly changes. (3) The changing environment selects the most suitable variety and (4) continuing change eventually produces a variety sufficiently different from the original to be called a new species" (p. 423)

What is the Origin of Life?

Evolution is a fundamental scientific theory that species evolved over million of years.

The theory of intelligent design says, life on earth is too complex to have developed through evolution implying that a higher power must have had a hand in creation.

The theory of evolution as also the concept of intelligent design are not supported by the fact a bitter debate about has ensued among the academicians and scientists.

In the past month, the interim president of Cornell University and Dean of the Stanford University school of medicine have both spoken on this theme warning in dramatic terms of long term consequences among the most significant forces is the rising tide of anti-science sentiment that seem to have its nucleus in US but which extends throughout the nation "geneo standard Phillip Pizzon".

Cornell acting president Hunter Rawlings in his State of the University address last week spoke about the challenge to science represented by "intelligent design which holds that the theory of evolution accepted by the majority scientist is finally flowed (taken as prestige issue by evolutionist.

Rawling said the dispute was widening politically, social, religious and philosophical rights in US society. Adherents of intelligent design argue that certain terms in nature are too complex to have evolved through natural selection and must have been created by a designer, who could but does not have to be identified as God. In the past five years, the scientific communities have often seemed at odds with both other issue as diverse as global warming, stem cell research and environmental protection.

Prominent scientists have also charged the administration with politicizing science by seeing to shape date to its own needs. Evangelical and fundamentalists Christians have built a purposeful position within the republican party and no republican parish can offer to ignore their views, but spoke the "culture of life".

Who Created Adam and Eve?

How did life appear on Earth? Did an intelligent force creat it or did it emerge out of a primordial solution of chemicals as claimed by Darwinians?

How did life form originate on earth and change their shapes, sizes and characteristics over time? Main stream scientific theory holds that species evolved through a natural selection. But recently the Darwinian theory has been challenged by a powerful group of scientists who proposed their own alternative theory called "intelligent design". At the heart of the debate is the question can a scientific explanation. of the history of life include the action of an unseen force or Gods? Similarly have Darwinians seen the selection process actually working in empirical situation? Do they have any evidence?)

Darwinian scientists contend that intelligent design (ID) does not have any evidence to support their claims. They say ID paints out seemingly week links in the evolutionary theory and concludes that designer is best hypothesis.

One of the main arguments of the ID theory is irreducible complexity, which they say some of the living forms and phenomena in this world are so complex that they could have existed only because of designer contemplated its function and thereby its existence. Their evidence for intelligent design is the elegant, complex, sophisticated molecular machinery that has been discovered in the cell – the foundation of life by science in the last 50 years. The cell literally is operated by machines made out of molecule, explained Michel Behe, author of *Darwin's Black Box*; the book that started the ID movement to *Delhi times*.

Many scientists say ID is a bogus theory and has no scientific supports. It is not backed by empirical data. Biologists of the evolution school, on the other hand, say they have evidence. 150 years of research has yielded fossils developmental patterns, bio-geographic distributions of organisms and genetic comparisons that support the theory of evolution, say Keneth R. Miller, a biologist at Brown Universtiy. Agrees V.K. Bhasin, HOD of Zoology of Delhi University. No doubt some life forms are complex but this complexity should not tempt us to abandon evolution and accept ID. Unfolding of evolutionary complexities should be taken as a challenge. Man in despair tries to evoke the ID short cut, he says.

ID and evolutionary are not contradictory theory but supportive to each other to arrive at the goal to origin of life or human beings. Evolutionary science should not make ID issue as prestige issue or anti-science ideology. Complexity issue may be accepted as ID planning. While every life forms originate at the wish or desire of ID through the process of evolution. The big-bang is the work of ID. Without his wish big-bang may not have occurred. He indirectly gave guidance to nature to function as he desires. Both these ideas are supportive in the origin of the universe and life.

Origin of Life

Life is "unique", "admirable" and the end product of 15 billion years of cosmic and terrestrial evolution and therefore is utterly complex. Life is a necessary and inevitable consequence of the way it would have originated and evolved. Indeed, the origination and evolution of life on earth were foregone conclusion sright from the beginning given the mass, the chemical composition and the physical and astronomical parameters of our planet. Other planets in our solar system are too hot or too cold or chemically unsuitable for the development of life. Life is not a miracle for earth, but its absence would have been rarely a miracle – earth is uniquely placed in the solar system.

Life is the set of molecular systems each one of which is capable of reproducing itself from generation to generation. A living organism is a molecular system capable of reproducing itself from generation to generation.

Life has had an important part in shaping the environmental evolution of the Earth. The Earth formed 4.6 – $4.5.10^4$ B.P.

There was asteroid bombardment and earth differentiated into core and mantle and degassed forming the earth atmosphere. It is this turbulent period that life on earth originated. It not probably originated not just once, but many times, and many different places only to be stormed or just wiped out but this might be asteroid impact. About $3.8.10^9$

asteroid bombardment thinned out and life then had firm hold on the surface of the young earth.

Life probably originated when methane was still the dominant gas in the atmosphere. Amino acids, the building block of protein, a mixture of methane and amino acids and liquid water with CO_2 and silicon to turn carbon and ammonia other organic compound formed condition favourable to their interaction which have helped in the origination of life on earth. In other words, "life arose simply from the workings of physical and chemicals laws" (p. 600, Asimov)

Life needs energy for its process. The earth has two sources of energy available of external energy (sun) and internal energy. These energies are sufficient to move electrons to higher energy levels upto ionization in the complex molecular system when photosynthesis occurs. The energy released as the electronic nature to the ground stall is stored in chemical bases that can be brokens through hydrolysis releasing energy for further processes. "The forms of energy that had brought it into being in the place of ultraviolet and radioactive energy were effectively gone or at least seriously diminished. For both these reasons, there is virtually no chance of any new and independent breakthrough from non file into life (baring some further human intervention". (p. 600 Asimov)

The only internal source of energy utilized for living process is the bacterial particles of compounds in vents along the mid-ocean ridges system and in hot springs.

The primitive earth was an immense laboratory rich in water reduced gases and a wealth of minerals with which liquid and gases were interacting and where energy for atomic rearrangements and the formation of complex molecules – radiation from the sun lighting and volcanic heat was plentiful. Submarine vents were more numerous and widespread than today, contributing to the formation of organic compounds. Under the conditions it would have been virtually impossible that the ocean would not have been infact a true primoridial soup, with a molar concentration of organic compounds in steady state equilibrium with the physico-chemical, environment. In terms of salinity that would have been about 3.5 mg per liter of water. The primordial soup was therefore a very dilute solution.

In order for the organic compounds in the primordial soup to interact with each other concentration was necessary. That could have occurred in a number of ways, including evaporation and the formation of brines in tidal pods. An efficient method of concentrating and preserving organics is foaming. In the primitive ocean, through foaming, organic compounds were concentrated in the open ocean and dumped on the beach and got energy supplied by the sun.

. The step from a micelle (roved up foam) with a mixture of organic compounds inside to a functional living cell is an enormous leap. The biochemistry of even the simplest bacterium is so extraordinary complex that it would seem impossible to believe that it came about by random steps and life eventually emerged.

Origin of Life (Recent Findings)

Development Scientists have identified the single chance encounter about 1.9 billion years ago to which almost all life on earth owes its existence.

It saw an amoeba like organism engulf a bacterium that had developed the power to use sunlight to break down water and liberate oxygen.

The bacterium was probably intended as prey but instead it became incorporated into its attacker's body – turning it into the ancestor of every tree, flowering plant and seaweed on earth. The encounter meant life on the planet could evolve from bacterial slime into the more complex forms we see today. "That single event transformed the evolution of life on earth." According to Paul Falkowsi Prof. of Biogeochemistry and biophysics at Rutgers University in New Jersey. "The descendants of that tiny organism transformed our atmosphere, filling with the oxygen needed for animals and eventually humans to evolve."

It had been thought that sub organisms emerged many times over the early earth, but the unique nature of the event has become clear from studies of chloroplasts, the bodies in plant cells that absorbs sunlight and use its energy to generate nutrients and oxygen. They show that the genes within chloroplasts and the proteins they produce are so similar in all plants, ranging from tiny algae to oak trees, that they must all be the direct descendants of a single cell.

It is an astonishing thought that a single random encounter between two tiny cells so long ago could have had such huge consequences said Ealleowski, who described the latest research in the meeting of American Geophysical Union. Falkowski's group at Rutgus is one of several groups in the world using powerful scientific tools such as DNA analysis to work out how life evolved after earth was formed about 4.5 billion years ago.

"ET's intervention may have hastened the emergence of life". They have also refined methods for dating ancient rocks using radioactive isotopes. This method can show as well how much oxygen was in the atmosphere when the rocks were formed. Such evidence suggests primitive life emerged upto 3.5 billion years ago but only as bacterial type organisms. Then more than 2 billion years ago, one group, the cyanobacteria, evolved the ability to use sunlight to break down water making nutrients and liberating oxygen.

This event was a breakthrough, but cyanobacteria were inefficient, so oxygen levels remained minimal. It took several hundreds million more years before the chance encounter that would lead to flowering plants. This took place in history showing how unlikely it was to happen at all.

Nick Lane, a researcher at University College London, said a picture of life evolving through a series of unique chance events was emerging. Oxygen energises all life, and makes it big, he said. Nothing else can provide the energy needed to fuel the demands of multicolor organisms. True polysynthesis evolved only once and the chance encounter that gave rise to plants also happened just once. These were two accidents in the 3.5 billion year history of life on earth. (TOI, *Sunday Times*, London.) Monday 10.11.2008.

Garden of Eden

(Study says life evolved faster in the tropic than elsewhere)

Now we know why there is so much more biodiversity in the tropic than anywhere else in the world. It is the tropical heat and warmth that helps life thrive and branch out via mutations into different species at a rate faster than in other regions. According to folklore, the Biblical Garden of Eden was set in the tropical paradise of Sri Lanka (India). For the farther you travel away from the tropics, the fewer the species you are likely to come across. In a paper published in the proceeding of the National Academy of Sciences, three scientists from the University of Auckland, New Zealand, propose the theory that heat is what has made life thrive and fast, in the warmer regions. Tropical conditions accelerate the rate of mutation, thereby creating a spectrum of genetic variation. Together with the process of natural selection, this further boosts fecundity and biodiversity.

Chemical reactions take place faster in higher temperature in turn increasing metabolic rates, generating free radicals, oxygen rich molecules which encourage mutation. More speciation due to natural causes in the tropical regions has given us a rich and varied flora-fauna heritage that is evolving constantly. Whether this is perceived as a God given gift or as a Darwinian natural selection processes is to be seen. There is no doubt that eco-biological riches place on us an onerous responsibility. The volumes and quality of inherited bio-wealth can easily destroy if conservation efforts and eco-allurement are given short shift in our zeal to get ahead with development project. Denuding forests, poaching, habitat destruction and plain insensitivity to other species could one day reverse the evolutionary process. This is happening already in the polar regions where polar bears and smaller species are facing extinction due to human induced climate change. Climate after all is what nurtures life and once natural cycles are tampered with in irrevocable ways it could compromise the pace of natural evolution. Some theologists contest the premise that the Biblical Garden of Eden ever had a terrestrial existence. Be that as it may, we nevertheless need to pool our efforts to conserve not one but many gardens in order to make life worthwhile for all of us.

Origin of Life

Liquids water is necessary for life to evolve. Simple chemicals must combine to form complex ones. Liquid water is an appropriate medium for these chemicals to dissolve, act and react.

Life has Never been Built by the Scientists

Chemicals building blocks : Receipt for life like carbon, oxygen and hydrogen, carbon can form long chain like molecules, integral for the creation of organic life. Hydrogen and oxygen can bond with carbon and they are present in water. Nitrogen, too is carbon friendly and stable. Other chemical ingredients that make life include Sulphur, phosphorus, sodium, manganese, iron, cobalt, copper and zinc.

Energy Source : To drive the chemical reactions, the sun is the primary source of energy, but extrainophile organisms living deep inside ocean beds and polar ice manage without the sun. They have survived like this for million of years.

Method : Earth ingredients are mixed to make primordial soup. Add energy, let them react forming molecules once these begin to copy themselves (re-produce) life has begun. Had there been no nature, there would not have been the universe and life.

Early atmosphere of the earth consisted of Carbondioxide, Nitrogen, Hydrogen, Methane and Amonia. One solution came from outer space. Asteroids, Comets, meteorites, and even specks of inter-planetary dust carry organic molecules, including amino acids or the ingredients necessary to produce them. Those extraterrestrial objects may have helped season earth's primordial soup with enough critical chemicals to permit the first strings of life.

Before DNA and proteins even before the simplest bacteria appeared life may have consisted solely of RNA, molecules floating in the sea, replicating, mutating and undergoing natural selection on their own. As DNA and proteins evolved, these more specialized molecules took over most of the critical work from the RNA. At some unknown point, life found a home inside a protective membrane, forming the very first cell. From these cell arose the three main branches of life – bacteria, orchoea and eukaryotes. When did this happen is shrouded in mystery. Scientists thought that life could not have developed until large comets and meteorites stopped pounding the planet some 3.8 billion years ago.

Those missiles from space may infact, have played a central role in the origin of life. A few scientists suspect that bacterium like cell evolved first on the planet and then journeyed to earth on an asteroid. Scientists have now confirmed that life on earth began in space.

Blue-green algae called cyanobacteria and seaweed has the ability to use sunlight to convert carbondioxide into energy-rich sugar, generating oxygen as a waste product such photosynthesis ancestor the food chain, producing sustenance for all higher organisms.

Eventually cyanobacteria started filling the atmosphere with oxygen, and started the growth of other microbes and other organisms. We inherits in our cells tiny power plants called mitochondria, oxygen harnessing from the bacteria which burn sugar and oxygen to generate energy.

Nickel Behind Origin of Life

According to a new study origin of life owe its existence to fluctuating level of a humble metal in the primordial sea. It is argued that the massive influx of oxygen into earth's atmosphere some 2.4 billion years ago that set evolution on a path to multicellular life was unleashed by a cascade of events in which nickel played a starring role.

What scientists call the great oxygen event "irreversibly changed surface environments on earth and ultimately made advanced life possible" beside the role of meteorite from outer space said Dominic Papinear of the Carnegi Institution's Geophysical laboratory and a co-author of the study. Scientists generally agree that this oxygen surge was made possible by rapid decline in the atmospheric levels of methane. But why methane dropped off has remained a mystery.

The researchers, led by Kurf Konhauser of the University of Alberta in Edmonton, Canada believe the answer lies in rocks that were formed before oxygen was abundant in the air or the sea. Analysing changes over time in the level of trace elements in these rocks, the scientists noticed that levels of nickel dropped just before oxygen level increased. (TOI April 11, 2009)

The Quest of Life in Origin

Seeds of life have come from asteroid belt but where did life begin? On earth and not on some other planet?

Saturn giant moon Cassin Mission to Titan hopes to answer why Titan, because its atmosphere and surface are believed to be dynamic and active. It is rich in hydro carbons and resembles past big-bang cosmic conditions before life began some 3.5 billion years ago. Titan is the only moon in the Solar system with an atmosphere. Its surface could be rich is methane and carbon molecules a pre-requisite for the creation of life itself. Scientists hope to find pre-biotic conditions here that proceeds the evolution of life.

Panspermia theory – several scientific theories have been mooted about our origins, the most popular one being the

Panspermia theory. It was propounded by Fred Hoyle and N. Chandra Wickremsinghe in 1970. According to it, "we are born of inter-stellar seedling when microbes got transplanted to earth as they piggy back on comets and meteors that collided with the planet. That would make us out to be the aliens, we are looking for not all microbes in inter-stellar space would survive of course", said Wickremsinghe. But the survival of even a minute fraction of microbes leaving one solar system and reaching the next site of planet formation would be enough for Panspermia to be overwhelming more probable than sharing life from scratch in a new location, S.Vante Archeries theorized that the universe in which life had always existed and migrated across space continually, colonizing new planets. Life traveled in the form of spores that escaped from the atmosphere of a planet by ransom movement and they were driven through space by the pressure of light from the sun. (p. 594 Asimovs – Arrchenivs)

Scientists are attempting to simulate cosmic conditions prevalent at the time following the big bang. The explosion stirred up primordial soup that somehow set about life. In this soup, single molecules combined to form more complex ones. As the basic molecules of life moved from space to planetary environment, Archeries further states that spores traveled on and on through interstellar space driven by light radiation this way and that until they died or fell on some planet, where they would spring into active life and compete with life forms already present or inoculate the planet with life if it was uninhabited but habitable. It is the ultraviolet light in interplanetary space that kills the bacteria. Thus, such seedling is not a solution to the problem of life but only shifts the problem elsewhere. (p. 594 Asimov Life on earth may therefore have originated when spores were carried to earth by comet tails. They began to interact and undergo chemical reactions that produced more complicated molecules. They were energized by lightning or volcanic heat to form amino acids. These went on to form proteins life building blocks.

If life evolved outside earth, the panspermia theory would explain how earth got inherited. If not, the same chemicals processes could well have taken place on this planet as pre-biotic conditions here, are believed to have been exactly what it is in Titan now. Scientists, therefore, hope the Titan Probe will confirm the primordial soup theory.

Creating life : To prove that who can be created from scratch, researchers at Harvard University have undertaken a multi-million dollar project that seeks to simulate like friendly chemical conditions in the laboratory. "We are trying to create a primordial organism in the lab." said Tack Szostak of Harvard Medical School. He and his team have successfully started an evolutionary cycle by randomly stringing together nucleotides to create trillions of RNA molecules, precursors of self replicating DNA. But they have yet to create a brand new RNA – a task that once achieved could be the link to the creation of life in the laboratory.

What is the catalyst that takes inert matter and transforms it into process capable of replicating itself, no matter how rudimentary? Even the lowest form of algae representing a process that can turn sunlight into nutrition and propagate the species. Over time, the humble algae will go up the evolutionary spiral on to more complex process or life forms unlike crystals which can replicate but are stuck in the same evolutionary groove forever.

One day we might stumble upon that magical something that breathes life into inert matter. It could be as ubiquitous and unglamorous as clay, or it could be a mystical part of faith. Either way the life will never be the same again.

Until then we will question, did life originate in the stars or on earth? Speculations abound. Astronomer Carl Sagan estimated that there were a million technical civilizations in our galaxy alone. Seeptres like Ben Zuckermann insist we are alone in this galaxy if not in this universe.

Still others, exobiologists, are delving deep into the earth, to study extremophile organism that they believe will tell us more about our origins, possibly on earth. Sunlight nor photosynthesis drawing energy from chemicals in hydrothermal vents beneath ocean fleas. How do a bunch of chemicals organize themselves into life? What are the conditions necessary to create this magic? With the Cassni probe help find answers to the questions where did it come from. Time will tell. Recent research has confirmed that Mars and Saturn were created from the clonis of the earth of the solar orbit where the earth originated.

Titan – Temperatures rarely venture above -179 °C the atmosphere is dominated by nitrogen and carbon – based compounds. It has a hazy atmosphere. Distance from Saturn – 1221850 km 512 in diameter 5150 km.

How Energy on Titan can be Tapped

Is there life on Saturn's moon Titan? David Grin Spoon a researcher at the Space Science and Engineering Division of South Western Research Institution in Texas says, "there is no shortage of energy source (food) because energy rich hydrocarbon are constantly being manufactured in the upper atmosphere by the action of sunlight on methane and falling to the surface."

The team suggests that acetylene which is abundant, could be used by organisms in reaction with hydrogen gas, to release energy that could be used to power metabolism, such a biosphere would be, at least indirectly solar powered.

Astronomers have long seen Titan as a place that had the pre-conditions for life, but many saw it as too in hospitable to actually contain biology today (Inspite of existed pre-conditions of life. Life did not flourish there? Why? Titan is barren of life why)

Titan Infused Life into Earth : NASA

Saturn's mysterious moon Titan appears to have an environment rich in the carbon based molecules that spawned life on earth and winds that etched streak into its icy surface NASA.

"On early earth there was organic materials and something happened to these molecules that gave rise to life."

Scientist Jonathan Lamine said, "We had to find a place elsewhere in the system where that process is being replicated." And it seems to be happening on Titan."

Images by the spaceship Cassini also suggested "an enormous amount of geology going on Titan indulging past eruptions of water vapour spawing volcanoes" an egg shell cracking on its surface, Lunine said. (still the Titan is not suitable place for life to develop there) Titan is life less). Cassini collected hundreds of images and radar data that pieced the veil of smog surrounding Titan for the first time. The radar images that showed streaks that resembled lava glows on Venus triangular up thrusts that could be rocks, and what could be a chain of frozen lakes containing organic matter. JPL Director Charles Eliachi, who heads the radar team said. The radar data covering just 1 per cent of Titan's surface also showed a deep surface layer of something that appears to be organic material rather than a rocky face, Eliachi said.

"We are seeing a place that is like geologically. According Eliachi . "We have read a couple of pages of the mystery book." Although Titan's equatorial temperature stays far below freezing, the water ice at its core may be mixed with ammonia, whose lower freezing point may allow it to throw and flow across the moon's surface in volcanic eruptions, scientists said.

Casini, which carries a piggy back probe called Huggens, is expected to fly by Titan 44 more times during its four year mission to explore Saturn and its rings and moon.

Huggens would parachute to Titan's surface to take readings of its dense atmosphere and soil.

The 51 billion mission has its launching in 1997, as per joint project of NASA and the European and Italian space agencies.

Titan Space Probe Suggests Life Began out there we are the Staff of the Entire Universe

Forty years ago, when Eric Von Daniken wrote chariots of the Gods and said extraterrestrials could have brought life to our planet, he was laughed out of serious science. Twenty years later, two mighty respected astronomer physicists with impeccable credentials, Sir Fred Hoyle and professor N. Chandra Wickrema Singhe said virtually the same thing. Other mainstream scientists thought they had gone off the deep end. Now that the joint NASA and European and Italian space Agency Space craft Cassini has begun bearing elementary images back from Titan, the massive planet sited moon of Saturn, no one is laughing any longer. This despite the date being acutely indicative of something similar. That is conditions on Titan resemble what our own planet was like for millions of years before life in carbon based molecules that are capable of sponsoring self replicating DNA. Panspermia literally meaning "seeds every where, is a theory which maintains that life bearing proto-spores are prevalent throughout the universe. Life on earth originated when some of them landed on its surface and propagated. It also suggests that life could have existed on another planet and moved to earth. Recent statistics have revealed a huge 7.5 per cent of all meteoric rocks blasted off from Mars for instance, eventually reach us. There are several other reasons too for considering the theory seriously. Studies of micro organisms have shown they can survive the harsh environment of space, including ultra violet radiation, proton bombardment and the prevailing near absolute zero cold. They can also exist unharmed for a long time in a "sleep" mode or in suspended animation, until revived by suitable conditions without suffering any damage. Finally, after they arrive safely from space, even pre-organisms can turn into protein from amino acids and eventually life growing and reproducing everywhere, to become creature like us one day.

Mother Earth is our only True Mother (Counter View)

The Cassini scientists hope to find evidence of the Panspermia theory of the origin of life. That life evolved out of a primordial soup, getting eventually dispersed through the cosmos via comets and meteorites. Saturn moon Titan could be rich in liquid hydro-carbon harbouring organic materials that resemble those of the primordial soup that generated molecular life. If we are indeed the result of interstellar seedling, that would make us aliens on earth creatures made of other worldly staff and then transplanted on this planet. Hoyle and Wickrema Singhe's work did popularize this theory. But an equally controversial and plausible explanation is also gaining ground. Given that the post big bang primordial soup scattered through the cosmos, available evidence shows that life is not all that universal. So what and where were the conditions available in order for life to originate?

British astronomer Heather Cooper has suggested that all human beings made Martians as meteorites from Red planet may have seeded life on earth billion of years ago. Mars is close to the solar systems asteroid belt though as and must have been hit by many more impacts. Some collisions blasted bits of Mars into space which circles the sun and fell on earth as meteorites, "it is possible life began on Mars and spread to earth through cosmic collision." TOI 1.19.2009.

All the conditions- environment required for life could well have been available on earth, itself not even on Mars or Titan, a product of chemical interactions of formal, dehyde, water, hydrogen, cynide, ammonia, and so on. As the nascent planet came together and solidified over millions of years, molecules brought together were pushed to surface, possibly forming the basing building blocks of life, through chemicals and mineral reaction and interaction. So while life evolved in other parts of the cosmos, it could have simultaneously come into being on earth and aided and abetted by further seeding from comets and meteors. Geological activity is often followed by bio-germination. Recent deep boring expeditions into polar and volcanic regions have unearthed evidence of molecular life that scientists believe evolved when life began on earth. Scientists are trying to replicate pre-life conditions in the laboratory combining nucleotides, fatty acids and water to form RNA strands, the precursor to the DNA has been found to be an essential link to assembling there chemicals something that is echoed in ancient thought, that we basically originated from dust. (Editorial TOI)

Primitive Worm (TOI 20 16/98 – Edi)

The discovery of fossilized tracks from the central India allegedly made by primitive worm 1.1 billion years ago, if confirmed, could push back the history of life on earth by as many as 500 million years. But it is unlikely the title, "cradle of life" will be confirmed on India in a hurry. Experts in such trace fossils are divided on the issue and some peers say the scientists still "have a lot of explaining to do". Meanwhile, three other Indian geologists have joined the fray with their own claim of fossils of organisms called "spriggine" reportedly discovered in Madhya Pradesh with all this, the history of life on earth seems to have suddenly slid into a series of regressions which could rock the very foundations of paleobiology. However, since the jung is still out on these discoveries, any display of jingoism will be both unseemly and unwise. For one, Akhand Bharat style India was non-existent when the first worms allegedly turned in the flooded ridges of the landmass which predates Gondwana land by a half a billion years. To say, that is not to slight the discoveries which could still lead to text book revisions of a different kind. For now, what should concern us is the fate of these primeval Rosetta stones in Churhat – known for an evolutionary lottery of another kind. The area where the worm tracks were discovered is said to be under development, with widening of roads and a proposed water canal for the parched district. The site also needs to be protected from depredations like of Indiana John.

Indian scientists should also be heartened by the fact that the Churhat discovery has been front paged by Science, one of the world's premier research Journals. However, our enthusiasm should be tempered by caution. First, because what looks like tell tale tracks could be the result of physical processes or inorganic traces. Then there is the question of accounting for the yawning gap of half a billion years between the present discovery and the second oldest fossil track record, recovered from China. When one is looking at processes of million years duration, the chances of finding good fossils which escapes the earth's epic upheavals and abrasions become slim indeed, which is why each discovery ought to be celebrated for the miracle it is setting aside momentarily the question, priority and credit which seem overwhelmingly to preoccupy scientists and their sponsors these days.

Seeds of Life from Heaven

Molecules found in a meteorite in Australia identified as uracil and xanthine – the two bits of genetic coding called nucleobases are present in human DNA and RNA. Zitamartin, a team leader of researcher at Imperial College, London said (TOI)

Life in space February, 2009 TOI

Three new species of bacteria not found on earth and highly resistant to ultra violet radiation have been discovered in the upper stratosphere by Indian scientists. Isro said the discovery will help explore the origin of life.

The species are – one Janibacter hoylec

Two – Bacillus Isronensis

Three – bacillus aryabata

It was a joint effort of the Pune based Interuniversity Centre.

Life on Mars

Chemical test used by Mars Viking Landers 30 years ago was not sensitive enough to detect sign of alien life even if they existed, a new study suggested.

Researchers analysed soil from several harsh Mars like environment on earth using the same gas spectrometry test employed by the Viking Landers. But even if in soil taken from areas teaming with microbial life, the test failed to register any sign of organic material. Thus, "the Martian surface could have several orders of magnitude more organics than the stated Viking detection limit." The researcher wrote.

The new study could also explain the detection of low levels of carbon dioxide in some Martian soil by the Viking Landers a puzzling finding that some scientists have used to argue for life on Mars.

In 1976 Nasa's Viking 1 and 2 Landers touched down on the Mars surface and carried three separate experiments to detect signs of life. One of these experiments was designed to look for micro organisms living in Martian top soil. In this test, no organic compounds were ever detected.

Life on Mars has been snuffed out early because the water there is salty. It was really salty and difficult for microbe organisms to survive in this water. One of the theory was that strong concentration of minerals take up the life. Robert backs up this theory. Another theory is that " a large meteorite may have sterilized life on Mars".

Origin of Life Impossible

One problem concerin is the complete lack of evidence for any possibly pre-biotic compounds that would allow evolution to occur. If these did exist they most certainly would be found in great quantities in oceanic sediments. But they are nowhere to be seen.

The first stage on the road to life is presumed to have been the built up by purely chemical synthetic processes occurring on the surface of the early earth of all the basic organic compounds (though basic components identified are imperfect) necessary for the formation of a living cell. These are supposed to have accumulated in the primeval oceans, creating a nutrient broth, the so called "prebiotic soup". In certain specialized environment these organic compounds were assembled into large macromolecules, proteins and nucleic acids. Eventually, over millions of years, combinations of these macromolecules occurred which were endowed with the property of self reproduction. Then driven by natural selection ever more efficient and complex self reproducing molecular systems evolved until finally the first simple cell system emerged. (Everything is assumed, but in reality, the urge of evolution is missing and we wait for the chance to happen which must be the edifice of evolution).

The existence of prebiotic soup is crucial to the whole scheme. Without an abiotic accumulation of the building blocks of the cell no life could ever evolve.

If the traditional story is true, therefore there must have existed for millions of years a rich mixture of organic compounds in the ancient oceans and some of this material would very likely have been trapped in the sedimentary rocks lash down in the seas of those remote times. But there is absolutely no positive evidence in existence, though rocks of great antiquity have already been examined.

Another problem concerns the presence of oxygen in the early atmosphere. Scientists agree this would prohibit evolution because it is thermodynamically impossible that reduced chemical compounds could have arisen in the presence of oxygen. Scientists agree that early earth was free of oxygen. Yet all the evidence tells us oxygen did exist. The evidence for an early oxidized atmosphere is increasingly so compelling that despite the far reaching implications, "it is becoming the new orthodoxy."

By natural process – controlled procedure of synthesizing chemicals by themselves is impossible in the absence of intelligent being. Scientists even today are unable to produce cell life though they know the life making elements and procedure in laboratory. "Life could no longer originate and develop from purely chemical evolution." (p. 600, Asimov)

Molecular evolution is not based on scientific authority. There is no publication in the scientific literature in prestigious Journals, specially Journalist books – that describe how molecular evolution of any real, complex, biological system either did occur or even might have occurred. There are assertions that such evolution occurred, but absolutely none are supported by pertinent experiments or calculations. Since no one knows molecular evolution by direct experience, and there is no authority on which to base claims of knowledge, it can truly be said that the assertion of Darwinian molecular evolution is merely bluster (p. 204). A conclusion is arrived at that molecular evolution never happened and is impossible, that all subsequent evolution never happened and must be considered impossible (p. 208). For years evolutionists have stated that the key evidence for evolution is found in the fossil record.

After an extensive evolution for human evolution, Dr. Duane Gish writes, "there is thus no evidence, either in the present world or in the world of the past, that man has arisen from some lower creature. He stands above as a separate and distinct created type or basic morphological design, endowed with qualities that set him far above all other living creatures. (p. 233).

Ramapithecus Australopithecus and pithecanth-ropus have all been heralded as transitional forms between ape and man. Ramapithecus is just one of a long series of creatures that have been suggested at one time or another as "missing link" but which when more complete evidence became available, were relegated to the ape family.

Neither is Australopithecus evidence of the man evolution. The view that the Australopithecus represent genuine intermediate has been challenged by the famous British anatomists Solly Lord Zuckerman and Dr. Charles Oxnard, formerly director of graduate studies and professor of anatomy at the University of Southern California Medical School. Lord Zuckerman led a research team for over 15 years that studied the anatomical features of ape, man, monkeys and the Australopithecus fossils, anatomical specimen from hundreds of apes, humans and monkeys were compared along with almost all available important fossil fragments of Australopithecus. Most evolutionists seem to clarify Australopithecus as a genus of the anthropoid apes. But Zuckerman replies, "I myself remain totally unpersuaded. Almost always when I have tried to check the anatomical claim on which the status of Australopithecus is based, I have ended in failure, and he concludes that Australopithecus was an ape and as such in no way related to immediate evolutionary ancestry of man.

Oxnard concludes that Australopithecus is actually not related to anything living to either man or ape, but was unique in certain ways. Dr. Gish concludes, "if Oxnard and Lord Zuckerman are correct, certainly Australopithecus was neither ancestral to man nor intermediate between ape and man.(p.233) with all the other extinct. Creatures certainly the Australopithecus could have been extinct ape that would today in the hope of finding evidence of human evolution be considered transitional between man and ape. After careful analysis Dr. Gish concludes the Australopithecus were justified extinct apes having no genetic relationship to either man or extinct apes.

Pithecanthropus or Homoerectus (Java man, Peking man) according to its discovered Dobias, was not a man, but a gigantic genus allied to the Gibbons. All the evidence from the fossil record and archeology indicate that the cro-magnon and Nuacdev people were however the same.

Meteorites may have Delivered Seeds of Life to Earth

Scientists have found evidence that meteorites may have delivered "left handed" amino acids the building blocks of life to earth.

Ronald Braslow, Professor, Columbia University as reported, thought earth was a hot, dry and lifeless planet three to four billion years ago, some scientists believe that a meteor slammed into desert plains at over ten thousand miles per hour planting the chemical seed of life.

Chains of amino acids make up the protein found in people, plants and all other forms of life on earth. There are two orientations of amino acids left and right which could mirror other. This is known as "charity". On order life to arise, proteins must contain only one chiralform of amino acids, left or right.

With the exception of a few right handed amino acids – based bacterial left handed "L amino acids – dominate on earth.

According to Braslow, these amino acids "seeds" formed in interstellar space, possibly on asteroids as they are carried through space, delivering to earth the left handed protein units. These meteorites were bringing the "seed of chirally".

Evidence of left handed excess was found on the surface of meteorites that have crashed in the earth even within the last hundred years landing in Australia and Tennesee Braslow simulated what occurred after the dust settled following a meteor bombardment, when the amino acids on the meteor mix oil with the primordial soup.

Under credible pre-biota condition desert like temperature and a little bit of water, he exposed amino acids chemical precursors to those amino acids found on meteorites. These amino acids could directly transfer their chirality to simple amino acids found in living things. On the pre-biotic earth this transfer left a slight excess of left handed amino acids.

Precursor of Life Found in a Distant Planet

The first detection of an organic molecule, methane in the atmosphere of a planet outside our solar system had been confirmed the presence of water there. Under the right conditions water can combine with organic chemicals like methane to make amino acids the building block of life as we know it. Existence of methane and water would be indicative that the planet was habitable. The extra solar planet known as HD 1897336 Jupiter like star about 63 light years from earth.

The temperature is to as 1700 dem of Farensity it is close to its present star.

Evolutionary biologists or scientists are in doubt that life on earth has not evolved but it was brought from outer space in the form of gem cell atom and hence a search in gigantic scale have been undertaken in out space.

lineage could go back billions of years. These saline tolerant [illegible] live deep inside a lake so saturated with salt that no fish, no plant, nothing or so we thought could survive here. These organisms extremophiles live in impossible conditions in extreme heat, cold, acidity, pressure radiation and salinity. There are anaerobes organisms that do not need free air or oxygen to live as opposed to aerobes which do. These creatures from the deep could even be our ancestors and possibly proto types of life on other planets.

The subterranean bacteria living independently of organic matter from the surface – eating and breathing geologic ingredients release methane in the process. Methane in the Martian atmosphere has hinted at the possibility that extremophiles [illegible] inhabit the red planet. A supposition that has made scientists less sceptical of finding extraterrestrial life.

All living organisms have DNA which helps in replication and survival. However, Jack Szostak of Harvard Medical school holds [illegible] with [illegible] that life [illegible] have existed even before DNA. But isn't DNA the fundamental building block of life? Deoxyribonucleic acid is the [illegible] molecule of life, [illegible] in a double helix [illegible] very [illegible] of an organism [illegible] DNA in order to understand its working [illegible] all the letters [illegible] in the human genome. [illegible] there was life before DNA, it has to have evolved from its precursor, the DNA [illegible] Ribonucleic Acid molecules, say [illegible].

The Harvard team is engaged in experiments which seek to create life from scratch as was done when the synthetic polio virus was created, [illegible]. However, this time round, it is not a synthetic life form that is being sought but the real Mc Coy. Scientists are trying to start an evolutionary cycle through random stringing together of nucleotides to create RNA molecules and specialized ribozymes when mixed with clay, the cell prototypes begin to grow and

4

Origin of Humans

Ascent of Man

Mankind is not descended from a single African Eve. Paleontologists have concluded studying a 15000 year old skull from Australia. A team from Michigan University found the skull had many features in common with that of a Homo erectus from Java, which had been assumed to be a distinct species displaced by modern humans.

According to new scientists, the researchers believe that modern humans are the product of continued world wide mixing of populations and gene flow between ancient homonids.

One study used genetic evidence that suggest "Munga man" an Australian skeleton dated between 40,000 and 60,000 years ago is genetically unrelated to African. The researcher Gregory Adcock of Australian National University and college said their findings showed the first modern humans evolved in Australia, not Africa.

Another research published in Journal Science analysed physical features of early human skulls to suggest there must have been inbreeding among the migrating Africans and resident Neanderthals and even Homo erectus species of pre-humans. "There never was a marauding band of Africans", University of Michigan Anthropologist Milford Wolpoff who led the second study, said in a telephone interview, "it certainly means that the Eve theory, the replacement, theory seem to be wrong."

Australian team and Wolpoff and colleagues belong to the matter regionalist school of human evolution. They believe humans evolved around the world at roughly the same time and that they probably mixed with earlier species such as Neanderthals and Homo erectus.

The out of Africa school says that all earlier humans died out and were replaced by a small group from Africa who quickly spread over the world. Some experts say. The two theories are not incompatible although they predict a fight over the latest studies.

But, Thorne, Wholedped author of the Alternative Theory of Regional Continents, said his findings, suggest that modern humanity developed from successive ways of people that moved out of Africa over the past 1.5 million years, not just the single group that figures in the out of Africa theory.

Thorne suggests. The successive waves of migrants from Africa and their descendants in different parts of the world remained on the same evolutionary path and eventually evolved into present day humans.

"What our evidence shows is that the situation is much more complicated than any of these supporters of "out of Africa" would have imagined. Dr. Thorne said.

They were arguing that because the earliest form of this particular gene in living people were found in Africa that meant that all people must have come from Africa.

Too Early to Dismiss out of Africa Theory

"Out of Africa theory is not dead. Anthropologists and others experts said, despite two studies that challenge the idea "we are all descended from a single African Eve."

US and Australian researchers published two reports that used physical and genetic evidence to suggest there may have been mixing of pre-humans with modern humans.

They said they had proved wrong the mainstream Out of Africa theory – that the ancestors of all living humans emerged from Africa some 50,000 years ago, and either killed off or out competed all other human like creatures who settled across much of the world.

Human Originated in Africa

The theory that modern humans evolved in Africa and spread across the world, got a boost with new research finding humans from diverse ethnic and geographical backgrounds back to that continent. Swedish scientists used mitochondrial DNA – genetic material in a cell that is passed unchanged from mother to child from 53 people who come from different continents and populations. Gyllenstein and his colleagues traced the ancestry of these people from DNA blood samples, the mitochondrial DNA is inherited only via the mother.

The biologists and geneticists at the University of Upsala said that even scientists who believe ancestors of modern humans who evolved simultaneously in several parts of the globe at about 2,00,000 years ago would now have to acknowledge that humans originated largely from Africa.

Origin of Man Theory

Debated after DNA tests

Australian scientists are challenging the theory of how modern humans originated after an analysis of the oldest DNA ever recovered from human remains.

The researchers recently extracted genetic material from a 60000 year old skeleton found near late Munga in New South Wales State in 1974. The material showed that Australia was a home to a group of anatomically modern aboriginal people much earlier than thought.

In a paper in the *American Journal* proceedings of the National Academy of Science, Anthropologist Dr. Alan Thorne of Australian National University said, the DNA findings last doubt on the so called Out of Africa model of human evolution.

It is remarkable that Anthropologist Alan Mann of the University of Pennsylvania in the US was quoted as saying by the Australian newspaper Tuesday about the DNA findings.

"What it says is that the more we know about human origin the more confusing the picture becomes." he said.

The Out of Africa theory proposes that all living people are descended from a group of modern Homo sapiens who left their African home land 1,50,000 years to 100000 years ago. The group and their descendants spread around the world replacing existing populations of older peoples including Neanderthals and Homo erectus.

But Thorne, who helped author the alternative theory of Regional Continuity, said his findings suggest that modern humanity developed from the successive waves of people that moved out of Africa over the past 1.5 million years, not just the single group that figures in the Out of Africa Theory.

The successive waves of migrants from Africa and their descendants in different parts of the world remained on the same evolutionary path and eventually evolved into present day humans, Thorne suggests.

He added: What our evidence shows is that the situation is much more complicated than any of these supporters of Out of Africa would have imagined.

They were arguing because the earliest forms of this particular gene in living people were found in Africa that meant that all people must have come from Africa. he said.

Individuals : A Sub-sets of a Higher Set

It is the ultimate goal of the self seeking to unite the God, where a drop of water merges into ocean, it loses its identity. The drop becomes part of a much larger whole. Much in the same way, individual soul seek union with God. There are different beliefs employing diverse practices to achieve this goal but ultimately it is only God's grace that helps us achieve success in this endeavour to merge with the supreme one.

At the highest level, all existence is one, God is the highest level of our combined consciousness also called the cosmic consciousness. Mathematically speaking as individuals, we are subset of a higher set.

The big bang created the material universe and, in the same way, eternally, the cosmic consciousness split itself up into different forms and levels. But this split does not mean that God has lost control. Far from it.

Due to the big bang galaxies recede away from each other and the universe is ever expanding. But gravity is still in control and after a critical line everything will fall back as gravity draws the universe back to naught. This is the cycle of creation. Just like the cycle of birth and death. In the same way, the super consciousness will know back all forms and levels of consciousness into itself.

Our sever of separateness from each other and from God is due to the fact that in our mental and sensory perceptions, we feel limited by our own individual bodies. This is because we as individuals, dwell as much lower level of consciousness.

Human Evolving to Perfection

Dr. Oliver Curry, a theorist of the Darwinian Centre of the London School of Economics said that he felt reasonably sure human evolution would result in humanity splitting into two sub species in 1,00,000 years. These would include a genetic upper class or gracile tall, slim and quick witted human, the other "robust" group, would be a squat, dim-witted and goblin-like under-class.

But Curry's most interesting projection was that the darker skinned of the world population may evolve to coffee coloured brown marker race will have symmetrical facial features, look athletic and have squarer jaws, deeper voices and bigger male organs. The women will have lighter, smooth, hairless skin and pert breasts. The uniform coffee coloured race will interbreed into sub species.

But thousands of years down the line, evolutionary theorist Oliver Curry says, coffee coloured humans will split into two distinct sub species best and worst. Haves – Top of the evolutionary tree will be lean, long limbed human, blessed with good health, intelligence and creativity.

The haves will be enjoying superior genes that give them symmetrical features, making them attractive.

Women of the next millennium will have clear eyes, pert breasts, glossy hair, and smooth, blemish free skin, thanks to cosmetic surgery.

Have nots – bottom of the heap will be an under class of unattractive, unintelligent, sickly creatures.

The have nots will be short, stocky and suffer from ill-health. They are also predicted to be dim-witted and ugly.

Spotted by the gadgets, humans will have lost the ability to communicate with their friends and family.

Love, sympathy and respect could be lost.

How our Brain Evolved

US and German Scientists launched a two year project to decipher the genetic code of the Neanderthal to help deepen understanding of how modern human's brains evolved.

Neanderthals were a species that lived in Europe and Western Asia from more than 2,00,000 years ago to about 30000 years ago. Scientists from Germany's Mak Planck Institute for Evolutionary Anthropology have teamed with a company in Connecticut to map the genome or DNA code.

"Neanderthal is the closest relative to the modern human, and we believe that by sequencing the Neanderthal we can learn a lot." said Michael Egholm, a vice president at 454. Life Science Corp of Branford, which will use its high speed sequencing technology in the project.

There are no firm answers yet about how humans picked up key traits such as walking up right and developing complex language. (these traits seem to be specific and natural to human and no copying to others) Neanderthals are believed to have been relatively sophisticated, but lacking in human's higher reasoning functions.

Neanderthal project follows scientists achievement last year in deciphering the DNA of the chimpanzee our closest living relative. That genome map produced a long list of DNA differences between humans and chimps and some hints about which differences might be crucial.

Chimp genome led to literally too many questions. There were 35 million differences between us and chimpanzees – that's too much to figure out. Jonathan Rothberg 454's said in a telephone interview.

By having Neanderthal, we will really be able to know the small percentage of differences that gain us higher cognitive abilities." he said. Neanderthal is going to open the box. It is not going to answer the question but it is going to tell where to look to understand all those higher cognitive functions.

5

Theory of Human Origin in Africa

In Search of Missing Link

Complete skeleton of ape-man species discovered

Scientists have discovered a remarkable, complete skeleton of a three year old female from the ape-man species represented by "Lucy".

The discovery should facilitate the contentions debate about whether this species, which walked upright also climbed and moved through trees easily like an ape. The remains are 3.3 million years old, making them the oldest known skeleton of such a youthful human ancestor.

It is pretty unbelievable to find such a complete fossil from that long ago. Said scientist Fred Spoor, it is a once in a life time find.

Spoor, professor of evolutionary anatomy at University College, London described the fossil the Journal *Nature.*

The skeleton was discovered in 2000 in North Eastern Ethiopia. Scientists have spent five pain staking years remaking the bone from sand stone and the job will take years more to complete.

Judging by how well it was preserved, the skeleton may have come from a body that was quickly buried by sediment in a flood, the researchers said. The creatures were a member of Australian Pithecus Afarensis, which lived in Africa between about 4 million and 3 million years ago. The most famous Afarensis is Lucy, discovered in Ethiopa in 1974, which lived about 100,000 years after the new found specimen. Most scientists believe Afarensis stood upright and walked on two feet, but they argue about whether it had ape-like agility indeed.

Climbing ability would require anatomical equipment like long arm that dangled down to just above the knees. The question is whether such features indicate climbing ability or just evolutionary baggage.

Spoor said, so far analysis of the new fossil has not settled the argument but does seem to indicate same climbing ability where the lower body is human-like, he said, the upper, body is ape-like, the shoulder blades resemble those of gorilla, rather than a modern human. The neck seems short and thick like a great ape's rather then the more slender version human have to keep the head stable while running. The organ of balance in the inner ear is more ape like than human.

Man-animal

Many critics have responded to the inadequacies of the new science of human nature by suggesting that the problem lies in scientific arrogance. Scientists, they suggest place too great a faith in human reasons and are insufficiently humble about the human capacity to understand ourselves and our world.

Most scientists, like most intellectuals today possess insufficient faith in human beings and human qualities. That is why they seek to reduce human beings to the state of animals or machines. The barbarous history of the 20th Century had left many people disillusioned about "what it means to be human? Such permission has also helped shape scientists view of what it is to be human. From the beginning of the scientific revolution to the beginning of the 20th century, most scientists took it for granted that human beings were exceptional creatures, not simply distinct from other animals, but superior to them because of out possession of reason and consciousness, language and morality. Such a view forced scientists to balance their mechanistic view of nature with a humanistic view of man.

The past century, however, has changed all this, leading as Rob Fokey observes to a loss of confidence in the extent to which humans could be said to be on a pedestal above the swamp of animal brutishness. In Fokey's words, "apes have become more ape like through the course of the 20th century, which humans have become more apish.

Chimp DNA Decodes Evolution Tale

Scientists have decoded the chimp genome and compared it with that of humans, a major step toward defining what makes people human and developing a deep insight into the evolution of human sexual behaviour, scientists sequenced the DNA of chimpanzee named Dint and compared it with that of human.

The comparison pinpoints the genetic differences that have arisen in the two species since they split from common ancestor some six million years ago. The realization that chimpanzees hold a trove of information about human evolution and nature comes at a time when they and other great apes are under harsh pressures in their native habitat.

Chimpanzees and people possess almost identical sets of genes. So the genes that have changed down the human lineage should hold the key to what makes people human.

Biologists suspects that only a handful of genes are responsible for the major changes that reshaped the apelike ancestor of both species into a human and that these genes should be identifiable by having evolved at a particularly rapid rate (can the scientists repeat the process practically?).

The comparison of the human and chimp genomes reported in the issue of *Nature*, takes a first step in this direction but has not yet tracked down the critical handful of genes responsible for human evolution. One problem is the vast number of differences some 40 million in the sequence of DNA units in chimp and human genomes. The study indicate that both belong to separate species and don't share DNA.

Evolution of 'y' Chromosome

After decoding the chimp genome and comparing it with humans, scientists are struggling to find an answer to the question of the evolution of human "Y" chromosome. The new finding implies that humans have led sexually virtuous lives for the past six million years at least in comparison with the flamboyant promiscuity of chimpanzees.

Some 300 million years ago, the "Y" chromosome used to carry the same 1000 or so genes as its partner the "X" chromosome. But because the "Y" cannot exchange DNA with the X and update its genes, in human it has lost all but 16 of its X related genes through mutation or failure to stay relevant to their owner's survival. However, the "Y" has gained some genes from other chromosomes because it is a safe haven for genes that benefit only men, "since it never enters a woman's body". These added genes, not surprisingly all have functions involved in making sperm.

The scientific world's leading student of the "Y" chromosome, David Page of the White Head Institute of Cambridge, may has been seeking to understand whether "Y" chromosome will loose yet more genes and lapse into terminal decay taking men with it. The idea of the "Y" extinction was so delicious from the perspective of gender politics, says, Page.

Two years ago he had discovered a surprising mechanism that protects the sperm making genes.

Chimpanzee's genes have been sequenced like humans. Comparing it with human genome could help determine what led to the evolution of humans some six million years ago. Since chimps and human came from the same stock, their genomes could reveal what sets us apart from other primates. Human and chimps seem to share 98 per cent of DNA and very few genes have spared changes that led to us evolving differently. If the similarities are striking the difference is fascinating. The chimps promiscuity and gene mutation, say scientists have rendered five of its 16 X chromosome related genes useless. The "Y" chromosome in most chimps has suffered fierce sperm competition from the few Alpha male chimps who often edged out other chimps in the mating game. The researcher say the competition enables the Alpha male produce more and better sperm. The survival of the chimp in terms of natural selection has come to depend upon the virility of the Alpha male.

Humans on the other hand, have lost none of their "X" related genes in the last six million years. Were we less promiscuous or did our chromosome behave that way out of sheer chance? That the human mating system did not depend on sperm competition for species. Survival is itself a revelation, probably even then, some unique faster began to differentiate us from other primates. However, more instance cannot form scientific theory. Paleontologists studies of human fossils, indicate that the practice of human pair bonding between mating couples perhaps evolved only 1.7 million years ago. But the genome studies show that even during the first four million years following the human chimp diversification, sperm competition was irrelevant human mating process. Primatologists offer that our ancestors might well have been gorilla – like rather than chimp like or bonobo-like. These question will continue to intrigue us. What matters is that international research teams engaged in different streams of studies in this case, biology, paleontology, mathematics, IT, and Evolutionary History are bringing us closer to understanding our relationship with other species.

Though scientists have compared the genome of ape and humans, but nowhere have they indicated that human genome or DNA have actually descended from ape? It also does not indicates common descent of ape and human. But it anticipated that human have descended from ape but no indication of inheritance of DNA from Ape.

Fossil-Human Link

In following the fossil tracks, human evolution scientists have for years searched for links between Australopithecus, the kin of famous "Lucy" skeleton and even earlier possible ancestors. Now they think they have found some connection in Ethiopia.

An international team of paleontologists is reporting the discovery of transitional species superimposed in sediments in the neighbourhood of a single site, Tim D White a paleontologist at the University of California, Berkley who was a team leader and his colleagues said the 4.1 million old fossil were anatomically intermediate between the earlier species – Ardipithecus Afarensis, the Lucy family. The new found bones and teeth are the earliest remains of the most primitive Australopithecus known as anamnesis.

This new discovery closes the gap between fully grown Australopithecus an earlier form we call Ardipithecus. White said in a statement we now know where Australopithecus come from before four million years ago.

The Scientists said the fossils supported the hypothesis that Australopithecus anamnesis was a direct ancestor of Afarensis, which lived 3 million to 3.6 million years ago. The Australopithecus genes, resembling apes in structure and brain size but unlike the great apes in that it walked on two legs – is thought to have given rise to our genus Homo.

Some later Australopithecus survived until about 1.2 million years ago, existing in Africa as contemporaries with Homo erectus, a predecessor of modern humans. The genes Ardipithecus, discovered by white in 1992 appears to have lived 4.4 million to 5.7 million years ago. It was even more ape like but also walked on two legs.

The relationship between Ardipithecus and Australopithecus, Scientists said, remains unclear because of the wide gap in their chronology. Still they suggest one probably led to the other.

White said, a key to interpreting the new anamnesis where it was discovered, in the middle Awash valley of the few region of Ethiopia. The area about 140 miles north east of Adis Ababa, Ethiopia's capital has also yielded critical evidence of the Afarensis and the Ramidus species of Ardipithecus.

Finding these three things in time sequence in a simple place, that is never happened before he said.

Missing Human Link

In following the fossil tracks of human evolution, scientists for years searched for links between Australopithecus, the kin of the famous "Lucy" skeleton, and even earlier possible ancestors. Now they think they have found some connections in Ethiopia.

The earliest remains – An international team of paleontologists is reporting the discovery of transitional species superimposed in sediments in the neighbourhood of a single site. Tim D White a paleontologist at the University of California, Berkley, who was team leader and his colleagues said the 4.1 million years old fossils were anatomically immediate between the earlier species Ardipithecus Ramidus and the later species Australopithecus Afarensis, the Lucy family, The new found bones and teeth the earliest remains of the most primitive Australopithecus known as Anamnesis.

"This new discovery closes the gap between the fully blown Australopithecus and earlier forms we call Ardipithecus came from before four million years ago".

Means primal development – The Scientists said the fossils supported the hypothesis that Australopithecus Anamnesis was a direct ancestor of Afarensis which lived 3 million to 3.6 million years ago. The Australopithecus genes resembling apes in stature and brain size but unlike the great apes in that it walked on two legs is thought to have given rise to our own genus Homo.

Some later, Australopithecus survived until about 1.2 million years ago, existing in Africa as contemperates with homo erectus a predecessor of modern humans.

The genes Ardipithecus, discovered by White in 1932 appears to have lived 4.4 million to 5.7 million years ago it was even more apelike, but also walked on two legs.

"Finding there three things in time sequence in a single place, that's never happened before." He said.

A Tree of Life (Evolution)

The mythological invented "Tree of Life" is believed to have its roots in heaven, since that is where the creator resides. Speakers of truth will have to first find their way through the many dense branches to get to the trunk and thereafter the roots. One can draw an interesting parallel from this in the latest findings of human evolution. The recent unearthing of six to seven million year old hominid skull could help link the huge evolutionary gap between the 10 million year old ape age and the five million year old find, believed to be evidence of the first hominids. A hominid is a member of the human family markedly different from chimpanzees, gorillas, orangutans, gibbons and other members of the ape family. Nicknamed "Toumai", the new found skull, "Saheleanthropus Chadensis" is thought to represent that point on the evolutionary time scale when hominds took shape, moving away from being chimps but still a long way off from today's human. Interestingly, Toumai has both ape like and human like features, a contradictory mix of the primitive and modern. While its brain case is like that of an ape, its prominent borrow ridges and canines are distinctly human like.

Toumai could therefore be the tip of that iceberg which could sink our current ideas about the nature of human evolution. Rather than a simple linear progression. Human evolution is now being viewed as being more like a bush whose branches are sometimes inter winged and sometime not with some ending as dead ends. We need to find our way through those various branches of evolution, which have their own distinct characteristics, but which are ultimately connected to the main trunk homo sapiens. Ancient theories of human creation range from the Biblical story of Adam and Eve to humans made of clay of the Munda tradition, Hindu ideas of progression from Brahma to fish, tortoise, boar, Narasimha on to more refined forms of humans. Ten Avtars of Vishnu provide an interesting analogy to modern theories of evolution.Exobiologists, on the other hand, have an out of the world creating story that we are born of the seeds sown by renegade debris from out space. But Toumai's discovery is not entirely controversy free the skull looks more like that of a female gorilla, says one scientists. While critics span over whose skull it is. Toumai could nevertheless prove to be a crucial place in the evolutionary Jigsaw puzzle. (TOI Editorial)

Early Humans Bred with Chimps

Our early ancestors interbred with chimpanzees after the two species drew apart millions of years ago, as suggested by a research paper.

The provocative idea is sketched by US genome experts, who have discovered that hominids and chimps diverged more recently and over a much longer time scale than anyone had thought.

During this time, the authors theorize, the two primates were rather more than kissing cousins, they had sex, swapping genes before making a final separation.

"The analysis revealed big surprises with major implicates for human evolution" says co-author Ericlander, Director of the Broad Institute of Harvard and Massachusetts Institute of Technology.

Until now, the belief was that humans and chimpanzees shared a common ancestor but went their separate ways around 6.5 – 7.4 million years ago. The basis for this is a carbon dated fossil called Toumai whose supports say is the oldest known human.

Are we the descendants of Toumai, or Homo erectus, or Lucy, or from the union of Homo erectus and Trobiandirs. We are not sure. We say that modern man evolved in sub-saharan region of Africa, but from whom.

Oldest Human Foot Prints Found

Scientists have confirmed that the oldest human foot prints even found, the devils, trails in Italy are 3,45,000 years old.

A team at the University of Padov had first found the foot prints in hardened volcanic ash atop Roccamontina volcano in southern Italy in 2003. At that time, it estimated that the marking were anywhere between 3,85,000 and 3,25,000 years old.

Now a French team has confirmed the exact year of the foot prints that belong to three early humans who were probably climbing down the side of the volcano, according to a report in the *New Scientist*.

In fact, the scientists led by Stephane Scaillet at the Laboratory of Climatic and Environmental Sciences used argon dating techniques to verify the prints age.

"Their more rigorous methods confirm that these are the oldest human foot prints ever found" said Paolo Miotto, who led the Italian team that first described the foot prints to the world.

According to him, the new findings also confirm that the owners of the foot prints were Homo Heidelbergensis.

Why Man is not an Ape/ Monkey?

A study has nailed the reason that differentiate us from monkey, for the matter, any other animal. Humans have more copies of a possibly important brain gene in their genomes than other apes, a new study finds.

Called MGC 8902, the gene is implicated in the function of the neocortex, the region of the brain that, in humans is responsible for consciousness, language, and other higher cognitive functions, lives science. com. Reported.

The researchers compared the genomes of humans to several ape species, including chimpanzees, gorillas, malagues and baboons. They found that the more closely, related the apes were to humans, the more copies of MGC 8902 they had in their genomes. Humans had 312 copies of the gene, chimps had 37 and malagues 30.

The study performed by Maydalena Poposco and colleagues at the University of Colorate, is detailed in the the Journal Science.

Gene duplication is important for generating evolutionary novelty. With two identical genes one continues performing its normal function, leaving the other tree to mutate into a new and potentially useful gene. One of the most dramatic instances of gene duplication occurred about 500 million years ago when cluster of gene, called the Hox gene duplicated several times.

Today, Hox gene are responsible for determining where limbs and other body segments will grow during the development of numerous organisms, ranging from fruit fling to human beings. Scientists recently figured out how to take Hox gene and use it to make up for defects in another.

Scientists also recently linked another gene, called Hari to the unique cognitive ability of humans. They found that Hari, a gene important for brain development in numerous animals, has undergone accelerated evolution in human, racking up many more mutations than would be expected by chance.

Researchers in the current study predict MGC 8902 encodes for multiple sections of protein, called DUF 1220 whose function is unknown but which is abundant in the neocortex and in particular sub set of brain cells. (by John Noble Wiford)

Ascent of Ape – Man

The discovery of ape man fossil believed to be the oldest in the world, by French and Kenya scientists in Kenya's great rift valley, bestows a bold new dimension on the unfolding saga of humanity's roots. Although the fossils themselves have not been dated, the rock from which they unearthed is known to be six million years old. This means, the Kenyan ape man promptly nick named "Millennium Man" could be at least 1.5 million years older than the oldest known hominid found earlier in Aramis in Ethiopia. This could profoundly alter the way scientists think about evolution and origin of species. The Kenyan ape man found at Kapsomin in the Jugen Hills in Kenya's Baringo district, seems to be in a more advanced state of evolution. The almost perfectly preserved femur shows that the ape man had strong back legs which enabled himm to walk upright, a characteristic which relates the creature directly to the line leading to many preliminary study on the arm and finger bones and teeth also show that the Kapsomin hominid was an agile climber of trees and probably subsisted on hard skinned fruits among other foods. However the fossil also bear remains of an ancient tragedy that occurred in the African Eden, it looks as though the Millennium man was killed dragged up into a tree and eaten probably by a large cat, in its usual resting place, another bits that fell into the water below was preserved perfectly in a fortuitous chain of events leading to last week's press conference in Nairobi.

To be fare, the discovery of the Kapsomin hominid does not mean that human descended directly from apes. Experts say, humans, chimps, gorillas, and other apes descended from a common ancestor and evolved independently. Although today there is only one species of human on the planet, in the hoary past there were several competitions. Since 1994, for instance, scientists have added four new species of hominid to the human family tree, the roots of which go now back to six million years with the latest find. This was the time when a crucial development bipedelism or two legged walking – occurred, separating the ape man from Korchaute like cohorts. The advent of tool making perhaps 2.5 million years before the present, marked the second advance. Then somewhere between two million and one million years ago, came the explosive growth of the brain and our ancestors began to emerge from Africa. Scientists have been painstakingly reconstructing this history by unearthing new fossils of known species. It could help them trace the complex relation among our sundry ancestors to further under mine the mythical account of Adam's creation. However, these discoveries do not in any way cheapen or devalue the ultimate mystery of life and its evolution. Indeed they only vitiate what the Jewish Doctor and Rabbic articulated in 12th century, the possibility that matter itself had the power to transform and guidance itself into intelligence seems far more awesome and divine than that of an angel quickening itself from outside. (Editorial TOI)

Fossil Ape could be the Ancestor of all

An ape that lived 13 million years ago in what is now Spain may have been the last common ancestor of all apes, including chimpanzees, gorillas, orangutans and humans, said the researchers.

The fossil provides a missing link, not directly between humans and an apelike ancestors, but between great apes and lesser apes such as gibbons, the researcher said.

The creature, named Pierolapithecus Catalaunicus, had a stiff lower spine and flexible wrists that would have made it a tree climbing specialist, the researchers write in this issue of the journal Science This probably is very close to the last common ancestor of great apes and humans said Moya-Sola of the Miguel Crusafont Institute of Paleontology in Barcelona, Spain, who led the study.

It would have looked something like a modern Chimpanzee and probably ate fruit, said his colleague.

The Ancestors we Never had

Nothing is ever quite settled when it comes to ancient hominids, and there unit a single claim in paleontology that Canile be used to start an argument. So, there will be people who will argue with Dr. Richard Klein of Stanford who has made one nostalgic statement for ancestors, he says, one never had.

If he is right, contact between modern humans and Neanderthals was fleeting at best, with no interbreeding. There has never been any conclusive evidence that the two species did interbreed but it has always been a possibility.

And just a few years ago in 1999 Scientists in Portugal found the 25,000 year old skeleton of a boy who seemed to have been a hybrid, the offspring of homo sapiens (modern humans) and Homo Neanderthalensis. But although there is still interest in this find. Dr. Klein, at least is unimpressed. In a paper, in the *Science*, he reviews the recent research and calls the find ambiguous at best.

DNA evidence is equally discouraging, he writes, several studies of both living humans and Neanderthals bones have found that every living person is descended from African ancestors who lived about 100,000 years ago. But the evolutionary branches that suggested that Neanderthals humans us split half a million years ago, suggesting that Neanderthals contributed nothing to the recently sequenced human genome.

But homo sapiens is a lonely species. We have no living relatives in our genus, and the thought that we might have spent some time with another human species, even it did go extinct, is comforting. A bit of gene swapping between species would seem to cement the link. These stories that fiction writers invent about Neanderthals have witnessed in the history of the earth than the emergence and spread of modern humans. Would require quite bit of time travel.

One has to hope around in time and place from about 300 000 years ago, when Neanderthals started to appear to about

Table 1
Evolution of Fossils

ERA		*PERIOD*	*AGE*	*EVENTS*
Archaeozoic		Achaean	4.6 Billion	Formation of earth, soil and weathering, sedimentation.
Preterozoic	PRIMARY	Algonkian	3.9 - 3.5 billion	Carbon –dioxide
		Ordovician	2.8 - 2.5 billion	Oxygen photosynthetic
		Pre-Cambrian	1 billion – 600 million	Single celled
		Cambrian	570 - 510 million	Multi-celled, marine life
Cryptozoic		Ordovician	510 - 439 million	Gondawana land mass – South America, S. Africa, Antartica, Greater India, Australia.
		Silurian	439 - 408 million	
Phanerozoic		Divonian	408 - 362 million 362- 322 million	Glaciations started at S. Pole, S. America, S. Africa, India, W. Australia, Madagascar.
Paleozoic	SECONDARY	Carboniferous	322-290 million	Abundant land and plant life at south pole.
		Permian	290-245 million	Sea level dropped, reptiles, Dinosaurs, birds, amphibians, Mammals, humans evolved.
		Triassic	245-208 million	
		Jurassic	208-145 million	
		Cretaceous	145-65 million	

(Contd.)

(Contd. Table 1)

ERA		*PERIOD*	*AGE*	*EVENTS*
Mesozoic	TERTIARYRY	Eocene	55 million	Fossil hominoids
		Oligocene	35 million	Agyptopithecus – 28 million
		Miocene-Neogene	30 million	Dryopithithecus – 20 million Kenyapithecus – 15 – 10 million
		Pliocene	10 million	Ramapithecus – 9 million Ramidus – 4.5 million Australopithecus – 4-2.3 million Afarensis – 3.5-3 million Afaricanus – 3.2 million Homohabilus – 2 million
Cainozoic	QUARTERNARY	Pleistocene	400000	Homoeructus – 1.64 million
		Holocene	12000	Homo-sapiens – paraesapiens Homoneanderthalensis – 250000-125000 yrs Homo-sapiens

30,000 years ago, by which time they were clearly gone. And one would have to visit Africa, Asia and Europe one would need a machine that moved instantaneously in space and time. The only such machine now in existence is fiction, and in it Neanderthals can indeed be visited. (TOI 16 April, 2003)

Descent of Man

There are two central concepts of evolution. The first in universal common descent – the idea that every living creation can trace an unbroken lineage back to the same primitive life form. Biologists armed with the powerful tool of molecular genetics overwhelmingly accept this view. The intelligent design proponents however, say that there is a lot of ambiguity and descent about the lives of evidence.

The second is natural selection which holds that the entire complexity and ingenuity of life has evolved due to acumulation of small random mutation. I.D. proposes an intuitively appealing alternative that the living world reflects the design of a conscous, rational intelligence.

Biblical theory – The most controversial debate over this creation story of the Bible relates to its time-span, as scientists have found 14 billion years history of evolution.

Darwinian theory – It propounds the theory of common descent, the idea that every living creature can trace an unbroken lineage back to the same primitive life forms.

Darwin reasoned that all creatures were continually developing minor changes that made them either more or less fit to survive in their ecological niches.

Those good chances survived, while those with less propitious ones were weeded out.

Over long period of time those small changes accumulated until entirely new species were established.

Intelligent descent – The theory argues that aspects of the natural world are best explained by an intelligent cause.

Not an indirect process. They argue that mutations happening over billion of years are impossible, which citing the example of eyes Evolutionary biologists respond that even primitive light sensitive spot has survival values and have tried to show how a series of small improvement could eventually build the complete organ. They call it irreducible complexity – meaning that all their parts are necessary for them to function at all.

Selfish Biocosm – This theory begins with the premise that the universe is life friendly and life on the earth was started by a very intelligent being. It says eventually life and intelligence will evolve to the point one is capable of figuring out how to create, or give birth to another universe just as earlier universe gave birth to our universe. As the progeny of an earlier universe, the cosmic equivalent of DNA is stitched into our universe, providing a recipe for development and a blue print for constructing off spring.

It is the changes in the gene that separated ape and human.

Authenticity of Missing Time Contested

A seven million years old skull gave its discoverer a headache as critics disputed his claim to have found the oldest human ancestor. Michel Brunet head of an archeological team that unearthed the skull inched showed off his find at the University of Pritiers in Western France which was published in the scientific journal *Nature*.

But the critics of the Paris scientist contested that Brunet actually had found the skull of an ancient female Gorilla. One critic Brigitti Senut of the National History Museum of Paris said the skull's short face and small canine teeth merely pointed to a female and were not conclusive evidence that it was a hominid. The characteristic taken to conclude this new skull is a hominid are sexual characteristics. More over other characteristics attached remained more of the Gorillas.

So little is known about the period of history represented by the skull. Ten million years ago the world had an abundance of apes and it was not until 5 million years later the first good record of hominids or members of the human family distinct from chimpanzees and other apes appeared.

Brunet said he could not approve that Toumai had walked upright, a crucial difference between ape and humans, because he had not found any leg and arm bone with the skull.

Senut contested the theory that Toumai represented the missing link of human evolution and cited the case of a skull discovered in the 1960 and accepted for 20 years as that of a hominid before experts finding agreed it was a female Gorilla. The skull had an ambiguous shape with the front looking pre-human but the back like that of a large monkey. Whatever it was a man or another type of primate can be determined by chemical research to establish Toumai diet or a reconstruction of the skull by computer imaging.

Evolution Apes

Primates are a group of mammals a scientific category that contains over 230 species of humans, Lorises Tarsiers monkeys apes and humans. All primates including humans share at least part of a set of common characteristics many of which evolved as adaptations for life in the trees, an environment in which the earliest primates evolved.

These characteristics include more reliance on sight than smell, overlapping fields of vision, allowing three dimensional sight, limbs, ánd hands adapting for dingling on, leaping from and swinging in the trees, the liability to grasp and manipulate small objects using fingers with nails instead of claws, large brains in relation to body size and complex social life.

Scientific classification of primates reflects evolutionary relationship among individual species and group of species. Strep Sirhina or wet nosed primates of which the living representatives include Lemurs and Lorises, are commonly known as Prosimians and they are the most primitive of living primate. They have all the basic characteristics of primates although their brains are neither particularly large nor complex and they have a more elaborate and sensitive olfactory system than other primates.

Earliest monkeys and apes evolved from ancestral Haplorhine or dry nosed primates of which the most primitive living representative is the tarsier, monkeys apes and humans, who share many traits not found in other primates together make up the suborder anthropeidea. Anthropoid primates are divided into the new world – consisting of South America, Central America and the Caribbean Islands, and the old world, which includes the African and Eurasian groups. Apes and humans together make up the super family Hominoidea, a grouping that emphasizes the close relationship among these species. In recent times in many areas of the world, another species of apes have been noticed which is supposed to be a link between man and ape is called "Big foot". It is said to exist in India, Canada and Malaysia. Its size is more than six feet and is hairy all over the body, Walks straight and survives from plants and fruits. Scientists are yet to study these species.

How Similar are Human to other Primates?

About 98 per cent of the genes in human and chimpanzees are identical making chimps closest living biological relatives. This does not mean that humans have evolved from chimpanzees but does indicate that both species evolved from a common primate ancestor.

Orangutans, the great apes of south east Asia differ genetically from humans to a great extent, indicating a more distant evolution any relationship. Modern humans have a number of physical characteristics indicative of an ape ancestry : shoulder's with a wide range of movement and fingers capable of strong grasping. Both humans and apes also have larger brains and greater cognitive abilities than most other mammals.

Human social life too, shares similarities with that of African apes and other primates, such as baboons and Rhesus monkeys that live in large and complex social groups.

However, modern humans fundamentally differ from apes. Peoples brains are much larger and more complex and people have intellectual capacity and forms of culture and communication.

In addition, only humans habitually walk upright, can precisely manipulate very small objects, and have a throat structure that makes speech possible.

Who were the first Humans?

At least 4.4 million years ago in Africa, an ape like species had evolved that had two important traits, which disguised from other apes: small canine teeth and bipedalism the ability to walk on two legs.

These are considered the first humans. There are many ideas about why the early humans split off from the apes, initiating the course of human evolution.

Virtually all hypotheses invoke environment change as important factor, specially in influencing the evolution.

Fossils from several different early humans species that lived between 4 million and 2 million years ago, show a variety of adaptations, that mark the transition from ape to human.

Missing Link in Evolution

A fossil of monkey like creature stated to be 47 million years old have been discovered by paleontologists which they claim may provide a missing link in human evolution, TOI reported on 21st Mary 2009.

The scientists said, it is the most complete fossil primate ever found, only missing part of one leg below the knee and could shed light on an early stage of primate evolution. Norwegian paleontologist. John Hurum, who led a team of scientists, who analysed the fossil in the past two years, said, it may resemble one of the earliest ancestors of humans but was not likely to have a direct ancestor.

The fossil is about 95 per cent complete, even including finger tips with nails, and lack only the lower portion of one leg. It also includes gut contents, showing the creature ate leaves and fruits in its rain forest environment. The animal was a juvenile female that experts believe died at 9 or 10 months of age. The fossil recovered from a mine about 25 miles south east of Frankfurt, is nicknamed Idea after Hurum's six year old daughter. Its scientific name is Darwinivs massillae where it was found.

The direct ancestors of humans "must have looked something like" Ida Hurum said. This is the only clue got to what they looked like" he said. But being cautious as scientists we are of course not stating that this is our direct ancestor. That is too much he added. Ida is linked to humans by the ape. Experts also said her opposable big toes and nails, not claws, confirm she was a primate.

The fossil was found by an amateur collector in the Messells pit, a dis-used quarry southeast of France fort where many fossils have been found. Ida was kept in a private collection until it was offered for sale to Hurum at the University of Oslo in 2006.

Scientists have discovered many fossils linking human ancestors, but not purely human. Human link of fossil is still missing and will remain so as the times pass on.

Human began Walking Upright 6 Million years Ago

As early as six million years ago, at the beginning of the human lineage, an ancestral species had already developed the transforming ability for upright walking, experts reported.

A fossil thigh bone found at Kenya yielded strong evidence that, the species Orrorin Tugensis stood and walked on its hind limbs. It was the earliest evidence of bipedal locomotion. It was reported in the journal *Science* by Brian G Richmond and William L. Jungers, Paleoanthropologist at George Washington University and the State University of New York, respectively. The research includes examination of original fossils and composition with skeleton of modern human, pro-humans and chimpanzees.

African "Little Foot" the Missing Link

Foot prints preserved in volcanic ash show that human ancestors in Africa were walking upright as early as 3.7 million years ago, showing this behaviour one of their first and most distinctive departures from all other primates.

But was bipedal walking the only way these proto humans got about? Were they still climbing trees, in the manner of chimpanzees for safety, sleeping and gathering fruits and nuts?

These questions have long puzzled and divided anthropologists study for crucial evolutionary changes in early hominids or human forerunner! After their divergence from the apes.

Now the discovery of four foot bones in South Africa has produced the best fossil evidence yet for the nature of ancestral locomotion, and many yield compelling answers or simply rekindle old debates.

The four little bones, rather than settling debate have already caused more fur to fly among the small group of experts who study the origin of man.

In a discovery, paleontologists describe as the most important in Southern African hominid exploration in recent decades, the four bones formed the in step and the beginning of the great toe of a hominid that may have lived as much as 3.5 million years ago, presumably a member of the Australopithecus genes.

This is the oldest set of connected foot bones of any hominid and the earliest evidence by more than half a million years for the existence of such ancestors south of tropical Africa.

But the greatest importance to the history of human evolution analysis of bones, dubbed "little foot" has revealed that this hominid combined human like and ape like foot characteristics.

The weight bearing hand and the springy arch of the foot were unquestionably adapted for upright walking much like modern man and paleontologists who examined the fossils which the great toe was set a wide angle to the other toes and was lightly flexible, presumably capable of grasping and climbing.

In particular, the shape of the joint forming the ball of the foot indicated that the big toe could rotate inward like the opposable human thumb, useful in tree climbing.

In a report of their research published in an issue of the journal Science, Dr. Roneld J. Clarke and Dr. Philip V. Tobias paleontologists at the university of Witwaterstand in Johannesburg, said the foot fossils were, "the best available evidence that the earliest South African Australopithecus, while bipedal was equipped to include arbored or climbing activities in its locomotive repertoire.

The Scientists said, little foot strongly suggested that this early ancestor was not exclusively bipedal as are modern humans, but must have been living both on the ground and on the trees.

The bones were discovered in 1980 but their significance was not recognized until much later. They were found in the deepest part of sediments in the Sterkfontein cave, which is near Johannesburg and has been the site of numerous early human discoveries.

The bones probably belonged to an early member of Australopithecus Africans or another early hominid species, the paleontologists said. They are the first connected bones found from the same foot of a single individual of such creatures.

"This may be the kind of foot that made Marg Leakes" foot prints. Mr. Tobias said in a telephone interview from Johannesburg.

He was referring to 3.7 millions year old foot prints embedded in hardened volcanic ash at the Lactoli site in Tanzania. This trail of foot steps, made by two or three individuals walking with an upright human like gait, was discovered in 1977 by scientists on an expedition led by Marg Leakes.

Missing Link – common Ancestor

Terrestrial lives share the same material and chemical composition, however they differ in their structure and thus fall in distinct and separate species. It does not mean that they share the same ancestor, they have different descendants. It is futile to term the missing link common ancestor. "Each and every species is distinct in itself. Species is a group of interbreeding natural populations, reproducing isolated from other such groups."

Similar in form and structure physically and biologically. Integrated form is no form, as such form do not survive on earth. ET have integrated form, and so they are super natural being belonging to out space. Since physiologically and biologically or genetically may share the body.

Science in Quest of Mankind (Dating Techniques)

Archeology has been invaded by specialists in the past molecular biologists and computing specialists, Now it is the turn of the Physicists who are bringing with them new ideas and newer gadgetry for reordering prehistory.

Within a little more than a decade their high tech methodology has revolutionized the way scholars described the emergence of man. The older view was that Homo erectus is an ancestor of modern man spread out of Africa several hundred years ago into Europe and Asia. On these continents it was believed man evolved slowly passing through transitional forms before they began to look like man. Neanderthal man who lived 35,000 years ago was believed to be one of these immediate forms.

But now the physicists on their new hunting ground have found other evidence. From a statistical study of DNA mutation rates they claim that the ancestors of all modern man lived in Africa. From experiment in accelerators and solid state physics they show that modern man was on the scene earlier than believed perhaps 90,000 to 100,000 years ago. If this is true then we must conclude that the Neanderthals were not humans in the making but human competitions that were swept aside as modern man established himself – a radical revamping of history.

Older paleontologists are reluctant to accept this. They prefer tracing evolution in the changing shape of the bones of fossils. But the new high technology dating techniques appear to be gaining ground.

Three techniques – electron spin resonance (ESR), thermoluminesane (TL) and mitochondrial DNA (mt DNA) studies lie at the heart of the controversy. All three are dating techniques that in theory at least provide absolute dates for the period that cannot be read by already existing techniques – carbon dating that reaches only 40,000 years into the past and KAr dating that begins counting at about 300000 years ago. ESR and TL are solid state physics methods that measure time by testing for minute radiation induced changes in crystal structure. They have been crucial in proving the oldest dates for prehominid fossils. Mt. DNA methods have provided the genetic data for the argument that modern man's origins go back to a single woman who lived in Africa 200,000 years ago.

This "Out of Africa" or "mother of all hypothesis was developed by Alan Wilson and Mark Stoneking of the University of California, Berkeley and is erased on the ESR, TL and Mt. DNA research. Mitochondrial DNA as averse to nuclear DNA is inherited only from the mother and so is unaffected by sexual reproduction. Mitochondrial DNA is believed to be relatively free from other selection pressures as well. On this basis the researchers assumed a constant mutation rate of two to four per cent per million years and projected back into time – Africa 20,000 years ago.

Archeologists opposing the mitochondrial DNA dating techniques cite differential mutational rates Mitochondrial DNA must have been affected by population extinctions in the past moving quickly in some periods and perhaps not at all in others.

If mitochondrial DNA methods have been at the heart of the "mother of us all" controversy, TL and ESR have held central roles in the debate on how Neanderthals and modern man are related. It was earlier believed that Neanderthals were the ancestors of modern man. TL and ESR research suggests that modern man existed before the Neanderthals. Many paleontologists including Richard Klein find the scenario of Neanderthals and modern humans living side by side in the middle East North Israel Qafzch, Tabir, Gkhul) difficult to accept. Klein points out that classical evolutionary biology rules out the notion that two types could share such a small territory. As a result he says, "I don't know what to make of the TL and ESR dates".

Is there something wrong with the ESR and TL techniques? Both TL and ESR date samples by measuring the number of electrons trapped at radiation damaged sites in the lattice of crystals in the fossil. The number of radiation damaged sites increase with age. In the TL process a sample is heated to excite the electrons which give off a visible flash when they leave the crystal lattice. The intensity of the flash which is proportional to the stored energy can be detected using a photo multiplier. By experimenting on samples of a known age. TL practitioners have built up a scheme that correlates TL values with age. ESR also measures radiation damage but it does so by exciting the electrons within the lattice not driving them out. The sample is put in a magnetic field and bombarded by carefully tuned microwaves. A sensor detects the response whose intensity correlates with the age of the sample.

The Achilles heel of both methods is that they assume that present day estimates of radiation dose rates which can be applied retroactively for tens of thousands of years. They are still superior to what is called the gold standard of archeology the C-14 dating methods which only goes buck to 40,000 years. ESR and TL as alternative dating methods came into use in the 80's. They have already delivered a potent message about the origin of mankind. The 90s will test these methods and say whether they will be applicable to the established order of mankind. (Review in TOI by Reena Pinto, 5 January 1992).

Neanderthals and Ancestors of Modern Man

Did Neanderthals and the first ancestors of modern men ever meet? The argument has raged among archeologists and paleontologists for decades.

Now a group of scientists claim to have proof based on radio carbon dating of artifacts finds in France – that the two distinct groups did indeed share the same space at the same time some 38,000 years ago.

These data strongly support the chronological co-existence and therefore potential demographic and cultural interactions, between the last Neanderthals and the earliest anatomically and behaviorally modern human populations in Western Europe, they wrote in their latest edition of the science journal *Nature*.

Some scientists have argued that Neanderthals and the first ancestors of modern man existed at the same time at least for a while but in different places, which others have argued that Neanderthals died out before modern man came along or vice versa.

Others still have suggested that they not only met but may even have interbred. Scientists believe they may settled the dispute.

Neanderthals

Neanderthals were Europeans. Most of their archeological remains have been found in Western France, though sites have also been identified as far as Central Asia. The population flourished in the Ice Age between 200,000 and 30,000 years ago.

The first skull of the Neanderthal was found in Neander valley in Germany in 1856 in a cave. After the first discovery at

Neander Valley other bones were found which clearly belonged to the same species. These finds proved that beyond doubt that the fist skull was ancient, but there was the certain who the Neaderthal were in relation to he inman species.

Nearly 500 Neanderthals have now been placed for study of which few decam are at most complete skeletons. Mitochondrial DNA has been extracted from Neanderthal bones and has provided a clearer understanding of their genetic relationship to us. We now draw an accurate and vivid picture of Neanderthalate. Neanderthal lived in the harsh climate of Northern Europe. Their anatomy reflect short limbs, skin interface area and conserved hear large noses maximized. Thus, brain growth facial and dental development was faster than in the Homo sapiens who eventually formed them out.

Neanderthal were also far more muscular than Homo sapiens. Studies of their vertebrate suggests that they carried heavy loads probably animal carcass for large distances. Healed fractures of their bones are cameron from a young age. Many died as adolescence, either of drill birth or as a result of injuries sustained in the hunt. Females also participated in the hunt which their injuries indicate.

Neanderthals brains were on average larger than ours, over this bulky size body. The remains of a nine year old boy of Teshik Tash in Uzbekistan show his brain capacity was 1500 ml., which is larger than the human adult average today. A study of as kull found in a cave on shount cewmd Israel suggests that Neanderthals could communicate verbally after a fashion, although probably did not possess the flexible language as we know it. A restructured jaw cavity was tested and the conclusion was that three distinct vowel sounds could have been uttered through it.

Seeing the hunting location of the Neanderthal indicate, how well they understood their landscape. They used trap of the land to kill bison, wild cattle and rein deer into valleys where they would be trapped woolly rhinos and mammoths were driven across country until they fell off, a whittled wooden spear found in the rib case of an elephant in Germany shows that they were prepared to confront their prey head on. Neanderthal did not lack courage. A flint knife presented with mammoth remains suggests they may have used this weapon to penetrate the stick skin.

Neanderthals did not wear rough skin. Awls for punching holes in pelts have been discovered, showing that they gathered clothes. They even made jewellery, piercing stones and teeth so that they could be hung on grass or strips of pelts.

The cave left by the Neanderthals have left trees are often high in hills where they would have had an advantage point from which to watch near by game. They also lit fires in the caves and sat around them because the remains of a dog found in a cave near Madvid in Spain show that it has been carefully placed as seating by the hearth.

Even more intriguing is the discovery of a prehistoric "tent peg" driven into the ground at one site in France. Neanderthals not necessarily "cave man" some preferred their own shelter to cave.

The Neanderthals have also invented during the course of their sojourn in Europe, they sought and found ways to make their short lives more meaningful. They were sociable people who lived in family groups. One Neanderthal skeleton belongs to an aged and disabled man who had obviously received constant care over many years.

But most strikingly of all, they had some degree of spiritual awareness. We cannot say, that they prayed to a Neanderthal god but we know that they took pains in the burial of their dead. The skeleton found in the Porgone region of France was lying on its side in a sleeping position with an arm supporting its head. Remains found in Porgone were accompanied by deposits of pollen suggesting that flowers had been strown on the body as part of some unknowable ritual of mourning.

The Neanderthals were not sub-humans they were singly a different kind of human, an adaption to the species that ended in Europe for 1,70,000 years. For the last 10,000 of those years our ancestors showed the world with them. We have to endure for many more million before we can say that they were as successful as the hairy, skulls people of the Neander valley.

Neanderthal John Noble Wilford

Ever since their discovery among the scientists there have been a controversy as to should they be seated with the closest kin, sent to the back of the room with the distant cousins or tossed out as rank interlopes, despite a family resemblance? In short, are the new extinct Neanderthals full members of the modern human species, a subspecies or an entirely different species?

Though many scientists think Neanderthals were a subspecies which could have interbred with Homo sapiens, new research appears to confirm the more widely held view that Neanderthals and modern humans were significantly different, enough to qualify a separate species.

The finding were based on detailed measurements of variation in the skulls of modern human and Neanderthals as well as 12 existing species of non-human primates. The research team, led by Dr. Katerina Harvati, a paleoanthropologist at New York University, reported its results during a proceeding of the National Academy of Science. "What we are really saying is that Neanderthals did not contribute to the ancestry of Modern Europeans. Harvati said.

Despite findings of some new research that suggest Neanderthals did not contribute to the ancestry of modern Europeans, there are still many who believe otherwise and that the Neanderthals were a separate species that did not breed with Homo Sapiens.

But another school of scientists who propounded the regional continuity theory say that the new migrants from Africa bred at least to some extent with the archaic populations they encountered, perhaps account for some superficial differences among people in different regions. In this view, Neanderthals were a sub species, and at least partly ancestors to modern Europeans.

Eric Delson a paleontologist at the American Museum of National History and Lehman College, both in New York City, said the new research was a mathematically rigorous approach to the question of Neanderthals human relationships. It is very convincing piece of work; Delson said. But not convincing enough, it seems to put the controversy to rest.

"This research will not change many minds said Erik Trinkaus, a specialist in Neanderthal studies at Washington University in St. Louis. His research has suggested that there was some interbreeding".

"We have known for a long time what these fossils look like", Trinkams continues, "We know that Neanderthals are distinctive, but this research does not change their underlying biology".

In the new research, Harvati and her colleagues, Stephen R. Frost, of the New York Institute of Technology in Old Westbury and Kieran P. Menulty of Baylor University in Waeo, Tex, used a technique known as geometric morphometrics to measure the degree of variation between and among living primate species, including chimpanzees, gorillas, baboons, monkeys and humans.

The researchers focused their analysis on some 15 landmarks on the cranium and face of earth specimen. They were examined in 3D to determine even the finest variations in shapes.

The purpose Harvati said, "was to devise a quantitative method to determine what degree of difference justified classifying specimens as different species."

The differences measured between modern humans and Neanderthals were found to be significantly greater than those found between the subspecies studied. The two living species of chimpanzees for example appear to be more closely related to each other than Neanderthals are to humans, the scientists concluded.

In a statement about findings, Harvati said, "the research provided the most converging evidence to date that Neanderthals are indeed a separate species within the genus Homo."

Neanderthals Skeleton remains found in Neander valley in Germany and Vin Diga cave near the creation capital zogrels, points that they were top level carnivores who lived in a diet of mainly hunted animals. The research is an analysis of 29000 years old bone. The isotopes of nitrogen procured in bones can reveal whether an animal had been consuming primarily animals or plants during the last several years of life.

Neanderthal DNA Nearly Identical to Humans

Researchers have sequenced DNA from the bone of Neanderthal man who died 38000 years ago and said that it shows the Neanderthals are truly distant relatives of modern humans who interbred rarely if at all, with our own immediate ancestors.

They estimate that modern humans and Neanderthals split from common ancestor at least 3,70,000 years ago, and possibly 500,000 years ago, although we share 99.9% of our DNA.

"We see no evidence of mixing 40,000, 30,000 years ago in Europe. We don't exclude it, but see no evidence" Edward Rubin of the US Department of Energy Joint Genome Institute in Walnut, Creak, California, who led one study told reporters.

This conflicts with some evidence from other researchers, including a team said earlier this month that humans may have inherited a brain gene from Neanderthals. The researchers reported their findings jointly in the journals *Nature and Science*. Rubin's team used one method to isolate and sequence part of Neanderthals DNA while another team, led by Svnate Paabo of the Max Planet Institute of Evolutionary Anthropology, Leipzig, Germany, used a separate method to sequence a much larger amount.

Paabo was the first scientist to find and sequence Neanderthal DNA in 1997 and first suggested that Neanderthal did not mix with modern humans.

"I think the sequence data will serve as a DNA Aime machine that will tell us about biology and aspects that we will never be able to get from their bones and a limbed number of associated artifacts." Rubin said. Neanderthal and modern humans are both descended from Homo erectus, which left Africa and spread around the world about 1.5 million years ago.

Neanderthals lived in Europe and the Middle East until about 30,000 years ago. Cromagnon people, the ancestors of modern humans, started a second wave of migration out of Africa about 10,000 years earlier.

One huge question is how they interacted. Paabo and Rubin's genetic analysis both suggest there was little sexual contact at least according to the genes from this one male found at the back of a cave in Croatia.

Paabo team started through to Neanderthals specimen before they found a bone well preserved enough to provide DNA. They know it was a male because the DNA has a "Y" chromosome, females have "X".

Neanderthals may have given Human Gene to Big Brain

Neanderthals may have given the modern humans who replaced them a priceless gift, a gene that helped them develop superior brains US researchers reported.

And the only way was interbreeding, the team at the Howard Hughes medical institute and the University of Chicago said.

The study, published in the proceedings of the National Academy of Sciences, for Hindus indirect evidence that modern

Homo Sapiens are so-called Neanderthals interbred at some point when they liked side by side in Europe.

The study demonstrate the possibility that interbreeding contributed advantageous variants into the Beckman gene pool that subsequently spread.

But the doubt prevailing is that Neanderthals who died out about 35000 years ago, ever bred with modern Homo sapiens. Neanderthals are considered more primitive with robust bones, but with smaller intellects than modern humans. Lahu's team found a brain gene that appears to have entered the human league about 1.1 million years ago, and that has a modern form, that appeared about 37000 years ago – right before Neanderthals became extinct. Both Neanderthals and Homo sapiens would have been benefited in use of interbreeding but the later became extinct after the episode. It shows that there was not interbreeding but excessive interbreeding by the Neanderthals there number was greatly reduced in course of time.

Lahu's team estimated that 70 per cent of all living humans have this type D variant of the gene. Buy no means do these findings constitute definitive proof that Neanderthals was the source of the original copy of the Dallete. However our evidence shows that it is one of the best candidates, Lahu said.

Researchers reached their conclusions by doing a statistical analysis of the DNA sequence of microaccephalin, which is known to play a role in regulariting brain size in humans. Mutations in the human gene cause development of a much smaller brain, a condition called microcephaly.

Humans are Strange

In a case where the differences may be more than skin deep, Neanderthals are often though of as the stray branch in the human family tree. But research now suggests the modern human is likely to live old age; Live Science.com reported.

What people tend to do is draw a line from our ancestors straight to ourselves and any group that does not seem to fit on that line is divergent destruct, unusual strange researcher Erik Trinkaus an anthropologist at Washington University in St. Louis told Live Science. But in terms of evolution of our family tree, the genes Home, we are the out liners and the Neanderthals are more toward the core."

Missing Link Search is Fruitless (Vain)

Humans are a special model. There is no similarity or identity with other living species (common ancestors.)

Humans are not at the inevitable end of a sequence, Trinkaus said. "it just happens examining fossil skeletons and Neanderthals the wrong way. Over the last two years he systematically combined through fossil comparing Neanderthals and modern human skull, Java, tooth, arm leg traits in terms of their shape."

To what extent Neanderthals are derived, that is distinct from the ancestral form is a big question. Also wanted to see the extent to which modern humans are derived relative to the ancestral form, Trinkaus said.

Trinkaus focused as opposed to any traits that might get influenced by life style, environment or wear or tear. When compared with our common ancestors, Trinkaus discovered modern humans have roughly twice as many uniquely distinct traits as Neanderthals. In other words, Neanderthals are more like other members of our family tree than modern humans.

In the broader sweep of human evolution, the more unusual group is not Neaderthals whom we tend to look at as strange, weird and unusual, but its us, modern humans, Trinkaus said, modern humans for example are the only member of our family tree, who lack brow ridges. Trinkaus said.

Neanderthal Women Joined in Hunting : Nicholas Wade

A new explanation for the demise of the Neanderthals, the stockily built human species that occupied Europe until the arrival of modern humans 45,000 years ago has been proposed by two anthropologists at the University of Arizona.

Unlike modern humans who had developed versatile division of labour (as well as occupations) between men and women, the entire Neanderthal populations seems to have been engaged in a single main occupation, the hunting of large game the scientists Steran L. Kuhn and Mary C Stiner say in an article posted on line in Current Anthropology.

Because modern humans exploited environment more efficiently by having men hunt large game and women gather small game and plant foods their populations would have outgrown those of the Neanderthals.

The Neanderthals endured for about 100,000 years, despite a punishing way of life. They preyed on the large animals that flourished in Europe in the ice age like bison, deer, gazelles and wild horses. But there is no evidence that they knew bow and arrows. Instead they used stone tipped spears. Hunting large game at close range is perilous and Neanderthals skeleton bear copius fractures, Kuhn and Stiner argue that Neanderthal women and children took part in the hunt along with the men.

Neanderthals were Cannibals

Skeletal remains found in Spain suggest human beings closest relatives Neanderthal went through rough periods which may have forced them into cannibalism. Past records of the world support that there were Rakshasas – Robust human like species who were cannibals particularly they had developed taste of flesh of human beings. And there was enmity and fight between these species. Neanderthals may belong to the Rakshasas species of the early humans. Researchers said after studying skeletal remains from North West Spain that Neanderthals suffered period of starvation and may have supplemented their diet through camibalism, reports Live Science. (Like Neanderthals Rakshasa were also totally dependent on hunting and gathering for livelihood and so that their fate was doomed). In contrast human beings were hunter gathers and resorted to agriculture and animal husbandry, for their livelihood and cope better to the environment. Humans used clubs, spears, pellets, bows, arrows, missiles as implements for hunting and battle.

Paleobiologists studied samples from eight 43000 years old Neanderthals skeletons excavated from underground cave in EL Sidron, Spain since 2000. The study sheds light on how Neanderthals lived before the arrival of human beings in Europe. Researchers found cutmarks and evidence that bones had been torn apart, which they say could indicate cannibalism.

There is strong evidence suggesting that the meat eaters Neanderthals were eater said the study lead author Antonio RO Sas of the Museo National de Uiencias Naturalls in Madrid. That is long bones and the skulls were broken for extraction of the marrows which is very nutritious.

According to Rosas, there is evidence of Cannibalism in Neanderthals remains from other European sites I would say this practice was general among Neanderthal populations, he said.

Teeth from the remains showed evidence of periods of starvation or minimal nutrition.particularly during difficult life transitions like weaning or adoloscence Rosas said. Teeth grow by adding their layers of enamel, but when some change in the natural development of the individual occurs, the enamel in deposited more slowly or stops altogether he explained.

Outside forces like climate or illness could also affect tooth growth, he said. So mostly harsh winters together with physiological difficulties in the life history of these people may explain what we found" Rosas said.

Skull Suggests Humans – Neanderthals Inbreeding

A skull found in a cave in Romanic includes features of both modern humans and Neanderthals, possibly suggesting that the two may have interbreed thousand of years ago.

Neanderthals were replaced by early modern humans researchers have long debated whether the two groups mixed together though most doubt it. The last evidence for Neanderthals dates from at least 24000 years ago.

The skull bearing both older and modern characteristics is discussed in a Paper by Erik Trinkaus of Washington University in St Louis. The report appeared in proceedings of the National Academy of Sciences.

The skull was found in Pestera Cuoass – the cave with bones in south western Romania along with other human remains. Radio carbon dating indicates it is at least 35000 years old and may be more than 40,000 years old.

The researchers said, the skull had the same proportions as a modern human head and lacked the large brow ridge commonly associated with Neanderthals. However, there were also features that are unused in modern humans, such as frontal flattering a fairely large bone behind the ear and exceptionally large upper molars, which are among Neanderthals and other early hominids. "such differences raise important question about the evolutionary history of modern humans said Co – author. Joao Zillhao of the University of British England.

It could reflect a case in which ancient traits reappear in a modern human, or it could indicate a mixture of populations, Zihhao said, or it simply may be that science hasn't been able to study enough early modern people to understand their diversity.

Nature The Lord of Creator

Flores

There is more and more evidence to show that nature has been working over time to create us humans in a variety of species spanning million of years. And this process may not have reached perfection in Homo – Sapiens as we would like to believe. A recent discovery has unearthed a completely new species of humans who lived from 90,000 years ago to as late as 12000 BC before apparently becoming extinct. This species almost certainly co-existed, if not actually interacted, with our cro-magnon cousins. Identified by Australian and Indonesian scientists from a find of fragmental bones buried in the sediments of limestone cave on the remote Indonesian island of Flores, it has officially been named Homo Floresiensis. This particular group of hominids were on average no taller than a meter or so, with a brain the size of grape fruit. None the less, they still managed to fashion delicate stone tools, light fires to cook food, organize group hunts for a dwarf species of elephant extant at the time, and possibly develop a proto- language of sorts along the way.

The discovery heralded one of the most important Paleoanthropological finds in the last 50 years, has the potential to drastically change all the received wisdom gathered till now concerning human evolution. As one spokes person of the Natural History Museum in London says.

Hobbits – small Brain – human

Hobbit sized humans have survived on an isolated Indonesian Island until 12000 years ago, were smart enough to make some tools even though they had small brains, scientists said.

Some researchers doubt that tools found with the remains of the species named Homo Floresiensis in cave on the island of Flores could have been made by the three foot tall creature whose brains were about the size of a grape fruit.

They believe that tools must have been used by modern humans.

Experts have also argued that the Hobbit people were modern humans suffering from an illness that caused their small brain and size.

But an international team of scientists said older tools dating back more than 800,000 years also found on the island showed the Hobbit inherited, their tool making skill from their ancestors.

Small brained or not, Homo Floresiensis were capable of making stone tools and therefore the standard story of the relationship between brain size and behavioural complexity was straight forward than currently assumed, said Alom Bramm of the Australian National University in Canberrg, who headed the team.

Until now, it was thought that the larger the brain the Smart the hominid Bruman said, his findings suggest that may not be the case.

The caused relationship between brain size and complexity of tool behaviour in humans is assumed, not demonstrated, said Bruman.

Until now, stone tools have only been found in association with large and relatively large brained hominids, but Homo Floresiensis changes that forcing us to rethink the way we associate big brain with sophisticated behaviour he added.

Bruman and his team who reported the findings in journal *Nature*, believe the tools found with the species dubbed "Flores man" were the end point in the tradition of tool making on the Island east of Java which was also home to Komado dragons, minature elephants and other exotic species.

The researchers said their findings, show the same type of stool tools found with the species were made by their ancestors when they arrive on the island at least 8,40,000 years ago.

Remains of the new species were found a few years ago which scientists discovered a partial skeleton of an adult female. The tiny creatures are thought to have descended from Homo erectus, which had a lárge brain, was full sized and spread from Africa to Asia about two million years ago. Scientists believe they became too small because of the environmental conditions such as food shortages and a lack of predates.

Africa to Asia migration was two million years ago and not 700000 years ago in Australia as told by Discovery.

Hobbits were predecessors of Trobrianders of Europe.

More Evidence to Bulk Existence of "Hobbit"

Scientists say they have found more bone in an Indonesian care that offer additional evidence of a second human species short and hobbit like that roamed the earth the same time as modern man.

But the vocal scientific minority that has challenged that conclusion since the discovery of human Flore scientists was announced last year remains unconvinced.

The discovery of a jaw bone represents the ninth individual belonging to a group believed to have lived as recently as 12000 years ago. The bones are in a wet cave on the island of Flores in the Eastern limb of Indonesian archipelago near Australia.

In 2004 scientists announced their original sensational discovery of a delicate skull and partial skeleton of a female, nicknamed "Hobbit" and believed to be 18000 years old in addition, they found separate bones and fragments of other individuals ranging in age from 12000 to 95,000 years old.

The findings have ignited a controversy unlike any other in the often continuous study of human origins.

The tiny bones have enchanted many anthropologists who accept the interpretation that these diminutive skeletons belonged to 9 remnant population of pre-historic humans that were marooned on Flores with dwarf appearance and other miniaturized animals, giving the discovery a kind of fairy tale quality.

If true, the discovery grafts a strange and tangled evolutionary brand near the very top of the human family tree.

The evolutional view of human evolution in that several type of primitive ape like ancestors appeared and faded over a span of about 4.5 million years. Modern Homo sapiens developed about 100,000 years ago, and quickly overtook other large brained competitions like Homo erectus and Neanderthals. Modern humans were thought to have roamed the earth without competition for at least the past 30,000 years.

Little People of Flores

Scientists from Indonesia Australia and Unites States weighed in with a comprehensive analysis based on their own first hand examination of bones and a single mostly complete skull. The evidence they reported strongly supports their doubt. The critic concluded that the "little people of Flores" were not a new found extinct species. They were instead modern Homo sapiens who resemble pygmies now living in the region and as suggested in particular by the skull appear to have been afflicted with the developmental disorder microcephaly which causes the head and brain to be much slender than average.

The International team of researchers who conducted the study was headed by Jenka Jacob of Gadjah University who is one of Indonesia's senior paleontologists. In the report Jacob and his colleague cited 140 features of the skull that they said placed it within modern human ranges of two jaws and some teeth that either show no substantial deviation from modern Homo sapiens or share features with – Rampa sas Pygmies now living near Liang Bua cave where the discovery was made. "We have eliminated the idea of a new species", Robert B. Eckardt a professor of developmental genetics Dipen State who was a team member said. Peter Brown, a paleontologist at University of New England said there is evidence that unique combination of features in Homo Florensil are found in the modern human.

Hobbits were Stunted Humans

Anthropologists were combining a bid to have the Hobbits enshrined as a separate branch of the human family tree. They argue the tiny cave dwellers were simple Homo Sapiens who came stunted and retorted as a result of iodine deficiency in pregnancy. Dubbed after the Wee foth in JRK Tolkins tales. The hominids – just a meter tall with a chimp sized brain lived around 18000 years ago on the island of Flores.

Indonesian Hobbits were Dwarfs not New Species

Palan skeleton of Indonesia which date to between 900 and 2800 years ago, appears to have belonged to so called insular drafts humans who grew smaller as a result of living in an island. The researchers said, the same thing happened on the Indonesian island of Flores where small skeletons dating back 15000 to 18000 years ago have puzzelled scientists. Some argue they are separate species called Homo Florensis, others say, they are small, because of nutritious deficiency, genetic factor or because they were similar to pygmies, dwarfs or other shorter type of people.

Is Flores Fossils a New Found Species?

Not all scientists agreed that the 18,000 years old "little people" fossil found on the Indonesian Island of Flores should be designated an extinct human – related species. Some expressed their opposition in news interviews and internal symposiums but Papers arguing their case were rejected by major journals.

Now the critics are getting their day in the court of scientific discourse. In the journal *Science*, researchers led by Robert D Martin of the Field Museum in Chicago, present evidence that supports their main argument that the skull in question is not that of a new found extinct species but of a modern Homo Sapien afflicted with microcephaly, a genetic disorder characterized by a smaller than normal brain and head size.

The researcher said the evidence used in previous studies to rule out microcephaly was flawed. They noted the analysis was primarily based on comparison with a brain cast made from poorly preserved skull of a 10 year old who was microcephalic, not one from an adult.

"Quite simply it could not have a worse example for such a study, Martin a Primatologist, said speaking of the fossil skull that was examined, tells us nothing about a microcephalic that is able to surprise into adulthood.

Indonesian Hobbits are a New Species

The tiny ancient humans dubbed hobbits whose remains were found in Indonesia in 2003, were previously unknown species altogether, a new study says report appeared in the 8 May, 2009 *TOI*. It reports, a team led by Willian Jungers of Stony Brook University in New York analysed the hobbits foot and found that it is startingly primitive in some ways; far longer than its modern human equivalent and equipped with very big toes, long and curved lateral toes and a weight bearing structure closer to a chimpanzee's. Recent archeological evidence shows the modern foot evolved more than 1.5 million years ago most likely in Homo erectus. So unless the hobbits became more primitive over time considered extremely unlikely – they must have branched off the human live at an even earlier date.

Species of Human – Florence

In the 1890s Eugene Bubois, an anatomist working as a doctor in the Dutch army, stunned the scientific world when he found the first fossil human remains outside Europe. Java man Homo Erectus, as it is now know threw ideas about human evolution into chaos by suggesting that Europe was not as most anthropologists had argued, the cradle of human evolution. As it turned out, neither was Asia.

The evidence now shows that all the important development in human evolutionary history from the appearance of Australopithecus (the first species generally regarded as human) to the emergence of Homo Sapiens happened in Africa. But Asia can still spring the old surprise in the field and few finds have been as surprising as that made last year on Java's Indonesian Neighbour Flores.

For Homo Floresiensis as the new species has been dubbed suggests that the ascent of man is not an evolutionary inevitability. Descent is also possible. That is because Homo Foresiensis was but a meter tall, and had a brain not much bigger than an apes.

In a truly ancient fossil human from, say, 3 m – 4 m years ago, those dimensions would be surprising. But the skeleton found by Peter Brown, of the University of New England, and his colleagues from Indonesia is a mere 18000 years old. That means it was alive at a time where Homo Sapiens had not only came into existence, but had already reached Australia.

The species is not, however, a descendant of Homo Sapiens. A tooth from a lower soil layer in the cave where the main skeleton was found shows it evolved before modern humans arrived in the area. The brain of Homo Florensiensis was a mere 380 cm. Nor is there any doubt that the skeleton is that of an adult (probably from the pelvic anatomy, a woman). Her teeth are worn, and some tell tale bones in the skull are knitted together in an adult way.

Species of human of course, a small animal will have a small brain. But what is noticeable about Homo Florensiensis is how small the brain is, even in comparison to the diminutive body. The species had regretted, more or less, to the brain body ratio found in Australopithecus.

As a result, astronomers said, the planet may already have lost a considerable amount of its mass.

6

Search of Missing Link

Origin of Humans

Scientists have now confirmed that modern humans no longer belongs to animal kingdom of ape but they have a separate and distinct species of their own species. According to unilateral descent of evolutionary theory, all modern humans have descended from one African women. Human origin is still a mystery. From whom the African woman descended? Was it the hominid or Homo erectus? We are not sure of it. We share the DNA from all living beings. The genecists have yet to confirm the descendant of humans. While the genomic researchers or biologists cannot go back beyond the African women because of lack of fossil materials linking her, as no fossil of such an antiquity is available anywhere on earth. Though Scientists have discovered that humans have been derived from bacteria that some genes haven't changed much since the very first single celled creatures who populated the prime zone. This single celled gene is found in all living creatures of the universe. We are in search of human predecessor beyond African women. The search will be continued in another chapter. At this moment, non-availability has prompted to explore the un-investigated area and throw some light on alternate assumption on the origin of humans, though like archeologists and paleontologists no fossil material for the sake of evidence could be presented. It is the stories and myths of the descendants of natural ancient people, inhabiting particular geographical region of the earth since millions of generations which of immense value which is no less important than fossil materials, have been explored and analyzed. World famous scientists like Carl Sagan and Eric Von Daniken have already made abundant references of these materials in their works. Though, all over the world the intelligentia and the scientists consider it to be a mere dream of the ancient people and fictitious. But unlike assumptions and theories of the scientists which are un-testable for verification, these stories and myths like fossil materials are based on facts and actual experiences, memories, events and their perceptions related to particular time. This remains in constant memory and folk-consciousness through such stories. "It is an impaired memory, the past's vague legacy to the future". (.33, 1995, Daniken)

Ancient Stories Relating to Origin of Mankind

In Eastern philosophy, as well as in other parts of the world, stories of creation of planet earth, mankind and other species are told by the ancient people. In India, besides the Hindu mythologies, the Austic speaking natural aborigines of proto-Australoid origins – the Santhals, the Mundas and Ho tell the stories with different background and styles of the origin of mankind which are worth nothing. These stories are still prevalent and are narrated during the traditional ritual performances.

(A) ***Humans birth from bird's Egg***

It is told by the Santhals aboriginals in their "Jom sim binti (p. 22 Hemrom ooz) the traditional narration during annual ritual that in the hoary past when the sun never set (indirectly indicate the place of habitation of the Santhals, in the pole region at that time), a beautiful swan laid a pair of eggs on the lotus leaf floating over the water. It is also stated that "Indus valley script are also used during the religious ceremony by the Santhals" (p.63, 1995 S.K. Biswas). The eggs were hatched and in course of time, a human pair – one male and one female baby came out from it. This dismayed the swan pair and made them quite embarrassed and depressed as they were expecting beautiful swan chicks like them. However the human babies were looked after well with all love and care. After a week or two the lotus leaf could not support the babies and the swan had to carry them away elsewhere. But as there was no dry earth, they could not alight and remained on flight for twelve long years. In the meantime, it was Lita who was responsible for all the creation, she saw them and felt great compassion on the swan. The Supreme God "Thakur" ordered him to make the earth where the swan can alight. As there was no soil and the earth was flooded with water, Lita look the help of water species and particularly of the amphibians to bring out soil from the bottom down the water with which he could make the dry earth. A number of creatures came for his help, but no one was successful but it was the earth worm who brought out the soil in its belly and put them on the tortoise back. Lita made earth platform from this soil and the dry earth came out. The swan with their human babies alighted on it, and life once again began here. The human children remained under the care of Lita and grew-up and the swan flew away to their heavenly abode. The human children grew up under the guidance of Lita and attained adulthood, established a family and eked out their living happily. The name of the human children were Pilchu Kora and Pilchu Kuri. And it is told that they became the ancestral parents of the Santhal people. When the human pair were able to support themselves, Lita one day vanished from their presence.

(B) *Humans the Descendants of Denosaurs*

The above story tell that humans took birth from bird's eggs. No intelligent and sentient human being can believe on this story but wait what the scientists tell about it. Scientists tell that "during late Jurassic period (220 million years ago) was an extraordinary time in vertebrate evolution when several major groups such as dinosurs, birds, crocodilee, squirrels, Lissamphibians and mammals first appeared in fossil records. This faunal diversification heralded the beginning of many major groups of Tetrapods that still persist today. (p. 205) The early and middle Jurassic (200 – 180 million years ago) was critical time for the evolution of several tetrapod groups of archosaurs and mammals (p. 221). The scientists say that birds descended from bi-pedal archosaurs (a species of tetrapod p. 303). The birds appeared in late Jurassic (p. 519). The above story of the santhal people of India, proposes another theory of human evolution from the bird's eggs or dinosaurs and not from Hominid as is theorised to be thought by the scientists. The early bird on record is Archopteryx from the upper Jurassic of Germany (p. 521 Ezniliani P.Earth). This break through in human evolution was achievedthrough hybridization and the process of rapid evolution and mutation combined with natural selection. In this case, it can be said that a stage was reached in birds' evolution when no further improvement in its body form or morphology was anticipated. Therefore, through rapid evolutionary process and multiple mutation and natural selection mysteriously a complete different form of species from the already existing species of birds to human evolved in one generation. Generally, it takes 5,00,000 years to change the form of species. In this case, it may have taken many more millions to achieve the human species and that would also be a mere chance. The genomic study suggest that as the genome are not programmed for specific model, the evolutionary may have taken to any form of the species. And in this case, it was through the abrupt development changes in gene multiplication that human species evolved.

Earlier we had cited the evidence of human mother giving birth to piglet or kid goat, here we have human species coming out from bird's eggs. In both those cases, no cross breeding are anticipated, only the evolution did work with the help of RNA or DNA gene. In both case, no model of the progenitor's species was followed. New species in multiplicity evolved twice after the mass extinctions – Permian and cretaceous periods. So we cannot dismiss that new species cannot evolve from existing species. The modern theory of evolution incorporate modern genetics concluded that new species may appear in very short time less than 10000 years (p.423)

(C) *Making Humans from Clay*

While the origin of humans through creation is now totally dismissed by modern scientists which the ancient people had accepted as a fact. It is the mental capacity and spirit which makes perfect human beings and Darwin sidelined the spirit. The scientists are unable to grasp the spirit and also the divine being which is a spirit. While the mental or mind is terrestrial, the spirit and divine are not, yet they reside terrestrially in human being along with the mind. Creation theory combines all terrestrial and heavenly objects along with spirit and divine and hence a perfect creature comes out a creative process of evolution.

The Mundas of the Austric speaking proto-Australoid people of India tell the creation story of human being as follows : One old man called "Haram" identified by the personal name "Singbonga" one day collected dust or soil from different locations of the earth and made clay images of a human pair – a male and a female and put them on an open space for sun bath. When the human images were in this state on the sun at a normal course of the day, a flying horse (people give no name of the creature) appeared from nowhere and destroyed the images to pieces. The first human pair were thus reduced to pieces at the initial stage before attaining the life. And first attempt of the "Haram" (old man) of making human pair abruptly came to an end.

In this pre-historic story there is a grain of truth and when pondered deeply, we notice three important points (1) collection of dust or soil and (2) the flying horse (reptile) (3) Haram (old man). We may analyse these three points in detail in the subsequent pages.

After sometime, may be a year or two, "Singbonga" the "Haram" once again collected the dust and with due preparation and care made human images from clay of the earth and put them as earlier, at an open space for the sun bath, and kept himself busy nearby in some other work, but remained vigilant towards the drying images. He heard a rustle, as the flying horse, this time in pairs, turned up again. But seeing the old man at the guard of the images, they stayed back at a safe distance and waited for a suitable chance to pound upon. The old man picked up a flack or two of the wood he was working upon and threw them towards the waiting flying horses. Instantly, a pair of fierce black dogs came into action and chased away the flying horses as directed. The flying horses flew away and never returned back again. The "Haram" put the obedient black dogs on guards duty of the images thence from. The dogs were dutiful and faithful.

The images were thus saved and secured and thereafter attained life. Under the guardianship and guidance of "Haram", the human pair started their family life, taught them to speak language and art of living. And when he found that the human pair no longer needed his protection and guidance, one day he left them and vanished. In this case there is no divine intervention in helping the imaged to gain life, but it was the creative natural process adopted by putting them on the sun to energize themselves and attained life naturally.

It is observed that in any image making job, ordinary soil is not used even in earthenware and pot making. Special care is taken for the selection of the soil. A variety of soil, not one type, is assembled for making the mixture of the clay. After proper mixing, the lump of the clay is put up for fermentation and synthesis for a week or two. Such care must have been taken by the "Haram" in the selection of the soil and mixing of it for the images. He may have collected dust of the clay which contained macro molecules, proteins and nucleic acids, etc. It may have been the primitive rare earth, star dust containing atomic dust and special water, of lives, phosphates, and nitrogenous molecules or meteorites and ammonia acids, etc. The mixture of these fine soil were added to make it the clay and thus synthesized. How these intracellular organisms or molecules or chromosal RNA and DNA were united. We don't know. We are not aware of the actual, component soil and chemical of the ingredients. But when the images were prepared, he must have taken utmost care the minute details which we are not aware. Before making the images he must have put the lump of clay for fermentation for a week or two and thus fully synthesized. When the images were ready, it was put up on the open sun. We know that source of energy for life is the sun or it is the solar energy which provide life to every living objects. Similar to the chloroplast of the plant which received life from solar energy, so the mitchondria gene in human body was activated from sun's energy. And the human body gained life through photosynthetic process. In laboratory to activate the chemicals, electric current is used, the solar energy did the same to human body. The human images of clay thus got its life. The "Haram" was scientist par-excellence. This pre-historic story carries the truth and first evidence of human creation from clay of the earth. We do not know how life originated on earth. But this story tells how life originated in clay images of the humans.

"Flying horse" of this pre-historic story is not a fiction, but it has been confirmed by the paleontologists as a reality and existed as reptiles or dinosaurs. The first flying reptile was known as "Rhamphorhynchus" (p. 520, Planet Earth). The "flying horse" in the Munda tradition of creation are actually the winged reptiles, lizard, dinosaurs, who the scientists say, were in existence during the middle and late Jurrasic time 180 and 168 million years ago. Flying dinosaur lived on earth between 65 and 230 million years back, they were pterosaurs who did not gather food but hunted their prey for food. The pterosaurs appeared in early Jurrasic 208 million years ago. (p. 519, Planet Earth).

It is reported that some 160 million years ago, those winged lizard were in existence in East Africa and dominated the earth. During Tertiary Jurrasic period placental mammals were evolving and placenta humans cannot be the later origin than this period. When placental mammals evolved, modern humans also evolved along with them. Existence of flying dinosaurs and origin of humans were simultaneous. Flying dinosaurs were predators as the Munda tradition clearly mentions. Human origin may have taken place during early Jurrasic to late Jurrasic period (208 to 160 million years ago) when flying dinosaurs were ruling the earth. Dinosaurs appeared on earth 227 million years ago and lived upto 65 million years.

Ancient Mundas were not the philosophers like the Greek who had the notion of flying horse. It is not known whether Greek and Munda people had any contact earlier and shared this idea. The flying horse of the Munda tradition is the notion of their own. Flying reptiles did exist in real history or pre-history at least in Munda history. We have now evidence of flying dinosaurs discovered by archeologists and paleologists. The Munda tradition therefore, is not fictions but it is real. Human origin is found in both Santhal and Munda tradition, though they belong to the same linguistic family, narrate two different stories of human origin, both the story however belong almost to the same period i.e. Jurrasic period when humans originated. Both stories, however, share the same ending. In Santhal tradition, after the completion of the work. Lita vanished from the sight of pitchu kora and pilchu kuri. In Munda tradition also "Haram" vanished from the presence of human pair. It may be assumed that the two were either people from outer space or extra terrestrial beings. Since the idea of intelligent designer have been dismissed by the scientists, we cannot say that they were divine being. In either of the absence, human evolution was not possible. Though we have the perception of E.T. We have no evidence of their existence. We have yet to detect their vehicle U.F.O. or their occupant E.T. but unable to dismiss their existence. The ancient people considered them as one of their own, or super human being, but not people of outer space, but in all these cases, they say, they went to heaven. So, it may be the ET who are helping the human since primeval time as Eric Von Daniken thinks. Scientists have the notion of self evolution or self origin of bacteria. Ancient people have the same notion with respect to their early man or even ET or "Haram" as Suigeneris. In case of the above two stories of the Santhals and the Mundas no divine explanation nor certificate from scientists is needed for their existence. Because in this area they are full of controversy regarding the place of origin of modern humans totally in capable of making any contribution scientifically or technologically humans from India or Gondwana land. Modern humans may have originated from Gondwana land and particularly from South Africa, India or Antartica is also one of the probable place of human origin. Gondwana land or India or Australia are of tropical climate and most suitable place for origin of life. Geologists now confirm that Antarctica was warmer than other place in primeval times but due to climatic changes, early evidence of life have all been wiped out. It is assumed Antarctica which was once a part of Gondwanaland linking South Africa, India and Australia having tropical climate, may have been the cradle of lives from where species spread to all parts of the planet earth. We have now accepted that African mother is the mother of all human kind. African origin of our mother is still an issue for the Australian scientists. The scientists now admit that after the dinosaurs extinction which occurred 65 million years ago, the Homo sapiens, the modern man flourished on the planet earth (Reader's Digest p. 232). The mass extinction of dinosaurs and survival of a human pair, before 65 million years ago, is supported by the story of the Munda tradition.

"Sengel da" – The Rain of Fire

In the earlier story of the Mundas, we have seen how the human beings survived from the flying dinosaurs. The progenitors of these early humans, however were perished along with the dinosaurs during mass extinction of 65 million years ago. This event of mass extinction is told by the Mundas of surviving descendants in the story of "Sengel da" or "rain of fire" (Encyclopedia Mundarica p. 3918, Vol XIII). The event of "rain of fire" caused by volcanic eruption, the earth plate cracked due to movement of earth's plate or crash of asteroid, is not a fiction, but it is a fact which occurred 65 million years ago in the Arabian ocean, in which a human pair – one male another female, both brother and sister, barely survived from this disaster. These surviving pair suggest, that it is they only survived and all living species perished from the rain of fire which engulfed the whole of planet earth. It was so gigantic and extensive that survival from this type of event, was a mere dream.

During the bygone era, when humans had barely adjusted to the earth's environments, there was a gigantic catastrophic event of "rain of fire" when every terrestrial creatures and plant lives perished. A pair of human beings – one male and one female, identified by the Mundas as Toto Kora and Toto Kuri (naked people) only survived by hiding in a crab's cave by the side of marsh or ocean helped by one spirit being called "Nage era" i.e. spirit of the marsh. In modern times fish like humans – half fish and half human in ocean is sighted. It is called water nymph. The human pair were saved by such water nymph. The Mundas say, "they are the descendants of these surviving pairs. Modern paleontologists have discovered tetrapod burrows in Antartica. The human pair may have used these type of burrows or cave for survival which was cool and comfort. There may be enough life saving materials like fish and drinking water. The cave or burrows of surviving pair may have been located away from the volcanic eruption zone, away from burning lava and intense heat and temperature, but there were the raining burning ash, cloud of ash and gas coverage zone. Reference of "Nage era" indicate that they were close to swampy areas or ocean's shore or close to Tethys sea in the north of the continent, in this case. There may also be river basin of India which indicates availability of fresh water such as Son-Koel – Damodar valley basin or Rajmahal – Purnea – Gulsi basin, Mahanadi valley and Godavari Valley which are away from volcanic eruption zone of the Arabian sea. Narmada, Satpura and Cambay basin fall directly under the volcanic eruption zone. However, it was only the presumption that the human pair may have adopted the cave for survival. We are not aware for sure where the humans were inhabiting in India when the volcano erupted. The place of habitation may also be either Srilanka or Antarctica or Ceylon or far Western or Eastern Indian continent.

The "rain of fire" or rain of burning ash from the sky was due to gigantic volcanic eruption in Western India at K.T. boundary some 65 million years ago. In this massive volcanic eruption, 5,00,000 k.m. territory of western India (Deccan trap) continent was covered by flood basalt. The separation of West and East Gondwana which started at the beginning of 160 million yeas ago, also producing vast outpouring of flood basalt in India and South Africa. "Just as the mid-ocean ridges were beginning to relax and biosphere seemed to have managed to control the CO2 problem with this with this separation impact, India split from Seychelles block and a giant outpouring of basalt emerged from the rift as stated above. The outpouring dated

66-10^6 million years, formed the Deccan trap in Western India. That outpouring of basalt lasted more than a million years. At the same time, it is estimated that 40 km. asteroid is stated to have crashed on the west coast of India which formed a crater named "Shiva" 600 km long and 450 km wide located at Carlsberg ridge on the Bombay high of the Arabian sea which added separation of India from Seychelles Island. India – Seychelles rifting originated the volcanic eruption and asteroid crashing shattered the lithosphere, outpouring of lava and CO2 gas cloud blocked the sky and rain fall of fire with high temperature devastated the flora and fauna with extensive dimensions.

Gondwana Assembly, INSA, New Delhi

It is this event which caused mass extinction of dinosaurs and many other large species of the earth. Its impact on earth atmosphere is stated to have lasted more than a million years which changed the global environment (p. 526 The Planet Earth).

The impact of the event of volcanic eruption and asteroid crashing 65 million years ago on Western Indian continent is narrated as follows. "The impact generated a force thousands of times more powerful than the explosion of all nuclear arsenal in the world. It injected a large volume of dust into the atmosphere that blocked sunlight for months and prevented photosynthesis, as a result plant died, followed by herbivores, and eventually the food chain collapsed, and all dinosaurs perished. The tremendous impact would have ignited global fires, initiated Tsunamis, destroyed coastal habitats, produced acid rains, turned sea water acidic, dissolved carbonate shelled animals, and devastated biosphere. Millions of organisms would have died instantly from the tremendous tremor and the global fire generated from the impact. It was a holocaust of unmatched dimensions in the geologic history." (p. 215 Gondwana Assembly, INSA)

It has been known for a long time that a great mass extinction occurred at the end of the cretaceous (65 – 66 million years ago), Perhaps 90 per cent of the cretaceous species were wiped out. Extinction was not indiscriminate. Organism that became extinct or almost so, were particularly susceptible to a tremendous temperature increase (1) they were already living in high temperature environment or (2) their eggs were laid in even such environment or (3) they had large bodies that could not efficiently dissipate body heat. Ammonites, Bohemmites, dinosaurs, and pterosaurs got wiped out, coral reats, Bony fishes almost got wiped out, amphibious, mammals, birds, snakes, sharks, Calaveras, Algae and plant almost survived". (p. 424, p. 527 The Planet Earth).

There have been doubt about the killing power of the volcano because until now researchers have struggled to measure just how much toxic gas would have been released. But after finding rare inclusion of gases in the deccan rock, a British based team has found vital preserved information about its original gas contents. Writing in the journal *Science*, they concluded that the massive amount of both sulpher and chlorine released would probably have had a "severe" environmental impact. There are several major mass extinction and most of these have uncannily occurred which one of these have flood basalt provinces was being formed. (TOI)

It is after the extinction of dinosaurs 65 million years before as recorded in "rain of fire" story by the Munda people of India, "the first modern humans appeared on earth" (p. 222, The Truth About History. Reader's Digest). It was the catastrophe when human beings were at the edge of extinction. Survival in such a disastrous environment which persisted for thousands or million of years was only a providential, and not chance escape. And the Munda assign this graceful act to Naga era a female divine nature spirit or water nymph of the water or swampy land where the pair had taken their shelter.

Human Genetics

The map of life unfolded by the genome explorers virtually abolished all boundaries of racial differences in the realm of a common human kind. Perhaps the most crucial revolution of the genomic project is that 99.9 per cent of all humans have the same DNA, the deoxyribonucleic acid which is the main constituent of the 23 pairs of chromosomes that carry genetic information. This effectively explodes "superior race" theories and myths. The centuries old "nature versus nurture" debate looks set to be tilted in favour of the latter. Indeed as the researchers say, there are no inherently "bad" or "good" genus. Similarly, it is a very slim line that divide the so-called "superior" of the species and those lower down on the evolution table. The human genome tots up just a little over 30,000 genes, a huge departure from initial estimates of around 100,000, just twice as much as these numbers of genes that make up a fruit-fly or a round worm. The crucial difference lies in better genetic organization in bio-governance as in corporate administration, style matters mere than more size. There are also vast areas in our genome that are deemed to be terraincognita, a genomic wasteland that forms the out back of the biomolecolar world within us. These genetic deserts appear to be of no immediate utility. However, we could eventually glean valuable information, say geneticists, from the numerous junk genes that dot our genome. In addition, we have squatter rogue genome that have somehow found their way into our genome during the complicated process of human evolution. The unique of the primordial amoeba, our long lost distant ancestor, apparently lives on us. We are a product of the unique orchestration of our genes, proteins, prehistoric bacteria and environment.

Mother of all Humanity

The human genome sequence show that every person on earth shares 99.9 per cent of the same genetic code with other people, which substantiate the theory that human kind has descended from one African mother, according to a report in journal *Science*. In fact, people from different racial groups can be more genetically similar than individuals within the same group. Individual variations represent about 0.10 per cent or 1 in 1,250 different "letters" in the entire sequence, the report in the the Journal has revealed. Some experts on the basis of these conclusions have announced that it proves the theory that human kind has descended from on African mother, all whites on earth, all blacks, all browns, all reds, all yellcws – whatever. The sequence sets the total number of human genes between 26,383 and 39,114. If the final tally lies somewhere in between around 39,000 then people have only about 13,000 more genes than the fruitfly, according to the Science Paper by lead author, J Craig Venter of Celera Genomics and 282 others. This range is surprisingly low as some researchers had predicted upto 140,000 genes in the human genome.

It raises the whole issue of what it is to be human or a member of the genes Homo, and shows how little we really know about our ancestry. The find also challenges our species specific anthropocentrism of posturing as the greatest kinds on the block to date. Because if it gets confirmed that a creature with so smaller brain was capable of such advanced behaviour including perhaps even communication skills then many theories about the evolution of our own intelligence might need to be hurriedly revamped. Actually, it appears, we never learn. Remember our collective chagrin when we discovered that low brow "bruts" like Homo Neanderthals buried their dead with flowers? Homo Floresiensis or Homo hobbits as he has been nicknamed because of his small size, reminiscent of JRR Tolkien's Hobbits – suggest that "there are many routes to what we call humanity. No single species can lay claim to the original patent. It is neither the brain size nor the body posture that determine intelligence, it lies even in knee. *TOI* November 20th 2004.

Human Genome

The human genome has been described as autobiography of the species because our combination of 3 billion DNA letters is what makes us human. But share a lot in DNA terms with other species. Only one percent of our sequence is shared with the humble yeast, 57 per cent with cabbage and whopping 28 per cent the chimpanzee our nearest relative.

Human beings need 46 chromosomes. When sperm and egg meet, a new cell is created with the proportioned number of chromosomes restored. Half of the chromosomes come from mother side, and the other half from father side. The chromosomes is a letters decided at the time when their pairs lives up for division."apart list of proteins needed to make a person research team led by J Craig Venter Celers Genomica stated.

Other team found how the "junk" regions of the DNA accumulated. The team has also found the small elements of the junk play a vital role in human life. In physical terms, the human genome is Lilliputian – two copies of it are packed into the nucleus of every ordinary human cell, each of which is about fifty the size of the smallest speck of the dust that the eye can see. But in terms of information contents, the Genome is gargantuan. Malt Ridley say – "the Genome is a piece of digital information written in genetist, composed of chemical symbols designated by a four letter alphabet of A's, T's C and G's. That works out to an agenetic epiphany which is 3.2 billion letters long. The biggest is sight emerging from the analysis of the letters that we have fewer genes than predicted, has surprising political and medical implications. The first is that the universal brotherhood of man calibrated to seers and sages in not mythical at all. For the biological difference between individuals works out to a mere fraction of the three billion letters in human genetic code. You and I differ by 2.1 million genetic letters from each other. Explains Venter, probably only a few thousand of these element for the biological differences between us, which means, we are all essentially chemical twins – even more than I thought.

In practical terms means that there is no basis for the concept of race. It means people from different racial groups can be more genetically similar than individuals within the same group reports BBC. Genetic studies show there is more availability in the Gene pool in Africa than out side. Scientists say the lower member of genes in the genome implies that the environment must play a crucial role in human development and we are not genetically hard wired or programmed. (Genetically programmed life or environmental effect – which one has effective role?) 3.7 billion long letters of human genome is far more than a mere sequence of chemical bases arranged on twisted strand of DNA.

Book of Life – Human Genome Project

Scientists have reached a landmark point in one of the world's most important scientific project by sequencing the last chromosome in the human Genome, the so called "Book of Life".

Chromosome – 1 contains nearly twice as many genes as the average chromosome and make up 8 per cent of the human genetic code. It is packed with 3141 genes and linked to 350 illnesses including cancer, Alzheimers and Parkinson's disease.

This achievement effectively closes the book on an important volume of the human genome project" said Simen Gregory who headed the sequencing project at the Sanger Institute in England.

The Project was started in 1990 to identify the genes and DNA sequence that provide a blue print for human beings. Chromosome – 1 is the biggest and contains per chromosome, the greatest number of genes.

Therefore, it is the region of the genome to which the greatest number of diseases have localized". Added Gregory from Duke University in the US.

The sequence of Chromosome -1, which is published on line by the journal *Nature* took a team of 150 British and American Scientists ten years to complete.

Researchers around the world will be able to mine the data to improve, mental disorders and other illness.

Chromosome, which are found in the nucleus of a cell are thread like structures that contain genes which determine the characteristics of an individual.

The human genome has an estimated 20,000 to 25,000 genes. The sequencing of chromosome – 1 has led to the identification of more than 1000 new genes. "We are moving into the next phase which will be working out what the genes do and how they interact" Gregory said.

The genetic map of chromosome – 1 has already been used to identify a gene for a common form of cleff lip and palate. It will also improve understanding of what process lead to genetic diversity in population, according to Gregory.

Each chromosome is made up of molecule of DNA in the shape of double helix which is composed of four chemical bases represented by the letter "A" (Aladamine), "T" (Thymine), "G" (Guamine) and "C" (Cytosine). The arrangement, or sequence of the letters determines the cell's genetic code.

Language Gene Traced

A study of the genomes of people and chimpanzees has yielded a deep insight into the "origin of language", one of the most distinctive human attributes and a critical step in human evolution.

The analysis indicates that language, on the evolutionary time scale, is a very recent development, having evolved only in the last 100,000 years or so.

The finding supports a novel theory advanced by Dr. Richard Klein, an archeologist at Stanford University, who argues that the emergence of behaviourally modern humans about 50,000 years ago was set off by a major genetic changes, most probably the acquisition of language.

The new study by Dr. Svante Pacbo and colleagues at the Max Plunek Institute for Evolutionary Anthropology in Leipzig, Germany is based on last years discovery of the first human gene involved specifically in language.

The gene called FOXP2 seems to be involved in the fall and jaw movements necessary for speech, the researcher said in the nature.

It is not the gene that made language possible geneticist Wolfgang Enard of Max Plund Institute said, adding it is probably one of many genes involved in speed and language which are complex abilities.

But the gene is clearly important, research last year found that people who lack two normal copies of the gene have considerable difficulty in speaking. They not only make mistakes in grammar but cannot always articulate words clearly.

The gene came to light through studies of a large London family well known to linguistics, 14 of whose 29 members are incapable of articulate speech but are otherwise mostly normal.

A team of molecular biologists led by Dr. Anthony P. Monau of the University of Oxford last year identified the gene that was causing the family's problems. The gene is known to switch on other genes during the development of brain, but it is presumed role in setting up the neural circuitry of language is not understood.

Dr. Paabo team has studied the evolutionary history of the FOXP2 gene by decoding the sequence of DNA letters in the versions of the gene possessed by mice, chimpanzees and other primates and people.

Dr. Paabo says the FOXP2 gene has remained largely unaltered during the evolution of mammals, but suddenly changed in human after the hominid line had split off from the chimpanzee line of descent.

The changes in the human gene affect the structure of the protein in species at two sites. Dr. Paabo's team reports. One of them slightly alters the protein's shape, the other gives it a new role in the signaling circuitry of human cells.

The changes indicate that the gene has been under strong evolutionary pressure in humans. Also, the human form of the gene with its two changes, seems to have become universal in the human population suggesting that it conferred some overwhelming benefit.

Dr. Paabo contends that humans must already have possessed some rudimentary form of language before the FOXP2 gene gained its two mutations.

By conferring the ability for rapid articulation the improved gene may have swept through the population, providing the finishing touch to the acquisition of language. May be this gene provided the last perfection of language making it totally modern, Dr. Paabo said (Nicholas Wade)

Genome Mystery

Several different proteins may be produced from a single stretch of DNA. Most of the molecules produced from DNA may not even be proteins, but another chemical known as RNA. The familiar double helix of DNA no longer has a monopoly on heredity. Other molecules clinging to DNA can produce striking differences between two organisms with the same genes. And molecules can be inherited along with DNA.

A gene was a specific stretch of DNA containing the instructions to make a protein molecule.

A gene was also the fundamental unit of heredity. Every time a cell divided it replicated its genes, and parents passed down some of their genes to their offspring.

Scientists discovered that when a cell produces an RNA transcript, it cuts out huge chunks and saves only a few smell remnants. Vast stretches of noncoding DNA also lie between these protein coding regions. The 21,000 protein coding genes in the human genome make up just 1.2 per cent of that genome.

A single gene, can make more than one protein, in a process known as alternative splicing, a cell can select different combinations of eyons to make different transcripts. But it turns out that the genome is also organized in another way, one that brings into question how important genes are in heredity. Our DNA is studied with millions of proteins and other molecules, which determine which genes can produce transcript and which cannot. New cells inherit those molecules along with DNA. In other words, heredity can flow through a second channel.

Much of the baggage in the genome comes not from dead genes but from invading viruses. Once these viruses invaded our genomes, they sometime made new copies of themselves and the copies were pasted in other spots in the genome. Yet some Carl Zimmer of these invaders have evolved into useful forms. Some stretches of virus DNA have evolved to make RNA genes that our cells use.

In order to define a gene, scientists must start with the RNA transcript and trace back to the DNA.

Genome Behind Mental Disorders

Two scientists have published a swaggering story of brain development that would change the way mental disorders like autism and schizophrenia are understood.

The theory emerged in pasts from thinking about events other than mutations that can change gene behaviour. And it suggests entirely new avenues of research, which even if they prove the theory to be followed, are likely to produce new insight in to the biology of mental disease.

Their idea, is broad outline straight forward. Bernard Crespi a biologist at Simon Fraser University in Canada and Christopher Badcock, a sociologist at the London School of Economics are both outsiders to the field of behaviour genetics, propose that an evolutionary tug of war between genes from the father's sperm and the mother's egg can, in effect, tip brain development in one or two ways. A strong bias toward the father pushes a developing brain along the autistic spectrum, toward a fascination with objects, patterns, mechanical systems, at the expense of social development. A bias toward the mother makes the growing brain along what the researchers call the psychotic spectrum toward hyper sensitivity in mood, their own and others. This according to the theory, increases a child's risk of developing Schizophrenia later on as well as mood problem like bopo disorders and daphnia.

Genome Music

Imagine the human genome as music unravel DNA's double helix picture. Its components lined up like piano keys and assign a note to each. Run your fingers along the keys.

Spanish scientists did that just for fun and produced what they call an audio version of the blue print for life. The team of Madrid's Ramony Cajal Hospital was intrigued by music on how it can make toddlers dance and adults cry and looked for hints in the genetic material that makes us what we can. They also led same microbial genes wax Niotobic.

The end product is "Genome Music" a CD out in February, 2003 known as Homo sapiens connexin – 26. It is a way to bring science and music closer together said Dr. Aurora Sanchez Sousa, a piano Paying microbiologist who specializes in fungi. It is the tribal way of incorporating science and technology and its development and achievement in magical time. The effort is praiseworthy.

DNA or deoxyribonucleic acid, is composed of long string of molecules called nucleotides which are distinguished by which of four nitrogen containing bases they contain adenine, guanine, thymine or cytosine, represented as A, G, T and C. These became the musical notes.

French born composer Richard Krull turned DNA sequence a snippet of a gene might look life AG & G TATAC GAGT into slal music. He arbitrarily assigned tones of the eight note do-re-mi scale to each letter. The nine became reform instance, Guanine is soadenine Land cytosinedo.

Ployet solo on percussion, classical guitar or the other instruments used on the CD the sequence would sound cute but rudimentary.

So the alphabet soup of bases served as just that base line to accompany melodies composed by Krull and his scientific colleague. They say the melding were influenced even dictated by the mood and rythm of the underlying genetic code.

In general, the genome music is an easy listening sound that is vaguely new age. One of the prettiest song is based on connexin 26, a human gene that causes deafness when it mutates. The DNA skeleton is expressed with tinseling bells and a flute melody does the rest.

Another song drums on a yeast gene known as SLT2, Sanchez sought the main author of the project if found of the sequencing because it features a stretch in which the triplet of nitrogen bases appears several in rapid the conjan a repetitive phenomenon that has a musical equivalent called abcbnato.

The DNA Cocktail

Genetics of happiness – is serotonin molecule – a neuropterans miter molecule in nerve cells.

The human genome has been described as the "autobiography of the species" because of our combination of 3 billion DNA letters is what makes us human. But humans share a lot, in DNA terms, with other species. Fifty one (51%) per cent of our sequence is shared with the humble yeast, 57% with cabbage, and a whopping 98% with the chimpanzee our nearest relative.

A human being needs 46 chromosomes, when sperm and egg meet, a brand new cell is created with the proper number of chromosomes restored. Half of our chromosomes come from our mother and the other half come from our father. The chromosome is lottery decided at the time when their pair line up for decision.

Mystery of Origin of Life

There are more things in heaven and earth, suggested Shakespeare long ago, the search for terrestrial life began.

Scientists examining soil and salt samples from Utah's great salt lake found them to be teaming with microbes whose lineage could go back billions of years. These saline tolerant homophiles live deep inside a lake so saturated with salt that no fish, no plant, nothing or so, we thought could survive here. These organisms extremophiles live in impossible conditions in extreme heat, cold acidity, pressure radiation and salinity. There are anaerobes organisms that do not need free air or oxygen to live as opposed to acrobes which do. These creatures from the deep could even be our ancestors and possibly proto types of life on other planets.

The subterranean bacteria living independently of organic matter from the surface – eating and breathing geologic ingredients release methane in the process. Methane in the Martian atmosphere has hinted at the possibility that exmophiles could inhabit the red planet. A supposition that has made scientists less sceptical of finding extra terrestrial life.

All living organisms have DNA which helps in replication and survival. However, Jack Szostak of Harvard Medical school holds a view that few concur with that life must have existed even before DNA. But isn't DNA the fundamental building block of life? Indeed deoxyribonucleic acid is the master molecule of life, manifested in a double helix. The nucleotides carry instructions the very vocabulary of life – vital to the replication of an organism. The human genome project sell to de-construct DNA in order to understand its workings by deciphering all the letters contained in the human genome. But if indeed there was life before DNA, it has to have evolved from its precursor, the DNA or Ribonucleic Acid molecules, say biologists.

The Harvard team is engaged in experiments which seek to create life from scratch as was done when the synthetic poleo virus was created, the better to understand the disease. However, this time round, it is not a synthetic life form that is being sought but the real. Mc Coy scientists are trying to start an evolutionary cycle through random stringing together of nucleotides to create RNA molecules and, specialized Ribozymes when mixed with clay, the cell prototypes began to grow and divide rapidly. Bio-technologists are already exploring how they can use them enabling enzymes to evolve formulations to help strengthen human survival.

But if RNA gave birth to DNA, what gave birth to RNA? Despite ongoing laboratory research with RNA and DNA, we have yet to answer the question. Where and when does life become life? In 1970 Fred Hoyle and Wickrema Singhe propounded that life on earth originated from building blocks transported through meteorite showers raining down from outer space. If so, that makes us literally star stuff, our ancestral root might be anywhere in the cosmos and to trace them would be as daunting a task as looking for a needle in a hay stack the size of infinity.

Writing on the mysteries of life and its origin biologist Lyall Watson in *Super Nature* conjectures that the fluid process we call life, began in the form of primordial sludge, in a "clay with plants." This clay could synthesize the geometric structuring of crystal formation with the dynamics of less rigid organic hierarchy. For life needs both logical structure and chaos to make it happen. Moreover, life tends to write its own definition of itself. For instance, futurologists predict a convergence of nanotechnology (super – miniaturization) and biotechnology which will create molecular machines capable of replicating themselves and evolving into more complex forms, so where do machines end and life begin? We cannot even begin to intuit an answer unless we first enlarge our tunnel vision of what life is all about.

We know that humans are only one of between 30 to 40 million questimated earthly species. But our etymology continues to be anthropocentric. The word "human" derived from "human" suggests that the virtues of "sympathy" and "compassion" are specific to our species. The concept of humanism is nothing more than a form of racism, a result of surface chauvinism. Despite the fact that all deep earth creatures were brought to the surface, they would far out number life on the surface.

A moral human being – whether survival of the fittest apply to human in the struggle to life by annihilating other life form from earth? Where the search for life end?

The seed of life supposed to have descended from outer space, would now be more dangerous if the extraterrestrial life fall again on earth. How the extraterrestrial seed of life survived on earth in hostile environment? Let us test the survival ability of life by introducing earthly members into alien environment of outer planet and see whether or they can survive or prosper?

The team of a returning robotic craft or manned mission importing an alien virus to earth that plays havoc without defenseless immune systems, thereafter is not the stuff of science fiction only. Which is why the Outer Space Treaty warns about the dangers of "adverse changes in the environment of the earth resulting from the introduction of extra terrestrial matter. It is a different matter that such a primordial introduction may have resulted in all life on earth.

Or even all life everywhere it exists according to the cosmic evolution version of Panspermia Theory which was revived in the 1970, by the British astronomers Fred Hoyle and Chandra Wickrama Singhe. The two worked together on the idea that complex molecules essential to life exist in interstellar clouds which, though regarded as controversial at the time, later proved to be correct. Amino acid molecules were even detected in space. They also proposed that comets which are largely made of water – ice, carry spores of germinal life across galaxies and protect them from radiation damage along the way. In sum they hold that life on earth was seeded from space. However, whether that event was a "directed" panspermia inasmuch as that something was in control of what was happening, or random, meaning a chance encounter is neither known nor deliberated, or whether the earth was at that time germinal life free or barren is also in dark. If the hypothesis is true, it can only lead into the conclusion that "contamination may be literally the germ of life and a bad thing after all. Eighty Four lacs forms of life beginning from insects seem to be true if we believe the views of the scientists that life stared by microbes. During the period of nine months of pregnancy human life passes through different life forms. Cosmic state to sperm and egg to human.

Evolution - Origin of Species

At the Digital Evolution Laboratory at East Lasting, Michigan, a team of computer scientists, biologists, and philosophers monitoring the evolution of digital organisms. A programme called "Avida" is working over time, creating a story of numeric commands and initially a cyber evolution revolution or real devolution? For by creating from scratch an entirely new species – evolution digitally, passing on to computers the wholly grail of genesis itself, delegating robots with what was hitherto believed to be the 5th copyright of the supreme being? The digital organisms may be very different from computer viruses, but all the same, they are made up of digital bits that can mutate in the same way. Deoxyribonucleic Acid (DNA) mutates and so are able to evolve. An Avida team member, Robert Pennock, who teaches philosophy say, An "Avida" is not a simulation of evolution, it is an instance of it.

Carl Zimmer, writing for *Discover*, points out that computer programmes and DNA are both sets of instruments. "Computer programme tells a computer how to process information while DNA instructs cell how to assemble proteins. The ultimate goal of the instruction by DNA is to make new organisms that contain the same genetic instructions", similarly a computer programme that contains instructions for making new copies of itself has taken a significant step towards life."

The intelligent Robotics Research Centre, Australia, reports that it has developed a series of artificial chromosomes that will give machines the ability to feel reason and desire thus paving the way for robots to reproduce in the way we understand, "reproduction". The essence is a computer code modelled on the human DNA, equivalent to a single strand of genetic code rather than the complex double helix of a real chromosome. Thus, it is conjectured to enable robot to feel connect and reproduce.

That is the crux of the evolution conundrum. Our understanding of life as being composed of DNA and chromosomes. The credit goes to Watson and Crick, who a half century ago, enthralled the world with their elegant double helix model that carries within its myriad molecules the chemistry of life. Their theory quite rightly so is roofed in the fact that we Homosapiens, are as Arthur C Clarke put is carbon based bipeds. Naturally since like us all other earthly beings are carbon based, we tend to define life itself as being composed of cells, amino acids and proteins. And this is what we look for when we hunt for signs of life in extraterrestrial location.

We assume that all life is DNA generated. The only concession we make is to acknowledge that life we find could be as simple as a microbe or as complicated as filth green men. But could not life evolve from a completely different system of molecules, the smallest physical unit of an element or compound? May be when we are looking for aliens we are looking for the wrong kind of life. What if life forms in other parts of the universe are non-DNA? And we are unable to locate them because we keep looking for familiar forms of life.

Amino acids are the building blocks of proteins and they require energy. Large amounts of energy are required to make Amino acids as is required to make humans, for example. Extra-terrestrial life could well be made up of compounds that are vastly different from amino acids. Like the organisms being created digitally by the team at East Lansing in Michigan. And non-DNA based life could be the only way for life to survive in a low or non-energy environment, a condition that is commonly observed in far-flung planets, where sunlight for instance is hard to come by.

Too far fetched an idea? May be but the ideas of Darwin and Alfred Wallan (the British Naturalist working in the

Malaysian archipelago who independently proposed a theory similar to Darwins even before the Origin of Species was published) were met with incredulity when they wrote about natural selection and the evolution of humans from apes, who in turn, evolved from more primitive life forms. That a number of species co-exist in the same environment only shows the individual rate of adaptation, among thousands of other contributing factors.

Scientists look for the following parameters to call something life : - (1) Growth through metabolism (2) Reproduction (3) and the power of adaptation to environment through changes originating internally. These attributes distinguish the organic from the inorganic, the live from the dead. The digital organisms display the last two attributes they can reproduce and they can adapt. And it could be only a matter of more computer time and number of crunching – and/or a teeny bit of divine intervention to initiate the first.

Human Organisms

(1) Human have somewhere from 26000 to 40000 genes.

(2) Earlier it was believed they have 100,000 genes.

(3) Men, more than women, produce genetic mutations that make evolution move forward.

To create the complex organism known as a human takes only twice the gene of a fruit fly or a round worm.

At the same time, scientists over described the overwhelming majority of the human genetic code as junk with little apparent purpose, it is actually brimming with remnants of long dead genes and bits of DNA that live amid the genes like parasites, re-shuffling and reshaping them over time. This suggests that junk actually plays a role in the process of evolution and deserves intensive study.

The researchers also concluded that men, far more than women, produce the genetic mutations that both bring disease into the human family and allow evolution to move forward.

The inherited material within most cells that controls basic cellular operations and playas role in most diseases.

In one surprising conclusion, the international team found that about 220 genes did not evolve in a straight line from all animals that come before humans. Instead, human ancestors adopted these genes millions of years ago directly from bacteria. In essence, this shows evolution making use of whatever material it found at hand as suggested by Collins.

Pilio Green of the University of Washington in Seatle, said it is more likely that gene transfer went the other way from vertebrate to bacteria.

The two teams also found hundreds of thousand of copies of mysterious DNA bits that act like parasites, detaching themselves from genome and reinserting themselves in a new location. Their existence had been known, but there are far more of them than scientists knew. More over one type of these parasites have the ability to move other pieces of DNA with them. The outer national team found that they could move more DNA than previously known suggesting that these elements play a role in re-shuffling genes to form new one. Another type was found to exist only where genes are plentiful, and it may help the body respond to extreme stress as per the international.

All this as well as evidence of genes that became inactive long ago, exists in the 98 per cent of DNA that does not produce proteins. One scientist considered vast material to be junk. Now they are finding that much of the material has or had, some kind of biological functions.

In addition to studying how genes work, the teams determined that genes are not scattered uniformly through DNA. Instead some areas of the genome, as the sum total of human DNA is called, one packed densely, while others are like deserts barren of genes.

The genome is the complex genetic information code about an organism. In humans, this information is contained in the deoxyribonucleic acid (DNA) sequence within chromosomes which are the major carriers of genetic materials.

Forensic Science of DNA

Every human being is a distinct specimen of creation. Both in case of external and internal specimen, the identity of person is distinct. Though Anthropologists and forensic scientists and new geneticists are engaged to create the identity problem with acuracy the process called forensic molecular photo-fitting, relies on mapping genes that are linked to skin pigmentation and in its more complex form, to groups of genes that control facial, structure such as corners of the mouth, eye brow pattern, nose and lip shape etc. so that a computer can then build a full image of a face based on the gene mix found in the DNA.

Scientists already know enough to closely estimate hair tint and texture, eye colour, the presence of moles, body size handedness, race and even if some ones ear wax is wet or dry. With facial reconstruction, the same science can be used to identify victims by piercing together an image of a person's face when the remains have been severely damaged or decomposed.

Besides forensics, however, the technology has other exciting implications too. It could be used to construct faces of people who lived before the advent of photography and by the same token, we might even be able to see what some famous persons looked like where no paintings of them are available or only with greater precision than ever before all the fossil skeletal remains of prehistoric and extinct animals who could have imagined that one day DNA research would allow us to take a camera back in time.

The Development of Human Speech

Prof. Tim Crow, Oxford university has proposed that there are genes that emerged late in human evolution and changed the way the brain developed, making one side dominant and giving us the ability to produce language. This gene would behave slightly different in men and women. Another group of researchers has announced that it has found a gene that appears to be capable of doing all these things. This gene is present in humans but not in apes. Says Dr. Bobed Affara of the dept, of Pathology at Cambridge University. This gene used to live on the X chromosome the female sex chromosome two copies of which are found in every female and one in every male. But in the human male, a copy has jumped over to Y chromosome the one found only in men.

"Apes don't have a copy of this gene on their Y further chromosome." Affara says. This means that the more must have come after humans split off from apes." It may also indicate the ape and humans have different root.

On the basis of latest molecular dating techniques, Dr. Chris Tyler Smith of the Dept. of Biochemistry at Oxford university, estimated that the jump could have happened about 3 million years ago. This was time when the size of the human brain was beginning to increase and tool usage was starting to appear. He admits through that there is a wide margin of error. "Genetic dating is far from a precise science. It could easily be a million years either way."

However, as circumstantial evidence it certainly fits in well with Crow's Theory and there is more. The fact is that this gene known as "PcDx" is found on the Y chromosome it likely that it is doing something important. That is because the Y chromosome is wild frontier of the genome. Genes that arrive here have nowhere else to go and the death rate is high.

Unlike all the other chromosomes, the X and Y don't normally exchange genes so once a gene arrives on Y via a rare freek event there it stays when it mutates, there are no healthy versions available to replace it. Most of the other genes here that we know about are involved in controlling masculinity and fertility and they stay stable because damaging mutations do not reproduce.

That PcDX has endured for millions of years, means it is important, though it has not remained unchanged for all that time and that introduces twist to this extra ordinary tale.

The block of genetic material that had come over from the X chromosome later split in half and reserved its position. According to Crow this most probably happened between 1,20,000 and 200,000 years ago. If he is right, that links PCDX to another crucial period of human evolution, when big changes in tool making and signs of symbolic ability began to emerge in Africa, leading to the appearance of modern humans. Thlersonish is more cautious, however. We have no idea what effect this second shift had on the way PCDX worked. He says, it is quite possible that it had none at all." He is also wary of dating events so specifically. "It must have happened after the first move and before the appearance of the modern Y chromosome about 100000 years ago. Circumstantial evidence is all very well, but what does the gene actually do? There remain more questions than answers, but nothing that has been found so far rules out the possibility that this is the gene or probably one of several involved in language.

"It is one of a family of genes known as Cadhedrins", Affara says. These genes make proteins that live on the surface of nerve cells and are involved in signaling. PCDX is active in the foetus and it is only turned on in certain regions of the brain. Once again these are all features you would expect to find in a language gene.

Still more impressive is the finding that PCDX behaves differently in men and women just is Crow suggested. Although PCDX originated on the female X chromosome, it is now slightly altered and it seems to have different effects. For instance, retinoic acid is an important molecule found all over the body, it turns genes on and off. Affara has found that while the version of PCDX on the Y chromosome responds to retinoic acid, the Y version does not.

What that suggests is that the male and female version are regulated in different ways, Affara says and there is a possible mechanism for a sex difference.

But PCDX was certainly not the only factor that allowed us to speak, but what is so new and exciting about this gene is a clear theory about one of the elements of language that can be tested.

Gene Function – pigmentation and Mutation

Human's have no links with chimps. In some species, a gene from one parent turn off the analoguos gene from the other. A new study of the phenomenon called paramutation may have finally elucidated how this works.

A team led by molecular biologist Vicki Chanller of the University of Arizona in Tucson looked at a gene known to determine the colour of a corn stalk. One version of this gene, called B – intense (B-1), produces a purple pigment. But it B-1 gets paired up with another version of the gene, called "B". If B-1 is silenced and produces very little pigment resulting in a mostly green stalk.

The effect is heritable B-1 stags turned off in the next generation, even it B-I is no longer there, an earlier work states that this paramutation effect required the action of a second gene, called mediator of paramutaion.

Intelligence Began with Women

Women may be responsible for the intelligence of human race by being attracted to quick witted man.

Scientists believe they have evidence that genes for intelligence are concentrated on the female "X" sex chromosome. Intelligence enhancing mutations would then show up most easily in men. This is because men have an "X" chromosome paired with a smaller male "Y" chromosome containing different genes. In women, who have two duplicate "X" chromosomes, such a mutation would be cancelled out by its corresponding "normal" genes.

According to the theory by preferring bright men, women would have driven human evolution forwards towards higher intelligence an accelerating rate. Crucial to proving the theory is showing that intelligence genes are usually numerous on the

"X" chromosome. The German researchers, Horst Hameister and Ulrich Zechner from the University of Ulm, claim to have found just such a pattern, scientist Nagazin reported.

Tradition of Munda tribe of Jharkhand, India, states that early invention or their improvement or better utilization of plough or design of house construction was done by the women folk, in the early history of human development.

Human brain evolving rapidly – gene show :-

(1) Human brain continued to evolve as recently as 5800 years ago and may be doing so today, suggest New research. Earlier theory was that human evolution stopped 50,000 years ago.

(2) It had been widely assumed until recently that human evolution more or less stopped 50,000 years ago.

(3) Scientists examined two genes connected to brain size using DNA samples from ethnically diverse population.

(4) They identified variations in each gene that occurred with very high frequency.

(5) Dr. Francis Collins, Director of National Human Genome Research Institute says "link between brain size and genetic changes is totally unproven."

Against the background as above humans have stopped evolving, but Anthropologists view in April 2009 TOI reported the whole process otherwise has been put on the fast track by our genes responding to rapid changes in the world around us. The thinking of the anthropologists is that the pressures of modern life may be speeding up the pace of human evolution. The idea nowadays is that human evolution is a continuing process and this idea is widely accepted by Anthropologist, Robert Wald Sussman, editor of the *Year Book of Physical Anthropology* at Washington university in St. Louis said. It is even conceivable that our genes eventually will change enough to create an entirely new human species, one no longer able to breed with our own species, Homo Sapiens, report Mc Clatchy Mews papers.

There was wide discussion on a controversial concept of ongoing evolution at the annual meeting of America Association of Physical Anthropologists in Chicago. Also a new book on "The 10,000 year explosion", by Anthropologists Henoy Harpending and Gregory Cochran of the University of Utah, Salt Lake city, appeared in which the authors had contended that human evolution has accelerated in the past 10,000 years, rather than slowing or slopping. The pace has been so rapid that humans have changed significantly in body and mind over recovered history.

Evolutionary changes result when random mutations or damage to DNA from such factors as radiation, smoking or toxic chemicals create new varieties of genes. Some gene changes are harmful, most have no effect and a few provide advantages that are passed on to future generations. If they are particularly beneficial, they spread throughout the population.

Any gene variant that increases our change of having children early and often should be favoured. Despite modern medical and technological advances, the pressure that leads to evolution by natural selection have continues. The massive AIDS epidemic that is raging in Southern Africa, is "almost certainly" causing gene variants that protect against HIV to accumulate in the African population according to Harpending.

Another Anthropologist, Joh Hawks of the University of Winsconsin – Medison, said, "our evolution has recently accelerated by around 100 fold," A key reason Hawks said, is the enormous growth of the world's population which multiplies the size of the gene pool available to launch new varieties.

Human Link with Colours

The human link with colours may be older than we thought. Evidence is emerging from Africa that colours were being used in symbolic way perhaps 200000 years ago, a Ute Scientist working in the region claims.

Lawrence Barham has been studying tools and other artifacts left by ancient humans at site in Zambia, BBC News Website reported.

He says, the range of mineral pigments or ochers found there hints at the use of paint, perhaps to mark the body. If correct, it would push back the earliest known example of abstract thinking by at least 100,000 years.

Being able to conceptualise, the ability to let one thing represent another, was a giant leap in human evolution. It was the mental activity that would eventually permit the development of sophisticated language and maths cells from Israel that were as strong as beads into necklace or bracelets are widely accepted to be the oldest un-equivocal evidence of such behaviour in humans.

But Dr. Barham said, it would be hard to accept that humans were not engaged in such activity much earlier in the archeological record.

As an archeologist, I am interested to find out where colours symbolism first appears because for colours symbolism to work it must be attached to language, the Liver Pool University researcher said. Colour symbolism is an abstraction and we cannot work this abstraction without language, so this is a proxy for trying to find in the archeological record real echoes for the emergence of language. Dr. Barham told at the British Association of Science festival. Dr. Barham has majored on a site known as twin Rivers, an old Cave complex in the South of Zambia over the past 10 years.

It was occupied by humans some 170,000 years ago, which type of human is not clear, however, there is a fragment of bone which could belong to Homo heidelbergensis the ancestor of modern humans, which like us had a large brain.

Dr. Barham said, the tools found at the Twin Rivers showed evidence of increasing sophistication with simple head axes giving way to smell blades and flakes that had to be attached to handles. The emergence of this composite technology combined with the systematic use of ochers. Ocher is a soft stone that contains iron oxides it comes in a range of colours.

At Twin Rivers, there are red, yellow, pink, black and even purple ochers. If they are scrapped they will produce a powder which can be mixed with animal fat, for example and used as a paint.

Women Existed before Men

A team of scientists in Stanford University have questioned the ancestry of man. Eve the original woman, was older than Adam, the original man, by more than 80,000 years according to the study. Genetic analysis of DNA samples from Y chromosomes of more than 1000 men from 22 geographic areas shows that their most recent common ancestor was a man who lived in Africa 59000 years ago. A similar analysis reveals that the genetic Eve lived 1,43,000 years ago. It is now possible to count generations by looking at genetic mutations in Y chromosomes. The scientists are explaining this away by saying that Adam and Eve had different molecular clocks and that fewer men participated in reproduction than women did. This may have satisfied them, but to the laymen all this sounds rather awry. At first, it would seem that Eve had not waited for Adam and devised their own means to discharge her biological obligations. Hang Bellfonte said. The women of today, is smarter than the man in every way. But this was trace all along when it comes to looking after the basics, women are much better than men who claim to be more cerebral and end up being clumpy. Nor does Adam give the impression of having been particularly up and doing. Geneticists would have believe that Eve had pre-emptied by arriving earlier.

Genes from one Parent Mute those from Other

In some species, a gene from one parent turns off the analogous gene from the other. In a new study of the phenomenon called paramutation may have finally elucidated this work.

The result could revolutionize future works into understandings the mechanism of apra mutation in plants and mammals, say Shiva Grewal a molecular biologist at the National Centre Institution in Bethesda, Merryland.

7

Migration of Humans on Earth

Theory of Human Migration

From a new analysis of a human skull discovered in South Africa more than 50 years ago, scientists say they have obtained the first fossil evidence establishing the volatively recent time for the dispersal of modern Homo Sapiens out of Africa.

The migrants appeared to have arrived at their near homes in Asia and Europe with the distinct and unmodified heads of Africans. An international team of researchers reported that the age of the South African skull which they dated at about 36000 years old, coincided with the age of the skull of human then living in Europe and the far Eastern parts of Asia even Australia. The skull also closely resembled skull of these humans.

The timing the scientists and other experts said, introduced independent evidence supporting archeological finds and recent genetic studies showing that modern humans left sub-Saharan Africa for Eurasia between 65000 and 25000 years ago, probably, closer to 45000 to 35000 years ago for Europe.

Until now, however, paleontologists had been frustrated by the absence of fossils to test the hypothesis of most geneticists that the people of sub-Saharan Africa and in Eurasia at that time were one and the same modern humans. The human fossil record in Africa from 70000 to 15000 years ago had been virtually blank.

In a report in the journal *Science* a research team led by Frederick E. Grine of the State University of Newyork at Story Brook concluded that the South African skull provided critical corroboration of the archeological and genetic evidence indicating that humans in fully modern form originated in sub-Saharan Africa and migrated, almost unchanged to populate Europe and Asia.

Grine and his colleagues said in an announcement by story Brook that "the skull was the first fossil evidence", in agreement with the "out of Africa theory" which predicts that "humans like those that inhabitate Eurasic should be found in sub-Saharan Africa around 36000 years ago". Ted Geobel, an anthropologist at Texas AIM University who was not connected to the research, said the skull opened the way to important insights about "the missing years of modern humans". The new findings pirated, on fixing the skull's age. When it was uncovered in 1952 near the town of Holmeyr, South Africa.

Human Migration the World Over

It was the discovery and dating of human fossils and stone tools that have expanded the story of humankind. Yet many regions of the world particularly India, Central Asia, West Africa, Antartica have not been intensively investigated. For now, it appears that the earliest Hominid to leave Africa the homeland (whether they actually did or not?) was Homo erectus a million or so years ago. One theory says, modern humans evolved from this early species in different locals at different regions of the world and not from African Hominids or Homo erectus. But an increasingly accepted hypothesis says "Modern Homo Sapiens arose in Africa some 100,000 years ago and made second great outward migration peopling the entire world". (p. 436)

We can convincingly assume now, as most scientists also agree without support of factual evidences that Africa was first peopled by Hominids, Homo erectus or archaic Homo Sapiens. The Europe was also first peopled by those Hominids or archaic Homo sapiens – the Cro-Magnon people before the arrival of Neanderthals. The archaic Homo Sapiens Cro-Magnon people – the Homo erectus – the early torch bearers of modern culture spread all over the world followed by modern humans. What made the early African or European Homo erectus so nomadic or adventurers when earth surface or atmosphere was not conducive or hospitable. How many homo erectus spread out from African Homoland to various locations of the world at a period ranging from two to one million years before. When movement from one place to another was a physical barrier at every step and Hominid or erectus were not so intelligent or physically agile like animals how they accomplished the journey. It is presumed that the means of communication – transport, no language, no survival technique or means of security, organization of family or social were absent. In such a situation, traveling in group covering hundred and thousand of miles with wives and children was almost impossible. Moreover, there were several varieties of predators lurking everywhere – dinosaurs, crocodiles, reptiles etc. Hominid or Homo erectus population may also have been reduced not only by predators but also through diseases. Food scarcity may be one of the primary reason of migration, but disease, volcanoes, earth plate movement, earth quake, are un-surmountable bottleneck to be over comes in undertaking long and hazardous journey. But looking at the fossil evidence of Hominides and Homo erectus which confirms such Journey, these early species had undertaken, it may be presumed that such journey was completed over millions of years.

Evolution of life through Panspermia theory or terrestrial molecular biologists proposes equal opportunity to all parts of the planet Earth for germination or origin of life wherever the suitable environment existed.

So, it was not only Africa, but even South America, Asia, Antartica, Australia (all Gondwana Land Countries) offered such opportunities and we got the evidences of life in these region in one form or the other. The evolutionist view of human evolution is that several type of primitive ape like ancestors appeared and faded over a span of 4.5 million years. Modern Homo Sapiens developed about 1,00,000 years and quickly overtook other large brained competitions like Homo erectus and Neanderthals. It is the brain or intellectuals, language and culture that made them superior over others, and the whole planet Earth was on their feet. Modern humans were thought to have roamed the planet Earth without competition from at least the past 30,000 years. Humans have faced the two major mass extinction (1) during the Permian period and (2) before 65 million years during the Cretaceous. Today, we believe our ancestors descended from African Homo erectus and created the story which is more a myth than reality that our evolution is unilinear. While the evidences show otherwise. There was multiple evolution at different locations of the Earth. The story of mankind is ever changing as we go on getting new evidence scientifically.

We have descended from evolutionary, ancestors of mankind which include Australopithecus, Homo habiis, Homo – erectus (pithecanthropus) Ramapithecus, and Zinzanthropus, Cro-Magnon, Heidelbergensis, Neanderthalensis, a Floresh (Hobbits) are also touted as evolutionary ancestors. These may be sub-divided into the Austric copithecus category as *Aetheopices, A. Boisei, A Robusties, A. afransil, A anamensis* etc. (p. 232 Darwin's *Leap of Faith*)

Homo-sapiens – modern humans "wise man" are stated to have appeared about 1,50,000 years ago. The earliest evidence of human species emerges from a fossil tracing human ancestor back to two million years.

In scientific theory, we generally accept that nature helped in the evolution of life. In that case, it is also observed that particular species or multiple of species evolved at a particular period. Homohabilis and Homo erectus may have evolved one after the other one better than the other in respect of adaptation to life. Homo archaic followed the Homo erectus and then the modern humans (Homo sapiens modern man), wherever the investigation have been undertaken. The above statement is justified by available fossil record. Except African Homohabilis, Homo erectus, Homosapiens archaic and Homo sapiens are found in Africa, Europe, China, Java and Australia and existed almost at the same period. If nature helps in the evolution of species, then there is migration too in large scale, which is not so is not justified. Every species evolved at his own place of availability i.e. African erectus in Africa, European in Europe, China and Java at their own place. As far as Homo Sapiens modern human is concerned, they are more agile, advance forerunner intelligent and have added advantage of culture. These qualities may have helped them to move around the world. So far the bipedal erectus and sapiens who lacked languages and culture did not move out from their place of origin. Because of the language and culture, modern Homo sapien, were more organized. They met the hurdles unitedly and efficiently and their population increased leaps and bounds with years, particularly in Asian countries.

Before the appearance of modern humans in Europe, the continent had been occupied by Neanderthals. They appeared also in the middle East. When the Homo archaic disappeared, the Neanderthals appeared. Neanderthals had great brow ridge. They had protruded face and big front teeth. His brain was like modern humans. He buried the dead and had few personal ornaments. They were less organized.

Homo Erectus "upright man" appeared some 1.6 million years ago and had a brain capacity of some 1000 milliliters come to modern Homo Sapiens of 1400. It is stated tht he was the first to control the fire and moved out of Africa into Europe and Asia.

Neanderthals appeared some 300,000 years ago and remained upto 35000 years. They disappeared suddenly and were replaced by anatomically modern humans. Neanderthals were of European origin. In South West Asia, they co-existed with many humans.

Origin of modern people in Africa (Gondwana land) was more than 70000 years ago, then they gradually spread, first to middle East, then to Europe and later to Far East Australia and America. The common ancestor of all modern people lived in Africa some 150000 years ago. This is after all a hypothesis. Fossil found in southern Africa (Gondwana land) tells that modern humans existed between 70000 and 100000 years tentatively. The DNA genetic code found in African women indicated her existence some 200000 years ago.

"Dr. Millard Wolpoff of the University of Michigan did not agree with those scientists who believe that there was a migration of modern humans out of Africa 100,000 years ago, nor that "these people were so superior to the indigenous populations elsewhere that they replaced them – bludgeoned them to death wiped them out or whatever. It goes against all historical evidence of migrations. Look, everybody knows that all humans alive today have common origin. And everybody agrees that in some fundamental way that origin was in Africa."

I am one of many who conclude that modern humans originated in areas all over the world and provided basis for further evolution. And that, basically, modern Africans originated in Africa, modern Chinese in Eastern Asia, modern European in Europe. And this happened to some extent because all those populations were interconnected by a flow genes, people were coming and going exchanging wives and so on (European world views think all humanity was connected in this way). Everywhere you get bigger brains, smaller teeth, all the peculiarities of modern people. How does this happen if there is not an exchange of genes all through human evolution? Seeds of human genes were sowed for particular period of time to grow all over the world.

As for the theory of mitochondrial Eve, he thought it flowed. You cannot ignore the male role in heredity. It is men who make invasions, kill the defenders, seize their property take the women as wives or concubines.

In the skull of early modern Europeans he was studying, Wolpoff saw no signs of African morphology, he saw instead evidence pointing to link with Neanderthals. There was above all else the nose "what a sol nozzle"? Dr. Wolpoff said, "we still see it in the Europeans of today."

The debate over the origin of modern human was sharpest in the Anthropological area, yet the resolution was not in hand.

Peking man represent Homo erectus feet, face specially the upper part and the nasal saddle. And also morphology of the area at the junction between the cheek bone and the maxillary bone, and the shovel shaped incisor as a very ancient history but was retained in China in high frequency.

Human first arrived in Australia 50000 years ago from Indonesia and Southern China. Homo erectus arried in Java about a million years ago change is slower in the tropic.

It is doubted, whether the modern man moved out to South Africa, then they have moved to Australia via Antartica about a million years time and arrived Tasmania and Mungo lake area of Australia. Some of the modern man may have branched to Indian Srilanka and Madgaskar, Andaman Island, Papua-Newguines, and even arrived to Aster Island.

Homo erectus, Latin for "upright man" arose in Africa 1.8 to 2 million years ago, migrating to Asia and Europe before becoming extinct about a million years ago.

Rats Hold Clues to Ancient Migration

Research into the common rats has revealed how people and certain diseases migrated around ancient world according to Australian Scientists.

A study of DNA from 165 black rats specimens from 32 countries have found six distinct family groups with each group coming from a different part of Asia. black rat carry a different set of diseases. Black rat or house rats or ship rats are one of the most common of the 56 species of rats, according to Alpin six different rats lineages originated in India, East Asia, the Himalayas, Thailand, the Mekong Delta and Indonesia. The Indian lineages spread to the Middle East aroung 20,000 years ago then later to Europe and eventually Africa the Americas and Australia.

The East – Asian lineage moved from Taiwan to Japan, the Philipines and Indonesia arriving in Micronesia about 3500 yeas ago. The other four lineages have not moved as far but could spread in future.

First People out of Africa

Homo erectus in Africa was a tall creature with long strides and a big brain, built much like us. Homo habilis, on the other hand, had short legs and long arms. Homo habilis lived only near reliable water sources. It did not seem inclined for migration.

Scientists had thought that complex stone tools hand axes and the likes found in Africa, were of the Homo erectus disclosed how early humans used to effectively butcher and process meat enabling migrants to take in more energy rich fat, grow bigger brain and build taller bodies.

Earlier assumption regarding migration was that it requires big brain, and ability to make complex stone tools, a long Homo erectus style gait.

Lord Kipanidze, called Dato is a paleo anthropologist at the Georgian State Museum in Tbilisi. Dato and his colleagues at Dmanisi in Western Georgia discovered several faceless skulls and mandibles – they seemed to be Homo erectus along with thousands of simple stone tools in sediments, undisputed evidence of humans outside Africa. In the early 1990 most scientists thought Homo- erectus didn't depart from Africa until around a million years.

Later, another skull was dug at the same site, usually fossils skulls are crushed almost beyond recognition but this one looked almost as complete as a skull as of today's. And did not look like Homo erectus. Its brow ridge seemed too thin. It didn't have much of a nose, and it had teeth looking like wolf canines, holdovers from our ape like ancestors. And its brain case was tiny less than two thirds of size of an average Homo erectus. If brain size is a measure of intelligence, as scientists have long believed, then this hominid from Georgia probably wasn't nearby as smart as a typical Homo erectus. The new skull had the chimp like face of Homo habilis, a small hominid with long dangling arms, who make primitive stone tools 2.4 million years ago.

The face of the newest Dmanisi skull suggests something of primitive man. As reconstructed, it resembled chimp like Homo habilis a 2.4 to 1.6 million years old homind with long arms and short legs proportion some have thought better suited for life in the trees than trekking from Africa. It had a thin brow, a small nose, and a brain less than half as large as a modern human.

The Dmanisi skull probably belonged to a teenager like skulls of young humans to-day, it is relatively thin walled and slender. Was it male or female? The skull size suggests it might have been a female, but its large canine teeth seemed masculine male apes today use big canines in sexual or territorial display. Either way, this human likely had plenty of facial and body hair.

Homo erectus in Java and China was heavier and more robust than it was in Africa. However, Asian creatures did not have hand axes. So it is possible that Homo erectus evolved from this primitive Dmanisi stock somewhere in Asia and then moved back to Africa. May be there were multiple migration back and forth.

At Dmanisi, the team found six individuals in the same layers. It is possible that there were several species of Hominids here. The fossils were found close to each other and different hominds species don't tend to bond together, hence they were of different species of hominids living at the same time. It is impossible that the species who have given now species name to every early Homonid with significant differences have made our family tree more completed than it really is?

Colonization of the World by African Tribe

Single tribe of about 200 people which crossed the red sea 70,000 years ago is responsible for the existence of the entire human race outside Africa, a new study has found.

Research by geneticists and archeologists has allowed them to trace the origins of modern homo sapiens back to a single group of people who managed to cross from the Horn of Africa and into Arabia. From then they went on to colonise the rest of the world.

The *Daily Telegraph* reported that while there are the ancestral populations in Africa it showed that one seems to have survived outside of the continent. The latest genetic research has indicated that it was not until around 70,000 years ago that humans were able to take advantage of falling sea levels to cross into Arabia at the mouth of the Red Sea, which is now known as the Gate of Grief.

At the time the 18 mile gap between the continents would have dropped to just 8 miles. It is not clear how they might have made such a journey but once a cross, the human were able to spread along the Arabian coast where fresh water springs helped support them.

It has long been assumed that human's success in spreading around the world was due to their adaptability and hunting skills. The latest research, however suggests that the very earth, human pioneers who ventured out of Africa owe far more of their success to luck and favourable changes in climate change than had previously been realized Stephen Oppenhcinur, a geneticist at Oxford University, said "what you can see from the DNA of all non-Africans is that they all belong to one thin African branch that came across the Red Sea. If it was easy to get out of Africa we would have seen multiple African lineages in the DNA of non-African but that there was only one which existed suggest it must have been very tough to get out."

The First Europeans

The most logical candidate for settling in Europe was Homo erectus, a species that probably evolved in Africa, about two million years ago. Erectus looked a lot like modern humans from the neck down but its body was more powerfully built and its head was more primitive, with protruding brow ridges, a backward slowping forehead and a smaller brain.

Although erectus may have spread as far as Java by 1.8 million years ago, many scientists believed that it had bypassed Europe. Some thought that the continents colder climate was too harsh for tropically suited erectus. But the major ice ages that wrecked Europe did not begin until around 900,000 years ago. So perhaps it was the intense competition for food that kept early humans out. Fossil evidence indicates that enormous carnivores prowled Europe between 1.5 million years ago, and they became extinct about 500,000 years ago. Scavonging Hominids would have been slim during that period and though small groups might have survived for a vocatively short time, that carnivores fauna might have kept the larger erectus population waiting at Europe's gate for millennia.

Some scientists believed that by the time Europe did become accessible to early humans, a nero species of Homo, better adapted for life there, had evolved. The first Europeans, they thought could have been a primitive form of Homo sapiens or even something entirely different. But there simply weren't enough fossils to determine which species arrived first.

The first species was discovered as Ceprano man by Italo Biddittu near Rome. The resembled skull which lack a lower jaw and face was a Home erectus but with some diminutive features. The classic home erectus has a slight crest along the centre of its skull. This skull has no crest at all. Ceprano man skull was larger than that of the classic erectus.

Antonio Ascenzi, physical anthropologist, University of Rome, believed that Ceprano man, belongs to same species as another human fossil the manor mandible, near Heidelberg, Germany. Some scientists assign that specimen to its own species of Homo. They believed that heidelbergensis migrated to Europe about half a million years ago from unknown parts and later evolved into the sturdy, cold adapted Neanderthals. The Italian scientist see more resemblance between Ceprano man and erectus fossils of about the same age that were found across the Mediterranean sea in Algeria. That suggest the origin of the people of ceprano might be North Africa. If so, scientists must figure out how these early humans reached Italy without leaving traces in Turkey, Greece or other points enroute. Aldo Sagre of the Italian Institute of Human Paleontology, wonders if in the past, Western Europe and Africa were connected by land. Although other scientists doubt that idea, some cite the discovery of early stone tools in Sicily. British paleontologist Alan Turner sees a potential passage from Africa through Gibraltar and Sicily. Even with a glacial sea level drop, such travel would have required a sea crossing. Evidence for the first routes into Europe remains scanty. In the meantime, early Homo fossil discovery were also reported by British scientists in Boxgrave England – a tibia or lower leg bone, about 500,000 years old, as well as stone tools of hand axe. According to paleontologist Chris Stringer of the Natural History Museum, London, the people of Boxgrave were Heidebergensis and may have migrated to Europe at about that time. The bone was massively thick with at least twice as much bone tissue as a muscular modern human. Its length indicates that Boxgrave man stood about five feet eleven inches tall. Large ridges along the back of the bone suggest that the muscles attached to them were immense and powerful. Stringer estimates that he would have weighed about 200 pounds.

British paleontologist Chris Stringer thinks that the Maner mandible (500,000 years old) Heidelberg, Germany, represent Homo Heildelbergensis, a species more modern looking than Homo erectus and perhaps the first species to populate Europe. According to Stringer, the jutting brow and rounded back of a 300,000 year old skull from Stenheim Germany place it on a branch leading from those earliest Europeans to the Neanderthals. Many scientists share Stringer's view of a multi-branched family tree. Others believe that just two species. Homo erectus and H. species account for the entire human fossil record outside Africa. The British scientists had hardly established the antiquity of the Boxgrove man as first Europeans. In the Sierrade Atapuerca in Northern Spain near Burgos, a site called Gram Dolina, fossils were discovered. This was a camp used by people who lived before the Neanderthals began to evolve. Aurora Martin Majera, an archeologist found three early human teeth. The fossils turned out to be much older than the team had anticipated, and some scientists believe that they represent a new species. Geologists analyzed the sediment at the site and determined that magnetic minerals in the layer above the fossils were oriented as if earth's current magnetic north pole were its south, and vice versa. The planet magnetic field which occasionally reversed last slipped poles about 780,000 years ago. The human fossil at Gian Dolina had to be older than that and thus close to the age of Ceprano man, which had been discovered a few months earlier. And primitive quartz tools found at a lower level of the dig proved older still dating back about a million years ago. These resemble simple cobbles and stone cores from which sharp flaks of hand axe were invented. Humans probably used such knife to butcher animals even to humans. Such sites were found from South Africa to Croatia to the U.S. South-West. Other teams of European paleontologists have discovered evidence that humans were butchering animals in Spain earlier than Gian Dolina people were. Paleontologists also think that presence of African fauna together with human tools and evidence of butchery at Micena ore support the theory that humans had made into southern Europe prior to a million years ago. The members of genus Homo not only reach Europe earlier than perceivingly believed, they seem to be capable of advances (hunting) behaviour. A deep sear across the brow ridge of Ceprano man justify it. They used throwing spears in hunting. They also used bone articles.

When the northern Europe was covered with ice glaciers by 350,000 years ago, the whole of southern Spain was inhabitate by humans. The fossils were found in underground cave at Lasima de los Huesos or pit of bones.

The discovery included three skulls, one of which had contained a brain as large as a modern human. Their face of structure, showed the beginning of Neanderthal features including a mid face that projected out "like a beak". They were as tall as we are. The Neanderthals were shorter. It is still unclear whether these pre-Neanderthals were archaic Homo-Sapiens, late Heidelbergensis or a new species altogether. There could have been a big difference of hominids living in Europe together. Diversity could have resulted from successive migrations of early humans into Europe. Such complexity was in Europe and in Spain, Germany, Italy, Britain etc. Europe was not the cradle of humanity but it was most creative workshop.

Theory of Human Migration in Europe Confirmed

From a new analysis of a human skull discovered in South Africa more than 50 years ago, scientists say they have obtained the first fossil evidence establishing the relatively recent time for the dispersal of modern Homo Sapiens out of Africa.

The migrants appeared to have arrived of their new homes in Asia and Europe with the distinct and unmodified heads of Africa. An international team of researchers reported on Thursday that the age of the South African skull which they dated at about 36000 year old, coincided with the age of the skulls of human then living in Europe and the far Eastern parts of Asia even Australia. The skull also closely resembled skull of those humans.

The timing the scientist and other experts said, introduced independent evidence supporting archeological finds and recent genetic studies showing that modern humans left sub-Saharan Africa for Eurasia between 65000 and 25000 years ago, probably closer to 45000 to 35000 years ago for Europe.

Until now however, paleontologists had been frustrated by the absence of fossils to test the hypothesis of most geneticists that the people of Sub-Saharan Africa and in Eurasia at that time were one and the same – modern humans. The human fossil record in Africa from 70000 to 15000 years ago had been virtually blank.

In a report in the *journal Science* a research team led by Fredrick E Grine of the State University of New York at Stony Brook concluded that the South African skull provided critical corroboration of the archeological and genetic evidence indicating that humans in fully modern form originated in Sub-Saharan. Africa and migrated almost unchanged to populate Europe and Asia.

Grine and his colleagues said in an announcement by Stony Brook that the skull was the first fossil evidence agreement with the "out of Africa" theory, which, predict that humans like those that inhabited Eurasia should be found in Sub-Saharan Africa around 36,000 years ago. Ted Goebel an anthropologist at Texas Africa University, who was not-connected to the research, said the skull opened the way to important insights about "the missing years of modern humans". The new findings pivoted on fixing the skull's age. When it was uncovered in 1952 near the town of Hobmegr, South Africa.

Gene Studies Confirm "Out of Africa" Theory

Two big genetic studies confirm theories that modern humans evolved in Africa and then migrated through Europe and Asia to reach the Pacific and America. The two studies show, the Africans have the most diverse DNA, and the lowest potentially harmful genetic mutation. Out of the studies show European – Americans have more small mutation, while the other show native Americans, Polynesians and others who populated Australia and Oceania have more genetic changed. The studies published in the *journal Native*, paint a picture of a population of humans migrating off the African continent, and then shrinking at some point because of unknown adversity. Later population grew and spread from this smaller genetic pool of founder ancestors – a phenomenon known as a bottleneck.

Population that remained in Africa kept their genetic diversity – something seen in many other studies, Bustamente's team has been looking at the DNA sequence of 15 African – Americans and 20 Europeans – Americans examining tiny one letter chages in the DNA code called "Singh – nucleotide polymorphisons" or SNP's (pronounced – 'snips')

Human Migration – after the Ice – Age

Ancient stone tools found on the Red Sea coast of Eritrea in East Africa are providing new clues about the evolution and migration of modern humans, scientist say.

The 1,25,000 years old tools unearthed by American and Eritrean researchers are the earliest well documented evidence of the modern humans adapted to marine environment and a new way to providing food.

They also support the "Out of Africa" theory that "humans evolved from a common ancestor in Africa and spread across the world." It represents a whole new kind of adaptation and feeding strategy that we suspect may have been influenced by climate change. Robert Water said in a telephone interview.

The Geologist at the Centre de Investigation Scientificade Education Superior (CIESE) in Mexico said the tools could indicate that humans were essentially forced out of their native habitat in the interior of Africa because of the glacial cycles at the time when the climate cooled and dried dramatically.

"We suspect this may have shrunk the fresh water environment forcing them into new habitate" he added.

Water who collaborated on the research with Yosephtibsakel of the University of Asmara in Eritrea and a team of International experts used uranium series dates to determine the age of the tools.

We were able to date the sequence of coral and shallow marine sediments in which the tools were discovered very accurately and very precisely to 1,25,000 years ago" he added.

So far they have found no evidence of who made the tools but they think human adaptation to a marine habitat spread quickly along the coast of Africa. We are documenting for the first time that coastal manned sites are viable place to search for early human activity." said Walter.

A research reported in the the Science Journal *Nature*, Also suggest possible routes for the migration of modern humans out of Africa. There are two ways this could have happened. The most logical way would have been northward along the coast of Red Sea into the Levant (the eastern Mediterranean Coast), Walter explained.

There could also have been a Southern route along the Red Sea close to the Arabian Penninsula, where modern humans could have crossed over a land bridge that may have connected the two continents.

"Either one of these two methods is viable" he added. In a commentary on the research, Chris Stringer of the Natural History Museum in London said, the research implied that at least, "one dispersal of modern humans from Africa must have occurred during the middle Paleolithic (100,000 years ago) and that characteristic elements of modern human behaviour existed by then."

Migrating People Camped out for 20,000 Years

People who migrated from Asia to new world camped out for 20,000 years off land now submerged under the Bering – Strait between Alaska and Siberia, according to genetic analysis.

A team at the University of Florida combined studies of DNA, archeological evidence, climate date and geological data to come up with their new theory which describe a much longer migration than most other researchers have proposed.

Connie Malligan's team proposes that the people who left Central Asia to eventually populate the Americas passed quickly through Siberia and got stuck in Berigia a former land that now lies under the frigid Bering Sea, where they stayed for 20,000 years until glaciers melted about 15,000 years ago opening a rock to America. There is no archeological evidence for that occupation as that the area is under water, Milligan said.

The researchers used sequences of methodical DNA taken from Asian and Native Americans for this analysis. This type of DNA is passed along virtually unchanged from mother to child. The small mutation that occur can be used as a genetic code to track the descent and the skin of ancient population. The university of Florida's Michael Miyomoto said the DNA suggest 20,000 years "waiting period" during which generation passed and genetic changes accumulated.

America

Migration to America most ancient artifact was discovered by Archeologist near Clovis in New Mexico in North America by 10,000 BC. There have been arguments about where the Clovis people came from, how they got there, and whether they really were the first people to set foot on American soil. The debate has been marked by a series of archeological finds or interpretations which appear to turn all previous theories on their heads.

The Clovis people it was said, came originally form Siberia at the end of the last ice age. At that time sea levels were about

90m (300ft.) lower than today and Siberia was linked to Alaska by a land bridge. The sinking of the ice exposed a thin peninsula a low rich grass land fall of game and edible plants allowing people to make their way on foot to the continent beyond.

So, far the earliest inhabitants of Americas are the people known as Clovis who descended from late Homo Sapiens from Siberia Pleistocene hunters wandered south from Canada and Green land probably through an ice free corridor they had opened by 12000 years ago. Skilled at taking mammoth, bison and other ice age animals, they used distractedly flatted spearpoids (Diuktai Calthral herigate) recovered at site throughout the America. Ininal digging at the Richey – Roberts Clovis Cache has exposed the largest Clovis points yet discovered.

Certainly someone came to America from the eastern part of Asia around that time. The archeological evidence is overwhelming. Findings revealed spear points very similar to the American forms have been found in Siberia, near where the land bridge was before it flooded Arctic artic ocean covered it at the end of the ice age. This part of Siberia was inhabited by a culture known as the Diuktai among the Clovis people.

There is no trace of them left today chromosol studies conducted in the last few years point to a different part of Eastern Eurasia as the origin of today's Native Americans. Their DNA shows close link with the people of Mongolia. This genetic evidence is backed up by a surprising piece of physical evidence. Some thing in the Mongolian tribe. Some Native Americans have a distinctive shovel shaped tooth that is probably found in present day Mongolians. This cannot be a coincidence, it can only be the result of a distant family resemblance.

But while some archeologists worked to find the people who wiped out the mammoth, others made in their business to demolish the Clovis barrier altogether. This new generation of researchers claimed that there is plenty of evidence of human presence in America long before the men with their two-edged spears arrived on the same. The argument has become so heated that American Palaeoanthropologists often define themselves as belonging either to the "Clovis" or to the "pre-clant" camp.

Not that the pro-Clovis advocates agree with each other. All they have in common is the connection that they were human in the America before 10,000 BC. Their thesis are about contradictions.

One theory holds that the Clovis people came not from Eastern Eurasia but from Western Europe in boats, across the Atlantic. Proponents argue that there are striking similarities between the Clovis spears and those made by the Solutrean people who in the stone age, lived on the Iberian peninsula – modern Spain and Portugal. They also claim to have identified a link between the languages of the Cree Indians and of Basque people of the Pyrenees. The journey across the turbulent Atlantic would have been possible during the ice age, they claim, because of the vast in flows which surrounded the sea like islands. People could have scrambled out of their boats on to the ice when the weather turned rough.

Most experts thought the Solutrean island far fetched. The islands were summarized as "Iberia not Siberia" and dismissed. But Spain is by no means the most distant location to be cited as the starting point for the people of America. Some scientists are convinced that the first Americans were Australians.

In 1999, Richard Neave, a British forensic artist, was given a skull and asked to reconstruct its face. The skull belonged to a skeleton found in Brazil and nicknamed Luiza. A 12,000 years old (a date which itself broke through the Clovis Barrier) she was the most ancient skelton yet found on the American land mass.

A shattering surprise came when Neave put flesh on Luiza's ancient bones, his reconstruction had features that were markedly Negroid, similar to modern day Africans, or Australian aborigines. Luiza's supposed face bore little resemblance to the historic people of Siberia or modern native Americans. So it is possible that some of the early humans who migrated out of Africa to reach Australia 40,000 years ago (via Antartica as also via Southern tip of South America) found their way to South America (via Antartica and South America)

There is a site at Mone Verde, in Chile, whose age could lend since weight to the Australia theory or Antartica South America theory. It appears to be an ancient place of healing. The site has been confirmed to be at least 14,5000 years old by corrected radio carbon dating. Some studies show that there are signs of human habitation below the remains at Monte Verde. This move ancient encampment, known as MVI, could be as old as 33000 years.

As the date mount at the foundations of the Clovis barrier crumble away. Before the Clovis people crossed the Beringia land bridge, other people came to South America from South Africa or from Australia or the South Pacific or most probably from Antartica to South America, or if they came from the north then they must have traveled in boats may millennia earlier there was believed – before the land route could be taken. In canon they could have hugged the coast, making frequent stop on the ice to hunt and last. This view has been confirmed by recent studies.

Another convincing study published in 2001 put the focus back on to the northern route. Anthropologists at the University of Michigan compared modern and prehistoric skulls from around the world. Key measurements such as nasal bone height showed that he Jomon the early indigenous population of the eastern part of the land mass that is now Japan, bore a close resemblance to some Native American who established in North America. Descendants of the Jomon, the Ainle, who are ethnically distinct from modern Japanese, still live on Hokkaido the north island of Japan, which at the time was part of the north-east Asian main land. Their American cousins are the tribes we know as the Sioux, the Black foot and the Cherokee.

Despite all the evidence – or rather because of the mass conflicting evidence – the question of who the first Americans were remains open. Some scientists prefer to think of the colonisation of the Americas not as an event with a single starting point but as a series of waves. It may be that some of the waves of people left no trace in the archaeological evidence. There is no simple answer to the question. Who came first to America? But we can give an answer to the question. Who are the truly native Americans. We can say that there is in a sense, no such person. Every one who has ever lived on the American continents from Alaska to Tierre del Fuego, from the stone age to the present day – is an immigrant on the descendant of an immigrant.

That is something on which all the archaeologists agree. Over the course of thousand of years, successive waves of people have made their way into North and South American. Some of the newcomers came on foot, others almost certainly, by boat.

It is now possible to use a range of scientific methods, - DNA profiling, linguistic studies, skull measurement to trace the origins of the different people. These findings an are being checked against the archaeological record to try to compile a time frame and a map of the people of the America.

The tribal people that we know today all hark back to different parts of the north eastern Asia, and they came in separate waves of immigration. If any people did come from South Africa directly or from Australia or even Europe they have vanished.

The ancient people identified by the scholars in both the Americans are as follows : -

(1) *Siberian* : some ancient Siberians probably crossed into north America, but there is no genetic evidence of their descendants today.

(2) *Mongolian* : The shovel shaped incisor tooth in modern Mongolian and also in some American Indian is proof of a genetic link.

(3) *Ainy* : An ethnic minority in modern Japan, it is currently proposed that the Ainy may share ancestry with the Sioux, Blackfoot and Cherokee.

(4) *Inuit* : The Inuit are related to the Chukchi who still live in a nomadic life in Siberia.

(5) *Blackfoot* : Skull measurements have suggested that Blackfoot Sioux, and Cherokee could have come from what is now Japan.

(6) *Alent* : A genetic divergence from Inuit around 9006 years ago shows that the Alent branched out soon after crossing Beringia.

(7) *Cree* : Apparent links between the language of the Cree and that spoken in the Basque region in France are regarded skeptically.

(8) *Apache* : Apache and Navajo are ethnically distinct from other Native Americans. One researcher suggests that their language has Sino-Tibetan roots.

(9) *Yanomani* : Genetic matches with Inuit of the north show that the Yanomani must have originated in north – east Asia and moved south to Brazil.

Genetic analysis published recently in 2008 October, give the following account of migration of people to America.

People who migrated from Asia to the New world camped out for 20,000 years on land now submerged under the Bering Strait between Alaska and Siberia.

A team at the University of Florida combined studies of DNA, archeological evidence, climate date and geological data to come up with their new theory, which describes a much longer migration than most other researchers have proposed. "We sort of went out onto a limb, incorporating all this nongenetic data" molecular anthropologist Conic Mulligan said.

Mulligan's team proposes that the people who left Ventral Asia to eventually populate the Americas passed quickly through Siberia, and then got stuck in Beringia – a former land mass that now lies under the frigid Bering Sea. There they stayed for 20,000 years, until glaciers melted about 15,000 years ago, opening a route to the Americas. "The reason there is no archeological Evidence for that occupation is that the area is under water" Mulligan said.

The researchers used sequences of mitochondrial DNA taken from Asians and native Americans for their analysis. This type of DNA is passed along virtually unchanged from mother to child. The small mutations that occur can be used as a genetic clock to trail the descent and the sizes of ancient populations, The university of Florida's Michael Miya Moto said the DNA suggests 20,000 year "waiting period" during which generation passed and genetic changes accumulated (Reuters)

Mexican Footprints 14.12.2005

Scientists who discovered the footprints said they were made by humans walking in volcanic ash 40,000 years ago. This seemed incredible since no human presence in the Americas had been established earlier than 13000 years ago. So geologists went to the scene near Puebla. They came to a more astonishing conclusion, the prints were in 1.3 million years old rock, meaning the prints were laid down more than a million years before modern Homo Sapiens evolved in Africa. It means either one of the view is wrong. If the dating of foot prints by geologist is correct, the dating of modern Homo Sapiens is wrong. The modern Homo sapiens may have evolved much earlier than we think today. The evolution process that we think today is very slow, which may not be correct. We have to think afresh on the slow process of evolution.

The surprising antiquity of the rock bearing the prints was determined by a research team led by Paul Renne, Director of the Berkolgy Geochronology centre in California. All the tests yielded the 1.3 million years date.

In the journal *Nature*, the team wrote "we conclude that either Homonid migration into the Americas occurred very much earlier than previously believed or that the features in question were not made by humans on recently erupted ash. In case of the latter, we have to question the authenticity of all the fossil evidences of Homo Sapiens.

The Niginal discovery was made in 2003 by Silvia Gonzalez of Liverpool, John Moors University. Renne questioned that there were in fact foot prints".There distribution is random, not like same thing made by early humans" He says.

Aborigines were the First Americans

The first people to inhabit America were Australian Aborigines – not American Indians. New archeological findings have uncovered evidence that they crossed the Pacific Ocean by boat and settled on the continent long before Siberians tricked across the Bering Straits after the ice age.

Scientists have reconstructed the skull of a young girl found in Brazil. At 12000 years old "Luzia" is the oldest human skeleton yet found on the American landscape. During the past four years 50 other skulls have been discovered in Brazil and Columbia, all pre-dating the invasion of Mongoloid peoples from the north about 9000 years ago.

Luzia's skull was discovered in the early 1970 by a French archeologist in a layer of sediments and was dismissed as insignificant. It was given away to the National Museum in Rio-de-Janeiro, where it remained until a few years ago when Walter Neves professor of Biological anthropology at the University of Sao Paulo heard about it and realized that it might provide vital clue for solving the mystery of Americas Anthropological heritage.

The procedure has revealed conclusive evidence of Luzia's ancestry. Neves is still shocked by his findings when we started seeing the result it was amazing because we realized the statistics were showing that these people were anything except Mongoloid, he said.

Luzia was constructed by Richard Neves, a forensic artist from the university of Manchester for *Ancient Voices* aBBC documentary to shown soon. Neves' reconstruction backed up Neves' calculation, "that to me is a Negroid face. The proportion of the face do not say anything about it being Mongoloid" Luzia's facial characteristics are similar to those of the people of the Islands of South east Asia, Australia and Melanesia. They are similar to modern day Aborigines and Africans and show no similarities at all with Mongoloids from east Asia and modern day Indians, said Neves.

The oldest signs of habitation in north or south America were previously believed to be stone spear points discovered at Clovis, New Mexico, in the 1930s. They were dated at 11000 years old charcoal a chipped stone stood and scraps of food found recently, however, have been dated at 110,000 years old. The remains, perhaps of a camp of ancient sea farers from Asia.

The theory that aborigines could have traveled by water to the Americas has been given further evidence by the discovery of a painting of an ocean going vessel in western Australia, which is 20,000 years old. The 4000 mile journey between Australia and South America can still be undertaken with relatively short island hops.

Dennis Standford, chairman of the Anthropology department of the Natural Museum of History, Wahsington, DC believes the "capability of pre-historic peoples has long been underestimated. Way back then they weren't really cave people, they were pretty sophisticated, he said "Neolithic people were doing a whole lot more than we give them credit for, they were just as smart as us, they just did different things" on the basic of the further evidence. Aboriginal invaders have been provided by computer imaging technology, used to interpret cave painting in Serra de Capivora in north eastern Brazil. The pictures show pregnant women and hunters chasing giant Armadillos, as well as what were initially interpreted by archeologists as human figures dancing. After more examination, however, the figures are now thought to be warriors spinning through the air with a spear illustrating battles between the aborigines and the invading Mongoloids from the north.

The American aborigines were almost entirely wiped out by the encroaching Mongoloids, but anthropologists believe that some of their descendants interbred with the Mongoloid peoples who preceded today's South American Indians, survived in Tierra del Fuego. Scientists believe that aboriginal descendants escaped to this remote island off the Southern tip of South America, where they prospered until European settlers arrived in the 20th century and brought illness to the area, which wiped out most of this remaining native Fuegans.

Rows of the crosses mark the graves of the Fuegans. Their skulls have now been analysed to reveal features common to Neve's skulls. Only a few Fuegans remain alive today, a falling anthropological link with the first native Americans.

Immigrants to India

"Human activity in India is found to have taken place between 400,000 and 200,000 years B.C. By the middle Paleolithic period (50,000 – 20,000 B.C.) man had spread to many parts of the Indian Sub-continents. Neolithic settlements (7000 – 5000 B.C.) are numerous in India and it appeared beyond doubt that Austric languages are descended from the Neolithic people". (P.P. Majumdar, P. 107 Vol.6, 1998, *Evolutionary Anthropology*). "Dr. Richard Klein, an archeologist at Stanford University argues that the emergence of behaviorally modern humans appeared 50,000 years ago was set off by major genetic changes, more probably the acquisition of languages". Evolution of modern humans is stated to have taken place in South Africa around 100,000 – 200,000 years ago, and Homocrectus leaved Africa by 1,00000 years which does not match with Indian history as there is a big time gap between the two. One assumption is that humans originated or evolved at different locations at different period on planet earth, but scientists disagree with this view, they say that humans originated in Africa only. How far this is correct, the search is on and the time will tell." The Indus valley civilization of culturally developed and advanced people flourished between 6000 B.C. to 1500 B.C are the gift of these Austric speaking proto-Australoid people of India.

During the period of earliest settlement of Baluchistan, the rest of the sub-continent of India was inhabited by various groups of these aboriginal communities (p. 112, *Bridget of Allchin*). They were pre-dravidian, proto-Australoid people speaking Munda or Austric languages and formed basic sub-stratum of the Indian population and culture. They resemble the Australian aborigines, except that they are considerably smaller. They are short and slender with dark brown skin, dark brown or black wavy hair and large dark eyes. They are long headed and have fairly pronounced eyebrow ridge and corresponding depression of root of the nose. The nose itself is often broad and the lips fairly full and there is a tendency to prognathism or protrusion of jaws. (p. 48-49, *Bridget of Allchin*). One of the outstanding pieces of Mohenjodaro-Harappa art is bronze figure of dancing girl. This girl seems certainly of proto-Australoid type, and if, as seems likely, she is indeed a representation of a Baluchistan type, one may note, in passing that, the very dark complexion associated with the proto-Australoid group would be in accord with the name given to Southern Baluchistan in classical times – "Gedrosia", the country of the dark folk." (p. 115, 148 Pigot). "The evidence of proto-Australoid people inhabiting the north-western region of Sind and Baluchistan of the sub-continent is enough to support the Austric speaking Kolarian people in habiting the N.W. regions known as Kolaria localy of the KOI (p. 274-286, 1906, Furlong). In Mohejodaro three skulls types are found which represent the primitive element of proto-Australoid group and are stated to be the dominant inhabitants of India (p. 16) evidence in burial. The evidences in Burials and Skulls discovered in Harappa civilization indicate the original inhabitants and subsequent occupants. There was first, the aboriginated proto-Australoid type, the second, the prominent

Mediterranean with that probably the short headed Alpine element and thirdly, Mongoloid type – a foreigner from north-East, the hill country of Nepal and Assam or beyond from China itself (p. 147 – 148)". The second and the rest skull types were of the immigrant people.

It is clear that in pre-historic times the earliest and original inhabitants of the north and north-western sub-continent of India, the builders of Indus Valley civilization were Austric speaking proto-Australoid aboriginal people represented today by Santhal, Munda, Hoet of Austric speaking aboriginals, the first people of India, whom the Rig-vedic people and later immigrants called them by the name of Dasas,Dasyas, Rakshas and Asuras, of course these were not the generic name of the people. It is noted that there were no Mesopotamians, Sumerians, Caucasians, Aryans, Asirians, Dravidians, Mongolians and Negritoes among them, when the culture and civilization originated and developed. The civilization was, thus built through the intelligence, talent, genius and foresightedness of the people. Had there been savage and barbarian as Darwin had imagined of ancient people, such an advanced civilization could not have been built. It was the only Agro based civilization Austrics. All the Austric speaking group of people used to address themselves by the genetic name "Horo" or "Ho" (Human). The Sind-Punjab aboriginal script have been traced in Bihar-Bangal border amongst the aboriginal of Indian Santhals. The Santhals and other tribes have their languages and script like olchites, Muandari etc. to be used for general purpose." (p. 63, 1995, S.K. Biswas). Among the aboriginal Santhal and Munda, Hihiri-pipri, Huriyappa or Harappa (this short of transformation in place names or personal names of the aboriginal people is not new in India), is said to be the abode of the aboriginal people in ancient time. When the Indus Valley civilization was brought down to an end in about 1500 B.C., the Indian Sub-continent was overwhelmed by immigrant people with different morphological, biological, cultural and linguistic characteristics in later history.

In about 4000 to 3000 B.C. plunderers, robbers, squatters, nomads, refugees, invaders of single ethnic and mixed groups and small traders crossed the Bolanpass either with wives or without overlooking the prosperous cities of Mohanjodaro and Harappa and except plunderers, robbers, nomads and invaders, who retreated, settled down in the cities, and mixed breed of population developed and the down fall of the civilization began. When the Indus Valley civilization was brought down to an end in about 1500 BC, the Indian subcontinent was overwhelmed by immigrant people with different morphological, biological, cultural and linguistic characteristics. The process of immigration continued unabatedly till seventeenth century. Thus, there developed a society multiplicity of linguistic group, religion group, cast group of different denominations, making themselves an amalgam of melting pot. The indigenous aboriginals, however did not mix many of the above mentioned groups and tribal endogamy was followed by them. Thus, a complete distinct identification was maintained by them.

"There are no monumental or public inscriptions known in the Harappa civilization, no hint of anything which could be regarded as business document, a private letter, a historical record, or a literary composition. When bilingual inscriptions are found,

And the script is eventually read by their means it is unlikely that we shall learn much about the life and thought of the people, certainly there will be no new literature revealed."

"As it stands, the Harappa script is unique, intrusive and without descendants. The script took on a characteristically local form representing a spoken language by a fixed set of symbols. The type of language likely to have been spoken within the Harappa kingdom is uncertain as the details of the script, except that we can definitely rule out any of the Indo European languages. The persistence of a Dravidian type of language "islanded" in Baluchistan among the Brahnis has given rise to the supposition that the Harappa language also belonged to this group, but the Munda group now largely spoken by proto-Australoids in India is another claimant. But Dravidian claim is only academic till the script is deciphered". (p. 180-181 Pigott)

"The language of the Harappans is at present still unknown, and must remain so until the Harappan script is deciphered. Broadly, there would appear to be two main contestants, that it belonged however improbably to the Indo European or Indo Iranian family; or that it belonged to the Dravidian family. In spite of the careful analysis of the corpus of Harappan inscriptions – now in the region of 2500 by Hunter, Langdon and others, the task of decipherment remains problematic. Numerous attempts have been and are being made but none so far can inspire much confidence. In recent years, the most significant advance has been the certain proof offered by B.B. Lal that the script written from right to left. The shortness of the inscription nearly all on seal or amulet further renders decipherment difficult. The uniform weights and measures another indication of the efficiency of state control throughout a large area". (p. 137, 1988 Bridget Aichin).

The recently published news item in *TOI* on April, 2009, reported "a group of Indian Scientists have conducted a statistical study of the symbols found in the Indus Valley remains and compared them with various linguistic scripts and none linguistic systems like DNA and computer programming". They found that the inscriptions closely matched those of spoken languages such as Tamil, Sanskrit and English. The result published in the *Journal Science* show that the Indus script could be "as yet unknown language". The Indus language and script is on unknown people and comparing it with modern known languages as above is not the wise decision. But no decipherment is yet completed as no detail is so far available.

The report further added that an article in 2004, claimed that "the Indus script does not represent languages at all, but just represented religious or political symbols. The claim was made that thc Indus civilization was not a literate civilization."

The above remark seems to have been given in response of the finding of Dr. S.K. Biswas referred on pre-page wherein he mentions that "the Sind-Punjab aboriginal script have been traced among the Santhal tribe who use it as religious symbols". And the remark on the script is that it represents religious or political symbols and since most of the Santhal aboriginals today are illiterate, the Indus civilization from where the script symbol perpetuate among the Santhals, the civilization itself was not of the literate one.

What Bridget and Allchin in 1968 had mentioned their observations, in the observation of Indian Scientists, but rather confirmed the script or language which resembled to Indo-European, Indo-Iranian or Dravidian family as stated above. The Indian Scientists are too patriot to follow the traditional value system and it seems could not come out from the traditional ethnic and linguistic prejudices but adopted a process of assimilation and integration to soften the issue or may have played dirty politics in favour of the government who already had denied the existence of indigenous people in India.

Rajesh Rao, lead author at the Washington University said, "at this point we can say that the Indus script seems to have statistical regularities that are in line with natural languages". Though the scientists agree that the Indus script or language belonging to Indo-European, Indo-Iranian or Dravidian family, they could not identify the Indus script or symbol with that to English, Sanskrit and Dravidian script or languages.

The scientists from Tata Institute of Fundamental Research in Mumbai Institute of Mathematical sciences and the Indus Research Centre in Chennai collaborated with Rao to develop models which helped comparing the symbols with present day languages. According to scientists, symbols in any language neither follow a random order nor a rigid one but have some amount of flexibility in choosing next letter or word. This flexibility also known as conditional entropy helps in analysis of a language structure. With this analysis they arrived at the conclusion that that the Harappans were likely "a literate civilization", after all.

It is clear that Indus script or language neither belongs to Sanskrit, English or Tamil, nor it belongs none to any known languages of the present world, the Indus inhabitants were not the Europeans, nor Aryans or Dravidians, they were a complete different set of people. The first inhabitants to be identified on the basis of skull findings on Indus Valley were proto-Australoid, the present day Astro-asiatic speaking, Santhal and Munda people. These languages are not the purview of research or analysis in the study of Indus script. Their language have different phonetic or sound system which the scientists are not aware of. It is futile to compare the Indus script with that of the present day English, Sanskrit or Tamil script or languages. It is assumed that Indus people had contact with Europeans, Indo-Iranians or Sanskrit speaking Rig-vedic people or Dravidians but it is strange that no reference of Indus people or script is found either in English, Sanskrit or Dravidian languages about the Indus language or script. This indicates the contact if any, was not peaceful, but hostile or there was no contact. The total neglect of reference by literate people indicate a complete denial of the local in this case the Indus valley people as the scientists today consider.

Unless the indigenous natural inhabitants of Indus valley civilizatioin are not identified, the language may remain un-deciphered, because the script or language belonged to these people.

Indus valley civilization were built by the indigenous Adibasi People (p. 67 S.K. Biswas) who were more civilized than the immigrants, but are stated to be non-literate, uncivilized and non human. Indus valley people are not identified but their identities were purposely hidden by calling them "Asuras" "Dasyus" and "Rakshasas" and by many other names. It will be a misnomer to call this "Asura civilization of India as "Indus civilization". The architect of this civilization were indeed the Asuras and Rakshasas of the ancient India according to Vedic texts who could not be identified. As with the script of these people, who are considered by the present day scientist as non-literate, whose script are still un-decipherable by scholars of the world; so also the word "Asura" and "Rakshasas" who were these people? Are they not foreigners? These two are riddle for the scholar to determine. In the absence of any authentic evidence, we may assign this civilization to un-known people like Indo-European (Aryan) or Dravidian or Tibetan – Mangolord people, but more to Astro-Asiatic language speaking people or proto-Australoids, because they are despised by the majority Indians. Neither the "Indus People", the "civilization", nor the "script" need to be identified, let it remain as "Ghost civilization". If need of identification arises, it will be European or "Iranian". The Harappa skull can be determined genetically. There is no question of inheriting the civilization, even the skeletons, culture and languages that were found in this civilizational region gives clear evidence of the identity of the people inhabiting there. But we deny to identify them. History can be blurred/ ambiguous and confused easily by archeologists and historians by giving biased analysis and interpretations of evidences. Interest of scholars in this civilization is totally absent because they are despised people. There is non-to-raise questions against this. All kinds of source materials of archeological and historical importance have quietly been allowed to be perished un-noticed and un-attended, those have not been preserved sequentially and carefully. All easily available sources of historic materials have been destroyed deliberately. (p. 43, 155, 1995, S.K. Biswas).

In the circumstances, it emerges out that the Aryans belonged to distinct ethnic group. They had come in small number and gradually mixed with the multitude of the earlier immigrant population in such a manner that their identity, from anthropological point became almost impossible to be detected.

India ultimately turned into a melting pot of racial admixture. The anthropologists when analysed found all the characteristics of Negrito, proto-Australoid, Dravidian, Mongoloid, Proto-mongoloid and Austric among the Indian races, it was the Nordic phenomenon. In 1931 census Nordic characteristics were found in minimal quantum, it is because demographically, Aryan were in minority (p. 175, 1995, S.K. Biswas) Even an atom is identified in melting pot. What is that atom? Our scholars knowingly deny to identify this atom. Originality of a race is identifiable genetically, but why it is not being done? Is it because the scholars themselves are knowingly avoiding to identify the original people obeying the secret order from administrative authorities of the country? Fear of compulsion is imminent among the authorities in identifying the original people who think better by not doing so. The fear is from the majority communities as they are presumed to unleashe the hatred and bloodbath. Much of derogatory remark have been written against the original people and history of India have already written of the indigenous aboriginal people of India from Indian scene. The fact, however, cannot be suppressed for long. The right of the aboriginals is knowingly denied by the authorities.

During 1931 census, Brajoshanker Guha, a physical Anthropologist classified Indian people in the following racial groups :

1. The Nigrito
2. The Proto-Australoid
3. The Mongoloid
    a. Paleo mongoloid
    b. Tibete mongoloid
4. The Mediterranean
5. The Western Brachycophols
6. The Nordic

Morphologically, the people of India may be broadly classified into four types (1) Pre-Dravidian or proto-Australoid

(2) Dravidian (3) Mongoloid and (4) Caucasoid. The Indian population lay between the Mongoloid population (China, Filipino, Malaysian etc) and Caucasoid, Scythian population group (Greek, French, Swiss, European-American etc.), Proto-Austroloid population (Munda, Ho, Santhal, Lodha, Goud etc.), African population (Nigrito) are genetically another distant from other global population."

The shape of head and nose are the two classic Anthropomorphic features that have been thought to be useful to characterize physical types among these various populations, so that extensive evidence have been collection in India over many years using these traits. These features are also known to be relatively less affected by environment with heritability of approximately 60 per cent. These characters are useful information on human evolution.

The Indian population due to its large numbers has a high level of genetic diversity which is in agreement with genetic evidence. In one of the studies, diversity in the mitochondrial genome in Indian population was estimated to be nearly as high as that of African and higher than in the mitochondrial genome of European and other Asians. "Indians are generally equidistant genetically from Europeans and Asians but quite distant from Africans". (102)

The Rig-vedic people were invaders and plunderers which is evidenced in Rig vedic texts. When they came to India in about 1500 B.C., they destroyed Mohenjodaro and Harappa civilization. The descendants of Rig-vedic people slowly established the new society, religion, culture, economic, political and linguistic system in the country and system of administration. During the long years of administration in the country there was no developmental work in the field of economy. These people were feudalistic in their attitude in every respect. Development was not in their mind till the Mughals and Britishers came to India.

Northern India has been a genetic melting pot due to large scale conversion from caste Hindus to Christian, which is when

Muslims of different areas of North India show close genetic affiliation with cast groups of different hierarchy. So genetic flow occurred across caste boundaries.

North-West and northern India also turned into a melting pot due to admixture of Hindus and Muslims. As stated earlier from 1500 B.C. and saw the entry of Indo – Aryan speakers from Persia and Iran. The entry began a long period of conflicts with and conquest of indigenous people. The immigrants often took wives and concubines from immigrant people, and also assimilated these people, so that within few generations their language and culture were considerably modified. (p. XI, D.C. Circar, *Austics of India*). A cast system was formed soon after the entry of the Indo-Aryan speakers. Linguistic imperialism was firmly established, resulting in submergence of Austic languages and culture. There was a great decline of indigenous peoples of the North to further and further South. The period from 520 B.C. to 300 A.D. was marked by successive invasions of Persians, Greeks and Scythians and was followed by until 1100 A.D. by invasion of Central Asian nomadic tribes (Huns), Arabs, and Turks. Thus, not only were there large movements of people (invaders) with diverse genetic backgrounds into India, but the entry of these people also resulted in trade contacts with China and South-east Asia. The north east of India also witnessed conquest of Kamarupa (Assam) by Ahoms, a Shan people in 1253 A.D. (107 p.p. Majumdar)

"Between 200 B.C. and 300 A.D. Roman and south-east Asian trade flourished and between 300 and 700 A.D. trade with the East-African coast peaked, and from 700 to 1300 A.D. flourishing trade continued with Arabs and Semitic people. Most of these early trade settlements were confined to the port areas of coastal India, particularly in Southern India. In more recent times, traders arrived from various parts of the world. The Portuguese came in 1500, the English came in 1610, the Dutch in early 1700s and the French in 1725." (107 Majumdar). Melting pot theory operated only among the immigrants and not among the indigenous aborigines. The findings of mitochondrial DNA studies and the extraordinary genetic diversity observed in India "land support to the weak Garden of Eden" model of human evolution. (107, Majumdar)

"Because genes move with peoples, the entry of diverse genetic elements into India must be a major reason for the extraordinary biological diversity of contemporary Indian peoples. The findings of the "Arab-Indian" haplotype at the B-globin gene cluster is a strong testimony to the movement of genes with peoples. Further, more than 90 per cent of the chromosomes bearing the sickle-cell mutation are linked to this haplotype in tribal populations from diverse regions of India. This indicates two possibilities – one is that the sickle-cell mutation arose in a restricted geographical area of India and subsequently spread to the Arabian region. In the event, the site of the Indus Valley civilization in the North-Western India-Pakistan border area that flourished about 6000 years ago before Christ is a strong candidate region where immigration had already taken place. The other possibility was that this mutation arose in Saudi-Arabia and moved to India with entry of the Arabs. The present day Indian aboriginals originated from this admixture of population in which the sickle-cell mutation arose or to which it was brought by the Arabs. (p. 107, Majumdar), is far from convincing as the process of mutation between Arabs and aboriginals is not conducive and admixture is not probable. Further, the practice of endogamy may have stood a major bottleneck for tribal-Arab mixture of population and is doubted. Arabs did not practice abduction of tribal women or keep concubines. Population mixture of Indian aborigines-Arab is only an imagination and not a reality.

"One study has identified a variation of a beta-globin gene tht arose more than 200,000 years ago in modern Asian population, among the indigenous aboriginal people of India. It is specific to that continent, so it cannot be from a common ancestral group. Yet this was before any Homo-sapiens arrived in the area, this study supports the assumption of origins of humans from India. One albeit contention- explanation, of course, is that the genetic material count have come from Asian – Erectus." (Truth about History, *Reader's Digest* p. 18). But neither the Homo-Erectus nor the Homo-sapiens existed by that time in India. It is, of course, a completely dubious contention.

"Another study of hyplo type of DNA Units has found minute traces of ancient DNA embedded in them. Geneticists still are considering the validity of the findings, but if they are accepted, they support the findings of beta-globin study, that there was a certain amount of inter-breeding between modern and ancient humans of India (p. 19). The first modern humans appeared on earth just after 65 million years." (Truth about History, *Reader's Digest*, p. 222). The beta-globin gene may have originated itself, taking into consideration the specific geographical location of the continent among the aboriginal people, without mutation such as sickle-cell emerged among the indigenous aboriginal people of India as a protection from Malaria menace. There is one more possibility, the aboriginal people may, already be carrying the traces of beta-globin gene and the inbreeding with Asian-Erectus or modern man was only the facilitator to help emerge the B. globin gene in the aboriginals.

Moreover, the sickle-cell origination or its existence among the Indian aboriginal population, is a defensive mechanism from malarial mosquito infection which exists among the African people. "Researchers have identified certain genes that confer resistance to malaria, and measured their presence in African and European populations. (p. 63 *Reader's Digest*). It further states that "the European variant only offers protection against milder forms of the disease. The mix of African and Mediterranean gene variants found in Southern Europe fits with the possibility that a virulent African malaria attached the Mediterranean in ancient times, weakening the Roman population but gradually giving rise to the resistant gene". This malarial resistance gene as known to sickle-cell is found among the aboriginal population of India and the aboriginal population did not come from Africa as is now reported by R.M. Pichappan of Madurai Kamaraj University, India, in *Genetic Jigsaw of India*, along with Ajay Rogura head of the computional Biology Research Centre IBM who said, that all of us have migrated from Africa. (TOI 9th November, 2008). Africa is the malaria infested region having tropical climate of hot and wet weather in which the mosquitoes flourish and India was also in the same region once. As with African population, Indian aboriginal population also developed this malarial resistance mechanism (sickle-cell gene). HIV and AIDS virus have also originated in Africa through apes and spread to the world.

HIV have developed no defensive mechanism like malaria disease have. HIV and AIDs are rampaging the Southern states of India, Kerala, Tamil Nadu, Karnataka, and Andhra Pradesh, the population of which was stated to have come from Africa.

"Gene 19130 is a marker of the first human migration out of Africa. Prof. R.M. Pitchappan, Madurai Kamraj University, Tamil Nadu tells, he found this in DNA of members of a community in a village near Madurai. The first human migration occurred 50,000-70,000 years ago, when we moved out of Africa into India, through the coastal region via the land bridge when the sea level was low".

"The hunter gathers body advanced to deal with the malaria menace. Tribal populations in India (indigenous people) have red blood corpuscles shaped like a sickle that inhibits malarial infection. This is a natural selection phenomenon for survival. "All of us are literally African". (TOI November, 2008).

The dominant prevailing view of the origin and spread of modern humans is that "Homo sapiens originated in South Africa around 1,00,000 – 20,00,000 years ago and that all present human populations outside sub-Saharan Africa are primarily descendants of a population that moved out of Africa about 10,00,00 years ago." We have seen the Indian position in the initial page of the article.

"Harpending and others (1993) have suggested after the migration of modern humans from Africa, there were many rapid population expansions following an initial period of isolation. Barllinger and others (1992) on the basis of data on Mt. DNA polymorphsons, suggested that such an expansion may have taken place in Southern China. Mountain and others (1995) using similar Mt. DNA have hypothesized that a centre of this expansion may have been in or close to India. Although, the high level of heterozygocity observed in African populations is compatible with a number of hypothesis that do not assume an African origin, the findings that root (ancestral states) of these Ales polymorphsons lies close to the cluster of African populations and that heterozygocities observed in African populations are higher than those predicted have been interpreted that (1997-1996) as evidence supporting the "out of Africa" theory and of a greater effective population size across Africa." (p. 444, Majumdar and others).

"Thus African population, most probably underwent large expansion before they moved out of the continent (though modern data do not support this hypothesis), and were to become the source of modern humans in other parts of the world. In the present study, we have presented evidence that with respect to the Ale insertion polymorphsons, the Indian show levels of heterozygocity (O.448 + 0.39) that are higher, although not always significantly, than most global population, including African populations (p. 445). Genetic studies show there is more variability in genetic pool in Africa than outside.

The findings of mitochondrial DNA studies and the extraordinary genetic diversity observed in India (among natural populations) lend support to the weak "Garden of Eden" model of human evolution (Harpending and others, 1993). It is hypothesized that modern humans coming into India, expanded Europe and other parts of Asia. It is reported that before the evolution of Homo-sapiens or modern humans 2,00,000 years ago in South Africa, modern humans in India had already made considerable cultural advancement before 4,00,000 years ago. (p. 107, 1988, Majumdar). Modern humans in India, particularly the Austric speaking populations are distinct origin and not supposed to be related to African populations.

A research study reported in TOI in 23rd July 2009, states that "Australian aborigines are genetically related to Indian aboriginal populations." This shared ancestry suggests that the aborigines population migrated to Australia via the so called "Southern rotate."

"The evidence was found by Dr. Raghavendra Rao, who worked with a team of researchers from the Anthropological survey of India, to find tell tale mutations in modern day Indian populations that are exclusively shared by Aborigines."

"For about 160-120 million years ago, when Madagascar, Seychelles, Srilanka, India, Antartica and Australia were parts of East Gondwana, and Gondwana Assembly (p. 197). no sea separated them but were land locked regions. The Mungo region of Australia and Tasmania were closely attached to Antartica. Australian Scientist say that Mungo man did not relate to Africa genetically.

From "Horn of Africa" as evidence indicates it is the Hominid only who crossed the bridge to Europe and middle East and not the modern humans at the early stage of migration. Modern humans originated in Europe, Asia, China, India and South-East Asia. Hominid originated in Africa.

There was another route of migration from Africa, called Southern route, it means the route emanating from South Africa from its Southern end, either towards the west or the east. Southern route towards the west goes to West Africa and South America. The eastern route comes to East Africa, India, Antartica and Australia and finally reached to Mungo region of Australia and Tasmania, Newzealand and Eastern Island.

When the Australians moved out from India on way to Australia via Antartica, some stayed back at 90° East ridge which is now called Andaman and Nicobar Island. At this period, there was no sea on the enroute and the aborigines traveled through land route only and became the early people of Australia. In course of time, Tasmanias were all wiped out by invaders but the Australian aborigines survived, and the present Government of Australia have offered them the status of "indigenous people" the "original settlers of Australia." It is unfortunate that the aboriginal people of India with whom the Australian aborigines of the later origins as stated have genetic link have been denied the indigenous status by the Government of India. The decision of the Government is prejudicial and not based on the fact. There are huge aboriginal population in India, and the Government cannot deny the indigenous status to them. The Australians who came out of Indian aboriginal population have the "indigenous" status which the Indian aborigines cannot be denied.

Human Foot Prints at Marcha

The foot prints on the sedimentary rock at Marcha, Jharkhand, India is of adult male human about five and half feet tall. He was leisurely walking down from north to south when his left feet slipped by the heel on the rock's boarder which was semi solid and scratched down about a feet down but stood erect balancing himself with the second feet. This made the left foot prints on the rock very vivid and clear as if it was made a little earlier. This sedimentary rock with foot prints was covered with layers of soils below subsequently, may be during Persian period or probably during the collision of Indian sub continents with Tibet or before by the Gondwana soils. This rock was unearthed from the rapid folowing water from the check dam which was built by the German missionary in about 1900 A.D. There was a drainage at the west end of the basement platform. The water flowing through the drainage, particularly during rainy season, slowly eroded the soil uncovering the sedimentary rock laying beneath ten feet deep below the top soil. The foot prints on the rock was first located by the cattle tending children of village Marcha during the period 1930 – 50. The drainage remains almost dry except rainy season when the dam is over flooded. With constant erosion during rainy season, it unearthed the sedimentary rock. For the first time, I saw the foot prints during the period 1950 – 1955 when I was in village school tending cattle in the dam located area. As a child we used to fit our feet on the footprints of the sedimentary rock. Numerous stories were told to us about the person who had made that footprints, but no story was near to the reality. There was no one in the villages or neighbouring villages who was knowledgeable enough to tell the reality of the foot prints. We as children used to see the foot prints daily uninterestedly. And when I left the village for urban area for higher education my contact with footprints was totally left till I completed the university education. After higher education, I joined Central Government service located in another State but my mind was alive to know the details of the footprints on this sedimentary rocks.

Village Marcha is located on the plateau region of Chotanagpur, Jharkhand, surrounded all around by rugged hills and ridges and valleys of Koel – amodar and Kar-Mahanadi drift river basins of the ancient Gondwana land in India. The techno-sedimentary evolution of the Indian Gondwana took place in two major cycles. The first cycle occurred in pre-breakup continental extension phase in Permian – early Jurassic time (255 – 200 million years ago) beginning with transgression of Permian Sea (Tethys Sea) through the intra-continental drift-system of Eastern India. The second cycle occurred during the continental break up in mid-Jurassic – early cretaceous (180 – 140 million years ago) when the young Indian Ocean transgressed over the emergent East – Coast. The Continent lower Gondwana sequence. (Sequence I & II) was deposited in the master basin in Eastern India during the first cycle. The scattered occurrence of the incomplete sequences of upper Gondwana sequences (III & IV) were deposited in varying environment during the second cycle (p. 61).

"It is interesting to note that Gondwana sediments in India and in other Gondwana land mass occurs only in drift Erabens, Pranhita-Godavar and Son-Mahanadi are also drift junction of deposition for Gondwana sediments" (p. 56).

In Eastern and Central India rocks of the Gondwana super group, ranging in age from early Permian to early cretaceous (255 – 140 million years ago) typically occur in a series of discontinuous graben basin along the Narmada –Son geofracture which transects the Indian shield in the middle. These East to West trending basins are Koel – Damodar, Rewa and Satpura. Besides these, Pranhita-Godavari and Mahanadi grabens trending NW-SE and N-S Purnea Rajmahal – Galsi grabens are other cogenetic important basins where Gondwana rocks well developed (p. 54). The sedimentary rocks were formed in Gondwana in Eastern and Central India rifted basins beginning of the early Permian to the end of the early cretaceous (255 – 140 million years ago) (p. 120)" Hence the sedimentary rock on which the foot prints of adult human of village Marcha had been located was in age prior to 140 million years ago. Modern humans in India were already in existence in India prior to 65 million years ago. The rain of fire event of the Munda tradition is a fact and not a fiction and confirms the existence of humans which occurred 65 million years ago with mans extinction of dinosaurs. It is stated a human pair survived this mass extinction indicate the human existence prior to 65 million years ago. The formation of sedimentary rocks is stated to be between the early Permian to the end of early cretaceous (255 – 140 million years ago), and thereafter no formation of sedimentary rocks took place after 65 million years. The Austric language group of proto Austraid people say that they have descended from this early pair of humans and are the first and original inhabitants of this sub-continent since the pre-historic times.

Very recently on Feb. 2009, John Noble Wilford reported in TOI an article on pre-human foot prints discovered in Kenya,

Africa, which is stated to be as old as 1.5 million years of the Homo-erectus, an earliest ancestral species which had already evolved the feet and walking gait of modern humans. He said that an international team of scientists who reported in *Journal Science*, said the well defined prints in an eroding bluff east of Lake Turkana "provided the oldest evidence of an essentially modern human like foot anatomy." They said the find also added to evidence that painted a picture of Homo-erectus as the pre-humans who took evolutionary strident – figuratively and now it seems, also literally. The finding supported the evolutionary principles.

Until now, no foot prints had ever been associated with early members of our long legged genus Homo. Preserved ancient foot prints of any kind are rare. The only earlier prints of a proto-human species were found in 1978 at Laetoli in Tanzania. Dated at 3.7 million years ago, they were made by Australopithecus afarensis, the diminutive species to which the famous Lucy skeleton belonged. The prints showed that the species already walked upright, but its short legs and long arms and its feet were in many ways ape like.

Wilford further writes, "studying the more than a dozen prints scientists determined that the individuals had been in steps and toes almost identicals to those in humans and they walked with long stride similar to human locomotion.

But modern human foot prints on sedimentary rock at village Marcha in age pre date the above Homo-erectus foot prints also.

8

Search of Alien Life

Shall we look for outer space for our birth or life? Is the earth not suitable for evolution of life? Do humans have capability to protect this unique ethereal life? How humans as intelligent being developed out of an amoeba or algae? What is responsible for this development? It is the atom that came out of the big-bang and atom created everything? Life was with atom and spread equally on every universe. Atom developed life on earth. We expect life to be developed on other planets, but it is not so, why it is only on earth. Why there is no earth-like planet on million of galaxies, when atom spread up equally everywhere? Why no life sprang up? Science must answer these questions. Why earth's environment is unique? Why the environment in different planets differ from each other, when the building block of the universe is one – i.e. the atom. What does the nature do in this respect?

If earth is not capable of giving birth to evolution of germ (life) and other planets have this why these are not giving birth to evolution themselves? It is the fact that they have sperm and earth have egg? Like Mars and Venus in mythical story. Then atom may not be the universal element. Or this case, only the life may have come from outer space (from other planet) and the notion of alien justifies itself.

We have no concept of diversified universe, because the 2500 galaxies or universe have evolved from one atom. So structurally all the planets of the universe should have the same. As on earth, life here is shared by all living species. We have come from one element. So it is expected that other planets of the universe should also share this feature, but that is not, why? Billion and billion of years have gone but there is no life, leave aside the intelligent being like human so far. What is evolution doing? Is the evolution in other planets defunct or sterile? Why earth is not bombarding other planets with its germs? Why earth is not exchanging its germs with other planets? Not even with its nearest moon? Why asteroids or stones are helpless to carry germ of life to other planets? Why evolution is dormant in other planets? Why there is discrimination in evolution of life in planets and universe? Why earth only is a lucky one to have lives and a scenic beauty? We all humans must ponder over these issues.

Search for an Alien Life Forms

The Allen Telescope Array – named for microsoft corporation co-founder Paul Allen, who put up 11.5 million dollars for the project will be "the world's most powerful instrument designed to seek out our signals from civilizations else where in our glaxyy". The SETI (Search for Extra terrestrial intelligence) Institute said.

Nothan Myhrold Microsoft Chief Technology officer said in one statement, "that the best scientific estimates tell us that the probability of intelligent life elsewhere in the universe is fairly high. There is great uncertainly and some controversy in the calculations. One thing however is beyond doubt. That is if we don't continue supporting projects like the Alien Telescope Array our chances of discovery will remain at zero.

Plans for the Telescope mark a turning point for the SETI Institute, the Silicon valley based none profit body which is the world's largest private organization devoted to the search for extra terrestrial intelligence. The Institute project phoenix, which spends more than four million dollars a year to buy time on large radio Telescope, is evidently held to be the inspiration for the 1997 live contact.

The telescope, which will be jointly administered by the University of California-Berkley- will be situated about 190 miles (464 km) north of San-Francisco at the University Hat Greek – observatory – remote that is "Radio quiet" with little static for man made interference.

Astronomers hope the new Telescope will be an important new tool in the hunt for alien life.

Finding of New Planets Spread up Search for Alien Life

Astronomers have found solar system in around five other stars and believe that they are on the verge of finding many more new stars.

The discovery is based on a survey of 1100 stars a tiny fraction of those visible from earth, suggesting that many others will also be found to have planetary systems. Scientists believe that one day life will be found in other planets.

The latest research was done by Debra Fischer at the University of California, Berkley, who studied system of the life stars already known to have orbiting planets. In each system planet was a large gas giant similar to Jupitar and hundred times bigger than earth

All the planets had elliptical orbits that tugged the star back and forth changing the quality of the light they emitted. They found, however that five stars inching 55 canan and HD 38529, showed further fluctuations whose leaning earth shrouded in darkness for years.

Scientist Scan Stars for T.V. Signals to Alien Life

Is there intelligent life on other planets? Astronomers plan to search 1000 nearby stars for Television broadcast and other signals that could indicate extra terrestrial life.

Current efforts to find extraterrestrial life for messages deliberately beamed across space- an approach that would miss any civilization that does not advertise its existence as earth's does.

The new effort would search a portion of the electro magnetic spectrum used on earth for more useful purposes radar, Televisions, and FM radio broad casts.

The electromagnetic spectrum spans radiation from high energy waves, such as gamma rays and X-rays to lower energy microwaves and radio-waves with visible light falling somewhere in the middle.

A new low frequency telescope under construction in Australia will be remote enough to avoid most radio interference. The project will be able to detect earth like radio signals within a distance of 30 light years which encompasses about 1000 years. The television antenna will begin listening for jingles of the early universe from billion of years ago.

To date almost all researches for extra-terrestrial civilizations have listened for elaborate radio beams from being reaching out for someone else. But there is no guarantee that aliens next door would want to broadcast their presence to the universe.

The Mileura wide field array is designed to hear the sounds of "reionization" when ultraviolet radiation from the first stars and galaxies blew apart interstellar hydrogen atoms.

Future larger antenna arrays could detect earth like signals from hundreds of light years away an expanse that would include 100 million stars would be powerful enough to start putting in some cosmic returns.

Unidentified Flying Discs

Cold dusty discs of debris have been clearly ditched around stars in other planet harbouring star system for the first time by Nasa Spitzer Space Telescope. The finding confirms standard theories of planet formation but raises questions about why the discs were found around some stars and not others.

The heavenly bodies of our solar system are thought to have begun as disc of gas and dusts about four billion years ago. As the planets and other large bodies gradually colsed, they swept up dust along their orbits, clearing a space around the sun. The sun also thinned out the original disc by sucking in dust or blowing it into space on the solar wind.

The new type of disc began to take shape as large objects occasionally smashed into each other and kicked up new clouds of dust. This debris disc is thought to be fed by collisions in the Kuiper belt, a band of ice bodies beyond the orbit of Neptune. Such debris discs had been seen around a number of stars, but none of these stars were observed to have planets.

Now a team led by Charles Beichman at Nasa's Jet propulsion laboratory in Pasadena, California, has used spilzer to search for the faint intravel glow of dust around 25 stars already known to host planets.

Alycia Weinberger at the Carnegie Institution of Washington said. "Prior to these observations, we really didn't know of any system that harboured both planets and discs other than our own star system."

"The fact that until now, astronomers had discovered 130 or so extra solar planets without seeing debris discs around any of them, is like knowing you formed a house but not being able to find the construction materials," she said. The new observations "complete the picture of the planet formation process." There are no obvious correlations yet" said Beichman. He suggested the six stars may have begun in larger discs of gas and dust as they evolved or perhaps large collision occurred recently.

Extra-solar Life

This exciting but not unrelated development continue the 44 year old STI (Search for extra terrestrial intelligence) movement is not a waste of time. For the first time, an earth like planet has been detected that could be life friendly. And, for the first time, Radio signals, have been detected from between the constellation of Pisces and Aries, some 1000 light year away. All the exo planets so far discovered have been gaseous giants. But now we have stumbled upon a planet only 14 times the mass of earth composed of rock, and which might have an atmosphere. Analysing the unusual radio-signals, those engaged in the search for ETS say they are the best bet so far for a contact by intelligent aliens. What would the aliens say to us? Would they mouth Arther C. Clark's famous live Greetings Carbon- based bipeds."

Clark is of the view that there are two aspects of the search for extra terrestrial intelligence – the technical and the philosophical. The first is the primary concern of engineers and the scientists. Where and how do we search and with what equipments. The second should be the concern of all of us, because it deals with the fundamental question. What is the status of that recent arrival on the scene, Homo Sapiens in the cosmic pecking order? The spectrum of answers preferred so far deal more with contact than detection because that has far greater dramatic possibilities, both in the realm of science and thought. The promise of finding ET's is far greater than its perils. In Clark's own words, it represents the highest possible form of exploration, and when we cause the explore, we will cease to be human. On the other hand if we are indeed these heirs to the galaxy, we must necessarily be its future guardians.

E.T. is no Like us

Even if an effigy E.T. existing, why should he be like us? The huge type surrounding the search for extraterrestrial intelligence and extra solar planet is nothing but the scientific equivalence of superstitions.

The same existential fears that one prompted us to clutch at any passing supernatural straw to imbue our lives with making has now given a higher test spin than before. The discovery of planets outside our solar system is literally, no earth shattering news because most modern theories of planetary development predict the formation of planets around stars any way. In fact Astrophysicists have long suspected the universe could in fact, be riddled with trillions of planets. The discovery, therefore of extra solar planets is not only not surprising but merely a function of technological advances that enables us to look for them with more precaution. The whole search should be recognized for what it really is, another show to dispel that familiar feeling of godlessness is being alone in the cosmos.

But, still does the discovery of a more earth like planet known so far which has been extensively studied is the closest one lying right next to us in our own solar system. Yet surface conditions on Venus are so hostile that no life could survive on it. Could then the latest finding of what is being touted as the first radio signals from an alien civilization portent the promised ET? Again not likely. For one thing, the part of the sky from where the pulses are emanating contains no stellar body, making the possibility of an astronomical anomaly far more plausible. For another, the signals are so weak and of such short duration that detailed analysis is impossible. Because even if they are from some intelligent source, what makes our anthropocentrism immediately guarantee them to be some carbon based bipedal biological structures with brain like ours with whom we could instantly become budding what if they are some mindlessly cybernetic silicon based entitles with whom we could never hope to communicate in a million years ?

Tracing E.T.

Two Australian scientists have made the hunt for extra-terrestrial easier. They have discovered that upto 10 per cent of the stars in the milky way the galaxy we inhabit may harbour conditions necessary for complex life to emerge.

Although our solar system has been in the most hospitable region of the galaxy for five billion years, the Scientists conclude that three quarters of the milky way is other inhabited solar systems if they exist would have have had taken one billion years longer, on average to be nature like.

The estimate come from a new map of the "Galactic Habitable Zone" an area of space whose boundaries are set by its safe environment away from exploding stars and marauding planets (Earth destroyers) and which has access to the chemicals necessary for building terrestrial planets similar to earth.

In a paper published in *Science Charles* live Weaver from the university of New South Wales and Yeshe Fenner and Brad Libson of Swinburm university of Technology, Melborune have identified regions where life is most likely to prosper among the 300 billion stars in the milky way.

What we have done for the first time is to quantify where planet life is likely to exist." Weaver said.

Waiting for the Alien Signals

For believers in life beyond planet earth, the SETI recording of SHGb O2+141 a possible signal from an alien civilization adds to the belief that ETS and UFOs are not figmentm of imagination. The latest radio signal from the darkness between the constellation of Pisces and Aries has drawn the attention of scientists worldwide. Is E.T. finally arriving for real?

From incredible to credible, The SETI discovery is certainly from a credible source. It can't just be dismissed as nonsense, says Nehru Planetarium director N. Rathnashree. According to Amitab Mukherjee of DU Science Centre. The radio interception has certain basic features that seem credible. Astronomers believe there is life beyond earth. It is all about finding the right signals, adds amateur Rahat Narang. This radio signal doesn't seem to be fake. If the same signal is recorded four or five times, we can be certain that intelligent life somewhere is transmitting it."

Wait and watch – certain scientists call the SETI signal picked up by the SET @ home project was received on three occasions and supposedly emanates from a part of the universe where there are no obvious planets or stars. Another factor putting a question mark against the signals relevance to aliens is that it was observed for just a minute. The signal is too short to have been sent by intelligent life. If a alien civilization wanted to get in touch with earth or advertise its presence, it would logically be in the form of an encoded message of a longer duration, says Atul Paranjpee of the Inter University Centre for Astronomy and Astrophysics adds Rathnashree, if this was a radio signal meant for earth, in those sending it would have corrected its drift.

Rathnashree feeds the SETI signal "could turn out to be emanating from hitherto unknown astronomical objects the same thing happened before we discovered Pulsar." says Paranjpee. We are sure that there is life beyond Earth in the universe but whether this life form is still evolving or intelligent is still to be seen.

Intelligent Life, at Home (Shekhar Bhatia)

"The beliefs that we are not the only intelligent life in the vast universe. UFO's and ET are supposed to exist in other intelligent life, scientists are engaged in search of terrestrial intelligence. It was about the possibility of locating something real about inter stellar signals about catching a flicker of a drifting voice in the universe. Like us human they are also looking for ETs." (Shekhar Bhatia)

Is there any Life out There?

By Richard Words and Christopher Goodwin

This week American Scientists will head for Areciho Rico site of one of the world's largest Radio telescopes when Jill Tarfer will scan the skies for signs of alien life.

As the Director of SETI, the search of Extraterritorial Intelligence, Tarfer hopes it is only a matter of time before we discover beings beyond solar system. Funded mainly by Paul

Allen, the Microsoft billionaires, SETI is joined an increasing number of scientists eager to be the first to find alien life of one sort or another. However, if the alien hunters hope to find intelligence beings they may all, according to a book that has observed the charts in America be wasting their time. Rare Earth written by an astronomer and a geologist, has turned on its head the view that in a universe teaming with billion of stars there must be other civilizations, Intelligent life not there as far as the finding, they claim.

It is a brave assault on a cherished belief. For more than 30 years the assumption has been that other beings with hightech civilizations are more likely than not. This view has seeped into popular culture, cherishing from star trek to the X Files has reflected a human fascination with, even a desire for alien company. But according to Peter Ward and Donald Brownlec, Arfeson at the University of Washington in Sealk, that view is about as crazy as a martian with dementia.

Earth really is a lovely planet. E.T. may never call home because he will never smile. The truth may be out there, but it is not what we hoped for : though simple life may be common in the universe, they argue intelligence is very rare. The SETI searchers look in vain and the best they can hope for to use the title of less successful film, is narrow from outer space.

Ward and Brownlee say, "our solar system has many special perhaps unique qualities. First, the sun is unlike most stars, it is more massive than 95 per cent of stars and it has remained stable for billions of years pumping out energy that has created a habitable Zone of acceptable warmth that is neither too near nor too far from it in comfort.

Earth however is perfectly positioned. It neither freezes like Mars nor boils like Venus, and has Guardian on constant patron. Orbiting further out is the giant planet Jupiter which say Ward and Brownlee, "acts as a comet-catcher a gravity sink sweeping the solar system of cosmic garbage they might otherwise collide with Earth".

We are also lucky to reside in what might be called a rural retreat of the Milky Way galaxy, quietly going about our business 25000 light years from the central hub. our region has relatively few stars. In other parts where stars density is far higher, we would probably have been gunned down by Super nova or nagged by black hole by now.

But surely, with zillions of stars, there must be other planets in similar lucky locations? Even if there are say Ward and Brownlee they "must also meet other requirements if they are to support complex life".

Our moon unusually large volatively to the size of its planets. It preserve has kept earth in a generally stable axis which other planets lacking moon have moved chaotically in ways that would have been catastrophic for life. Our solar system also has unusually large amounts of metals which are pre cursor to complex life.

"Earth core is molten and surface – the mantle – slides about on its such plate tectonics are vital to life, say Ward and Brownlee. They create mountainous continents and gaping oceans that have kept water on the planets surface. No other planet in the solar system has plate tectonics." (earthquake) Ward and Brownlee further argue that the conditions that combined to create complex animals which emerged only 600 m. years ago, are rare, if not non-existent elsewhere.

The battle of five suggest that SETI chicks kept in a fridge at their headquarters may never be opened to celebrate the discovery of other beings if Ward and Brownlee are correct. This implies more than disappointment at a lack of life like situation. They should make us stop and think.

"What if the earth, with its cargo of advanced animals is virtually unique in this quadrant of the galaxy – the most adverse planet, say in the nearest 10,000 light years? write Ward and Brownlee. "What if it is utterly unique the only planet with animals in the visible universe a bastion of animals amid a sea of microbe infested worlds? If that is the case, how much greater the loss the universe sustains for each species of animal or plant driven to extinction through the careless stewardship of Homo – Sapiens.

Star Dust

The inter stellar dust deep space one eminent particles of material dust and distant comet will be collected by Appolow rocket to study the evolution of the solar system and how life began on earth. The solar system was created about 4.7 billion years ago, the study of star dust indicated.

We have come from a similar cloud in stellar dust and gas that condensed to form the planets. The cometry material may have brought the life sustaining elements – the carbon and water based chemicals to earth. Tony Manuonel Prof. of Space Physics at the University of Kent, Canterburry, said.

Bringing star dust back to earth for analysis could help to explain the evolution of life.

"The building block of life have been thought to have come from further out in the solar system, but farther away from the sun and then would be materials from asteroid comets," he said.

People have long suggested the commetry play a role in the origin of life, no one really knows because no one knows how life began."

But we know that comets are the most carbon rich materials in the solar system and unknown they are full of organism compounds and they fall on the earth all the time."

Apple rock for star dust created Feb. 6, 1999, will land back to earth on January 15, 2006.

Star to be Probed for Alien Life

Astronomers say a star called 37 cm offers the best chance of finding alien life.

The star a little hotter and brighter than the sun, is on a list of 30 to be investigated by a future generation of life seeking telescopes situated at relatively close 42 light years away. It is the 37th brightest star in the constellation of Gemini. Scientists are looking for targets for the Terrestrial planet finder and Darwin telescopes planned by NASA and European Space Agency. Both are due to be launched in about 10 years and will be capable of finding habitable planets outside the solar system. Astrobiologist in Tueson, US complies a set of criteria for choosing which star to be observed. These included the amount of heavy metals present when a star formed and its age. Young stars emitting bright X-rays were excluded as were small, "double stars". Turnball narrated the 5000 or so stars within 100 light years of earth to a short list 30 and presents the light to scientists.

Nasa's Kepler satellite has distilled 1235 potential planets orbiting nearby Satellite stars with 68 planets that are roughly the earth's size and 54 planets in the so called habital zone a region continue to life as we know. There Earth-like Planets are work to be probed for alien life(TOI 9-2-2011).

Hunt for New Worlds of Planets

The masses of these new planets are comparable to those of Neptune or Uranus in our solar system, ranging from about 14 to 20 times the mass of earth.

The previous planets found around living stars other than the sun have been giants like Jupiter or Saturn at least 50 times the mass of earth, composed of gas at crushing pressures and scorching by high temperatures and undividedly, abodes for life. Astronomers said the new planets might be "ice giants" like Uranus and Neptune or even giant humble of iron and rock dubbled "Super Earth". Like those, previously discovered planets, the new ones are circling too close to their stars to be viable for life.

But their discovery, astronomers said, is an encouraging sign that planets are plentiful and varied in the galaxy and a new generation of planets, hunting space missions planned for next decade will find planots as small as Earth. "We are getting closer to answering the golden question of whether there is life out there" said Dr. Geoff Marky an astronomer and long time planet hunter at the University of California, Berkley.

"We are trying to find our own roots, chemically and biologically in the stars."

Dr. Paul Buntler of the Carnegie Institute of Washington, said, "we are prepared unexpectedly for next step in planetary science finding truly earth mass planets."

One of the new planet is part of a system around a star 55 Concri already known to harbour three larger planets making it the first planet system to be found beyond the solar system and likely target for research.

Dr. Barbama Mcarther of the University of Texas said, "we are on the way to finding the first extra solar planet Earth and it is an exciting road to be on."

Dr. Butler and Dr. Mc Arther were the leaders of the two overlapping teams who announced the discovery of two of the planets at a news conference at *NASA* headquarters in Washington on Tuesday.

The third team composed of European astronomers led by Dr. Michel Mayor of Geneva Observatory in Sauverney, Switzerland, announced the discovery of a third small planet in a news release on (Friday 2nd Sept 2004.)

Cosmic Rays Changes Planet's Like Pattern

The acceleration in the production of stars or the stellar body boom period of the milky way sparked a flowering and crashing of life here on earth, a new study suggests.

Some 2.4 billion years ago, when the milky way started pouring on to our planet, causing instability within the living, report space.com. Population of bacteria and algae repeatedly speared and crashed in the oceans. The researchers counted the amount of carbon – 13 within sedimentary rocks the most common rocks exposed on the earth's surface when algae and bacteria were growing in the oceans, they look in carbon – 12 so the ocean had an abundance of carbon – 13.

Many sea creatures use carbon – 13 to make their shells. If there is a lot of carbon – 13 stored in rocks, it means life was booming. Therefore, variations in carbon – 13 are a good indicator of the productivity of life on earth. The researchers found that the biggest fluctuation in productivity coincided with star formation, which had an affect on earth's climate and therefore on the productivity of life on our planet.

According to one theory, when a star explodes far away in the milky way, cosmic rays penetrate through the Earth's atmosphere and produce ions and free electrons. The released electrons act as catalysts and accelerate the formation of small clusters of sulpheric acid and water molecules, the building block of clouds. Therefore the cosmic rays increase cloud covers on Earth, reflecting sun light and keeping the planet relatively cool.

The data reveals that biological productivity kept oscillating between very high and very low. The reason the researchers suggest is that stronger winds daring icy epochs stirred the oceans and improved the supply of nutrients. "The odds are 10,000 to 1 against this unexpected link between cosmic rays, and the variable stone of the biosphere being just a coincidence, and it offers a new perspective, on the connection between the evolution of the milky way and the entire history of life over the last 4 billion years, said study author Hanrik Stang Mark.

Artificial Intelligence

Can one believe that everything we call "human" such as Intelligence emotions values and even self awareness really evolve from physical processes that can in theory (and increasingly in practice) be duplicated or surpassed by non-biological systems – namely machines? Some people believe so. Their argument is that which our evolution has taken the water and carbon based approach to development intelligent automata have advanced along the silicon and metal route. How different can one be from the other that we prefer to give pride of place to the former? That is a question humanity must now increasingly begin to address – especially since the staff of science fiction from Frankenstein to robotics pressing forward every day into reality. Not only that truly scurry part is that while "blind chance" and things like natural selection took million of years to produce brain power that interpret as intelligence, computers have taken less than 60 years.

But will computer even have soft realization like one school of thought which reckons that considers not as a function of complexity maintains that while an individual computer can compare no where near the connectivity of a 100 billion nerve cells, the human brain has, the internet on the other hand could when the Net's inter connectivity level begins to equal the one inside our heads then it's possible, they say, it could shake in mechanical existence aside and slowly arise into awareness. However, what is generally overlooked in this scenario is that it doesn't necessarily mean this entry would automatically also be aware of us or for that matter, anything else, including the reality of the entire external world of phenomena. What for instance, can a living brain do by itself if it lacks a body and more importantly, a sensory apparatus of very little actually, except think. A living internet would possess an astonishing memory all the knowledge of the world and the ability to process any amount of data at the speed of light, but it would be totally ineffectual in protecting itself in any way to impinge upon us. In other words, when we finally, manage to create another form of life with its own siliconized awareness we would never be able to know about it.

Bibliography

1. Ashok Sahni and R.S. Loyal, Edited Academy, - Gondwana Assembly: New Issues and Perspective. Indian National Science New Delhi 1999
2. Asimov Isaac - Asimov's New Guide to Science. Penguin Books 1984
2. Bridget and Raymond Allchin - The Birth of Indian Civilization, a Pelican Origined, Penguine Books, 1968
3. Bernad Wood - Human Exhortion : a very short introduction. Oxford University Press, Oxford, New York, 2005
4. Carl Sagan - Cosmos. Ballen Wine Books, New York, 1980
5. Cesare Emitiane - Planet Earth. University of Cambridge Press Paper back 1995, 1997
6. Dr. E.K. Victor Pearce - The Origin and Destiny of Life. Om Books, Secunderabad
7. Erich Von Daniken - The Return of the Gods. Element Books Limited, 1995

8. Glen Barcley - Mind Over Matter, beyond the bounds of nature. Pan B Books Ltd., London, Sydney, 1975

9. Irfan Habib - Pre-history, People's history of India – I Aligarh historians saciety

10. John Maynaid Smith - The Theory of Evolution. Cambridge University Press Reprinted 1995, 1997

11. John Ankerberg and John Weldon - Darwin's Leap of Faith : Exposing the False Religion and Evolution Om Authentic Secunderabad, 2005

12. John C. Greene - Darwin and the Modern World View. Mentar Book, The New American Library 1963

13. John Cowper Cowys - The Meaning of Culture Rupa & Company, Delhi, 1960

14. Lee Strobel - The Case for a Creator Om books, Secunderabad, 2004

15. Naval Viyogi - The Founders of Indus Valley Civilization and their later history. Vol.I

16. Patrick Moore and Lain Nicolson - Indian National Historical Research Council, Ludhiana, Delhi, 1995
Black Holes in space Orbaol and Chambers Ltd., 1979

17. P.C. Hemrom, Dr. - Santhali, a Natural language U Hemrom, New Delhi 2002

18. Paul Copan and William Lane - Creation Out of Nothing Om Authentic Books, Craig Secunderabad, 2006

19.	Partha P. Majumdar	-	People of India: Biological, diversity and affinities Evolutionary Anthropology, Vol. 6, 100-110, 1998
20.	Partha P. Majumdar Biyut Roy, Sanat Banerjee Madan Chakrabarty, Badal, Dey, Mamita Mukherjee, Mamoni Roy, Piyati Guha Thakurta, Samil Sil	-	Human Specific insertion, deletion polymerphisons in Indian populations and their possible Evolutionary implications European Journal of Human Genetics 435-446, 1999
21.	Partha P. Majumdar Nitai Pada Bhattacharya, Priyadarshi Basu, Mahusudan Rajat Banerjee, Biyut Roy, Samank Roy Choudhury		Negligible male-gene-flow across ethnic boundaries in India, revealed by analysis of Y. Chromosomal DNA polymorphism Das, Srivink Pramanik, Genetic Research Vol. 9, p. 711-719, 1999
22.	S.K. Biswas	-	Autochthon of India and the Aryan Incursion Genuine Publications and Media Rit Ltd., New Delhi 1995
23.	Sem Topno, Dr.		Musical Culture of the Munda Tribe. Concept Publication, New Delhi, 2004
24.	Staart Piggott		Prehistoric India. A Pelican Book, Penguin India, 1956
25.	Sankara Nanda Mukhopadhyay		The Austrics of India. K.P. Bagehi Company, Calcutta, 1995
26.	Stephen Hawking		A Brief History of Time, from the Big-Bang to Black Holes. Spaa Time Publications, 1988

27.	V. Rami Reddy	Physical Anthropology, Evolution and Genetic of Man 1995 Reader's Digest
28.	V. Indira, Tinupati DP	The Truth about history London How new evidence is transforming the story of the past 2009 National Heographic
29.	Rick Gare	The first Europeans p. 96 - 112 Vol. 192, No.1 July 1997 National Heographic
30.	Ricl Gare	The first steps pp. 72 - 99 Vol.191, No. 2, Feb. 1997 National Heographic Skull 1470 Vol. 143, No.6, June 1973 pp. 819 -829
31.	Richard Leakey	Vol. 168, No. 2, Aug. 1985 (1) Continents adrift life triumph (2) Origin of earth and lifes (3) Annals of life written on rock fossil David Jaffery pp. 142 – 197 Vol. 192, No. 3 Sept. 1997 National Geographics The dawn of human the trecking first of kind pp. 92 – 99
	Rick Gare	Vol. 193, No. 3, March 1998 National Geographics The Rise of Life on earth A 54 – 81
	Richard Moncasterksky	Vol. 193, No. 4, April 1998 National Geographic Life grows up the rise of life on earth 100 – 114
	Richard Moncasterksky	Vol. 194, No. 2 Aug 1998 Dawn of human – reducing Our Family Tree 90 – 99

Lee Berger	Vol. 174, No. 4, Oct. 1988 National Geographic The Search of Modern Humans p. 38 – 477
John J Puckman	Vol. 196, No. 4, Oct. 1999 The Unveiling the Universe p. 8 – 41
Kathy Janger	Vol. Aug. 2002 National Geographic The first Pioneer of New Kind Feb 2003 Galaxy hunters p. 4 – 29 April 2003 Rise of mammals p. 4 – 37
Leakey, Richard	The origin of human kind. Phoenix, 1995
Leakey, Richard and Roser Lewin	Origin Reconsidered. Abacus 1993

Index

Q

R